Enter Rabelais, Laughing

ENTER RABELAIS, LAUGHING

BARBARA C. BOWEN

VANDERBILT UNIVERSITY PRESS

NASHVILLE & LONDON

Publication of this book was supported by a subvention from the
Graduate School of Vanderbilt University.

This publication is made from paper that meets the minimum require-
ments of American National Standard for Information Sciences—
Permanence of Paper for Printed Library Materials. ∞

Library of Congress Cataloging-in-Publication Data

    Bowen, Barbara C.
      Enter Rabelais, laughing / by Barbara C. Bowen. -- 1st ed.
      p. cm.
      Includes bibliographical references (p.) and index.
      ISBN 0-8265-1306-9 (alk. paper)
      1. Rabelais, Francois, ca. 1490-1553?--Criticism and
    interpretation. 2. Comic, The, in literature. I. Title.
    PQ1694.B63 1998
    843'.3--dc21   98-8865
                                                             CIP

Manufactured in the United States of America

To Otto's Group
in aeternum floreat

Contents

List of Abbreviations

CL	Rabelais's *Cinquiesme Livre* (Fifth Book)
EC	*The Critical Edition of Rabelais,* begun by Abel Lefranc and his team in 1913, and never finished
EOV	The *Epistolae obscurorum virorum*, 'Letters of Obscure Men'
G	Rabelais's *Gargantua* (Book I)
MM	Pulci's *Morgante Maggiore*
MRTS	Medieval and Renaissance Texts and Studies
P	Rabelais's *Pantagruel* (Book II)
PMLA	*Publications of the Modern Language Association of America*
QL	Rabelais's *Quart Livre* (Book IV)
RQ	*Renaissance Quarterly*
RH	Rabelais, *Oeuvres complètes*, ed. M. Huchon
RQ	*Renaissance Quarterly*
SATF	Société des Anciens Textes Français
TL	Rabelais's *Tiers Livre* (Book III)
TLS	*Times Literary Supplement*

Prologue

"Ah!" said the man with the violin,
"that's what the trouble is. People
don't seem to laugh now like they used
to. I don't know why it is."

A.G. MACDONELL
(*England Their England*)

This book is addressed to readers already familiar with *Gargantua and Pantagruel* by François Rabelais, preferably but not necessarily in the original French. It is in one sense a general study of the four books we know Rabelais wrote, but for reasons explained below its chapters will focus on certain specific aspects of his comic art. The book is not, like most critical works, an exposition of *a* basic point of view, but on the contrary an attempt to explore the multiplicity of a writer so many-sided that no one reader could completely understand him. And again, unlike most critical works, this one is primarily about Rabelais the comedian; about why his writing caused uproarious laughter in his intended sixteenth-century readers. I have chosen to deal fairly briefly with the two most obvious François Rabelais, the comic narrator and the comic playwright (chapter 2), and at more length with aspects of him that are less accessible to the modern reader: humanism (chapter 3), rhetoric (chapter 4), medicine (chapter 5), and law (chapter 6), always with a view to explaining what is laughable in his giants and their adventures.

These are not by any means the only possible or necessary subjects; if I knew more, and if my readers liked enormously long books, I could add chapters entitled "The Comic Logician," "The Comic Gastronome," "The Comic Costumier," "The Comic Physicist," "The Comic Astronomer" . . . But this book does at least try to present a many-sided comic writer, to counteract the very numerous one-sided portrayals of Rabelais in twentieth-century criticism (see chapter 1).

Readers should be warned at the outset that the author will make no apologies for what is today considered an old-fashioned approach to writing about literature. I think of myself as a scholar rather than a critic, less interested in the latest debates on identity and selfhood, the validity of deconstruction or gender studies, or whether Rabelais should be labeled a grotesque, Mannerist, or Menippean author than in Demerson's discovery that the verbs *fleurer*, *sentir*, and *estimer*, used of the dog attacking the bone in *Gargantua*'s Prologue, refer to Bonaventure's explanation of how to read the world (Demerson 1996, 20). With regard not just to these labels, but to labels in general, I call myself a skeptic. Although both life and criticism would be simpler if we all meant the same thing when we use the terms *comedy*, *irony*, *parody*, *satire*, and so on and so forth, the obvious fact that we do not mean the same thing suggests to me that such terms should be either avoided, or very carefully defined.

The training of scholars, in my generation, was implicitly based on the concept of objectivity, in which I still believe to a large extent. That is to say, the ideal reader's initial attitude should be, not "Let me see if I can find misogyny in Rabelais," but "Let me see what I do find there, and relate it as far as possible to what I know about the intellectual climate of the time when it was written." But scholars age, rather faster than masterpieces of world literature, and I am well aware that how I read Rabelais today has been much influenced by the person I now am: middle-aged, English, and a university teacher at the end of her career. I also have my own sense of humor, not so far removed (I like to think) from Rabelais's, but perhaps not the same as yours, or your students'. So I make no apologies either for the use as analytical terms of words like *joke*, *funny*, *goofy*, and *trivial pursuit*, which may well shock more sober-minded critics. These terms will, I hope, be seen as justified and necessary, in a book on one of the world's great funny writers, by a *Rabelaisante* who believes as he did that laughter makes the world a better and saner place to live in, in the twentieth century as it did in the sixteenth.

The ideal book on Rabelais's comedy would be comic throughout, but this one cannot, alas, make such a claim. Because most of its chapters are dedicated to recovering lost intellectual contexts, a good deal of space is necessarily devoted to explaining how a particular context functioned; this means, especially in the chapters on medicine and law, long and perhaps tedious summaries of basic information. I hope that these passages will be found worthwhile, and ultimately illuminate the comedy, which is incomprehensible without them.

Because I hope that the book will be of interest to general readers, I have tried to keep the notes to a minimum, and I have translated passages longer than a few words in a foreign language. I have also tried to take into account as many different critical views as possible, and to attribute these views accurately; but the book has no pretensions to completion or to complete objectivity. Every critical work is by necessity based on the books, whether primary or secondary sources, that the critic has read. My perception of Rabelais changed when I reread him after reading Bakhtin, or Folengo's *Baldus*, and it will change again if I live long enough to read all the relevant works on my "still-not-read" list. Because I have been reading, and thinking about, Rabelais for many years now, I may sometimes attribute to myself an idea I found elsewhere, and if this is the case I apologize in advance.

Quotations from Rabelais are taken, unless otherwise specified, from the most recent critical edition, by Mireille Huchon (Pléiade, 1994). Since I began writing this book, the problems of understanding Rabelais have been greatly facilitated by this edition, and by the editions of individual books published by the Livre de Poche in its Bibliothèque Classique: *Pantagruel*, *Gargantua* and the *Quart Livre* edited by Gérard Defaux, and the *Tiers Livre* by Jean Céard. Readers of French now have access to much valuable information that was previously available only in scholarly articles for specialists. The problems of translating Rabelais remain, in my opinion, insoluble, but the Donald Frame translation, most often used here, is better than nothing. I have translated nearly all the Latin used in this book, and most of the French, but my translations aspire to accuracy rather than elegance.

A complete list of the people who have helped, inspired and encouraged me, argued with me, corrected my errors, and asked me to please go away and stop pestering them, would fill a chapter, but I must express my warmest gratitude to David Bright, Terence Cave, Joan and Arthur Crow, Tom McGeary, Tom McGinn, Darryl Phillips, Charles Porter, Anne Lake Prescott, Florence Weinberg, and my heroic research assistant Christie St. John; the librarians of the Bibliothèque Municipale (Lyon), the Centre d'Etudes de la Renaissance (Tours, especially Mlle Simon), the Bibliothèque Méjanes in Aix-en-Provence, the Rare Book Room at the University of Illinois (Urbana), Houghton Library (Harvard), and the library of Vanderbilt University (especially Yvonne Boyer, and Marilyn Pilley and Tom Toplon of Interlibrary Loan); the National Endowment for the Humanities, for a Senior Fellowship in 1988–89; the techno-whizzes who taught me how to use the computer: Josette Amsilli, Tracy Barrett, Dan Church, Bill Longwell, Margaret Meggs, and Mary Nell Snoddy; and the kind and patient people of the Vanderbilt University Press, especially Bard Young. All the members of Otto's Group sat heroically through sections of this book and helped me to improve them; special thanks to Vincent Bowen, Errol and Jean Elshtain, William and Kaaren Engel, Walter Harrelson, John and Pat Post, William Race, Matthew Ramsey, Hans and Lottie Strupp, and Barbara Tsakirgis. They should feel no obligation to read the book in its final form.

CHAPTER I

Rire est le propre de l'homme

Nothing like a little judicious levity

R.L. STEVENSON

How Rabelaisian Is Rabelais?

Poor François Rabelais. With Epicurus and Jean de Meung, he must surely be one of the most consistently misunderstood writers of Western Europe. From his time to ours, the four books of *Gargantua and Pantagruel* have been synonymous with hyperbole, overindulgence and gratuitous obscenity. Much of his text, said George Saintsbury in 1917 (108), is "mere nastiness, which is only attractive to a very small minority of persons at any age, while to expert readers it is but a time-deodorised dunghill by the roadside." I wish I could remember whether it was Saintsbury or Tilley who deplored in 1905 the fact that women would never be able to read him. In 1938 Ringling Bros. and Barnum and Bailey billed their gorilla as Gargantua the Great; a 1967 Japanese monster movie was called *War of the Gargantuas*; who knows how many gourmet French restaurants are named "Gargantua" or "Pantagruel"; and a computer called the Milliard Gargantubrain figures in *The Hitchhiker's Guide to the Galaxy* by Douglas Adams. In 1963 Brewer's *Dictionary of Phrase and Fable* still defined "Rabelaisian" as "coarsely and boisterously satirical; grotesque, extravagant and licentious in language."

In 1994, a Rabelais centenary year in France, one would have expected the French to have absorbed some of the information available, since M. A. Screech's groundbreaking research in the 1950s, on a more complex and interesting Rabelais: the Evangelical Christian humanist, follower of Erasmus, campaigner for good government, good education, healthy intellectual curiosity, and humorous Stoicism. The special Rabelais number of March 1994 of the *Magazine Littéraire* does include some solidly erudite pieces by knowledgeable scholars (Demerson, Jeanneret, Demonet, Smith, Céard, and Joukovsky), but it also contains several contributions by enthusiastic nonspecialists who fundamentally misunderstand their beloved author (cf. the claim by Michel Onfray on page 18 that Jesus would not be welcome in the Abbey of Thélème). It is to Rabelais's credit that he can still fascinate large numbers of readers who have very little understanding of his text, and my intention is not at all to disparage those readers. But for those of us who would like to understand, to the extent that is now possible, what Rabelais's own intentions might have been, and how his first humanist readers understood him, enthusiasm is not a sufficient qualification.

Specialist readings of Rabelais may be more complex, but they are also much more confusing. Twentieth-century academics have "discovered" a bewildering multiplicity of François Rabelais. Although most critics nowadays accept Screech's Rabelais the Evangelical Christian humanist, our author has also been firmly labeled an atheist (Lefranc), a Freemason (Naudon), a proto-

Marxist (Lefebvre), a social subversive (Bakhtin), a hesuchist (Saulnier), an esoteric (Masters and Gaignebet), a Cornucopian (Cave), a Menippean (Coleman and Blanchard), a Dionysian (Weinberg), a sophist (Defaux), a misogynist (Freccero and Glidden), an *angoissé* (Nakam, Randall), a coherent book-structurer (Duval), a deconstructionist (Schwartz), a Platonist (Gauna).[1] Some of these Rabelais are undoubtedly authentic (whereas others exist only in the fertile minds of their expositors), but even when authentic they are usually, for my taste, too exclusive. Most readers are at least partially conscious, not of *a* Rabelais, but of many different Rabelais, and of the four books as belonging to a multiplicity of literary genres: pseudo-epic, theatrical farce, mirror-of-princes treatise, and humanist encyclopedia, to name only the most obvious.[2]

Some recent Rabelais criticism attempts to solve the problem by claiming that Rabelais is deliberately enigmatic and open-ended, and that we should not try to pin him down (Schwartz, Demerson sometimes), because he "purposefully thwarts the reader's desire for completion" (La Charité). This is an appealing critical stance in today's uncertain and threatening world, but I believe it is unfair to Rabelais. Like Erasmus (whose *Praise of Folly* can also be read as light entertainment, with no awareness of what it is really saying), Rabelais expected his very serious religious and humanist messages to get through to their intended audience, even while they were enjoying the story on other levels.

I believe that the first step to reading Rabelais as he wanted to be read is to look for multiplicity, not for unity. Sometimes this multiplicity will involve an abrupt change of tone from one chapter to the next—from the humanist educational treatise of P 8, say, to the hilariously gratuitous linguistic display of P 9. At other times a switch occurs within a chapter; in P 29 we jump from a comic pseudo-epic flight of fancy to an entirely serious Evangelical manifesto and back again. But many of the most satisfying episodes are those belonging simultaneously to several genres. Grandgousier's prayer in G 28 is *at the same time* a charmingly naïve plea to God by an old-fashioned father-of-his-people, and a Renaissance humanist depiction of the Ideal Prince. The battle with the Andouilles (QL 35–42) is *at the same time* a spoof of Homeric and Arthurian epic, an anthology of sausage jokes, a compendium of learned references to Erasmus, the Hebrew Bible, and other humanist sources, and a serious comment on Carnival and Lent.

Not only do the four books belong simultaneously to different genres, but their author, like many Renaissance intellectuals, was also a man of (by our standards) staggeringly broad knowledge and interests. He writes, very often, as a humanist; less often but quite clearly as a Christian; always, I think, as a devotee of classical literature; and episodically as a doctor, jurist, architect, jeweler, costumer, military strategist, zoologist, royal propagandist, sailor, etymologist, mythologist, botanist, falconer, historian, and meteorologist.... Whether the erudition displayed in all these domains is his own, or copied from some contemporary manual, is beside the point; for a chapter, or for a sentence, he speaks with the voice of authority on that particular subject.

Rather than focusing on *a* solution to the enigma of Rabelais, I believe it is more productive to ask as many different questions as possible of his text. This may be partly ethnic bias; I can still remember my Oxford tutor, W. G. Moore, saying: "You know, the English seem to be better at asking questions than at answering them." In this book I will ask one big question: Why did Rabelais's first readers laugh? I will ask this by way of a number of smaller questions: What did it mean, in sixteenth-century France, to be a storyteller/dramatist, humanist, orator, doctor, and lawyer who was also a comedian?

I like to encourage my students to look for multiplicity in Rabelais with the following analogy. Imagine, if you will, that three celebrated European authors have decided to collaborate on a work of fiction: Aristophanes, P. G. Wodehouse, and Umberto Eco. Eco will provide the plot, an extended and convoluted quest with ramifications spanning many years and many countries, frequently interrupted by extended forays into abstruse intellectual domains, or philosophical reflections on how language holds the world together. Aristophanes will add ferocious satire of political, social and intellectual sacred cows (including tyrants and bad education), outrageous puns and word-play, a delight in obscenity, and characters who are sometimes real people and sometimes completely fantastic. (After writing this passage, I chanced upon the French translation of Aristophanes by Debidour [Folio], whose introduction refers a number of times to Rabelais.) And Wodehouse will contribute what the French call *comédie gratuite*, a kind of inspired, poetic goofiness with no philosophical, political or social content.[3] Would not such a tripartite collaboration be quite likely to produce something rather like the four books of *Gargantua et Pantagruel*?

Laugh, and the World Laughs with You

But to mention Wodehouse is to raise an immediate problem: not all readers find Bertie, Jeeves and their friends laughable. To appreciate the humor of their fantasy world one may need, somewhere in the sober intellectual soul of the scholar, a touch of unrepentant youthful frivolity. Wodehouse describes Pongo's elderly Uncle Fred as a man who "still retained the bright enthusiasms and the fresh, unspoiled outlook of a slightly inebriated undergraduate" (*Uncle Fred in the Springtime*, chap. 3); there is a definite strain of this "undergraduate humor" in Rabelais, which many sober intellectual scholars either cannot or will not recognize. Wodehouse characters like Uncle Fred cheerfully demolish the conventional world around them, and the conventional language used in that world; a Wodehousean young man's immediate reaction, on hearing that someone hasn't a leg to stand on, is "Awkward if he wants to roller-skate" (*Money in the Bank*, chap. 1). The Rabelais of Panurge's practical jokes and stream of incomprehensible languages, and of the play with metaphors in the *Quart Livre*, would have enjoyed this. He would also, I think, have enjoyed the librettos of W. S. Gilbert, who shared with Wodehouse an unusually developed sense of the absurd, which I like to call the goofy, and which Cicero and Pontano labeled the *sub-absurdum* (see chapter 4).

This book has probably already lost some readers, for, as we all know, individual senses of humor vary so widely that no consensus seems possible. The only conclusion to be drawn from this century's voluminous writing on humor is that no rules apply to what makes people laugh; there is, apparently, no such thing as a class sense of humor, an educated sense of humor, or a gender-based sense of humor.[4] National and ethnic wit may be partially identifiable; I have heard a Jewish friend and an Arab friend roaring with laughter as they exchanged dinner-table jokes unfathomable to the Anglo-Saxons present, but I have never seen a satisfactory attempt to distinguish between French and British, or English and American, humor.

"Laughter is the best medicine," *Reader's Digest* assures us; "Laugh, and the world laughs with you," asserted Ellen Wheeler Wilcox. Such clichés might lead us to assume that laughter is a definable, or at least a graspable, entity, like Romanticism or measles. Unfortunately, it is apparently impossible to identify joke motifs or subjects that will invariably raise a laugh. Many people find irresistibly comic the *Far Side* cartoons which have hardly ever made me smile. Arriving Britons find laughable American place-names like Chillicothe and Schenectady, which were certainly not comic to the Native Americans who first used them.

Every Sunday, in my Nashville church, we pray for our president, governor, mayor, and bishop, whose names as of this writing are Bill, Ned, Phil and Bert—all mildly humorous to the English, who do not usually shorten the names of public figures (unless in affection or derision, as, for instance, Winnie or Maggie).

Are there any motifs or objects universally accepted as comic? In old vaudeville there were at least two, chamber pots and mothers-in-law, but chamber pots are extinct, and speaking as a mother-in-law I do not find the old stereotype side-splitting. Similarly, tripe and sausages were by definition comic to Rabelais's first readers, but probably are not to most modern readers (my students grimace with distaste at the mention of tripe). I have polled colleagues to try and discover *anything* generally perceived as hilarious: cuckolded husbands? (not in today's world); bossy women? (not to today's women); monkeys with brightly colored bottoms? (not if you don't like animals); a very small kitten chasing its tail? (not if you're allergic to cats); two clowns hitting each other in the face with cream pies? (not if you think physical humor is vulgar); and so it goes. A character in Lilian Jackson Braun's *The Cat Who Said Cheese* claims that "a plate of sardines is funnier than a slice of bread. . . . A donkey is funny; a horse is not. Pants are funny; shoes are not," but would everybody agree? We should all like to think that laughter is a universal language; alas, the facts say otherwise.

This is, I think, the major obstacle confronting seekers after a definitive theory of the comic. Whereas agreement has been fairly general, ever since Aristotle, on the basic elements of tragedy, over two thousand years of earnest discussion have not produced a universally acceptable theory of the comic. I doubt that any one researcher could find the time to read the huge number of authors who have made the attempt; certainly I have not tried to do so. Each of them, especially in our century, combines debt to previous theorists with a personal viewpoint, and each bases that viewpoint on a particular category of the laughable, ranging from Molière comedies (Bergson and Meredith) to Jewish marriage-broker jokes (Freud). And each has a different number of categories of the comic; four in Monro, eight in Gutwirth, three in Raskin, five in Favre, and so on and on.

Monro's four categories provide an apparently useful overview of the problem. He divides theories of the comic into: 1) superiority theories (Hobbes, Bain, Leacock, Ludovici, Bergson, Feibleman, McDougall); 2) incongruity theories (Kant, Schopenhauer, Spencer, Eastman); 3) release-from-restraint theories (Kline, Freud, Gregory); and 4) ambivalence theories (Greig, Krishna Menon). Unfortunately, this leaves out a good deal of recent theory by anthropologists (Douglas), linguists (Raskin), philosophers (Morreall) and psychoanalysts (Flieger), to name only authors known to me.

Of the very numerous modern writers on the nature of laughter, I have read probably a couple of dozen, and have often found specific insights and examples which struck me as more satisfactory than any sweeping general theory. Peter Tiersma, in a short paper, brilliantly analyzes the verbal wit of Marx Brothers movies, via a detailed discussion of techniques including simple puns (the beard sent by hairmail), decomposition (Leavenworth/Twelveworth), puns on idioms (idle roomer), structural ambiguity ("You try my patience"—"You must try mine some time"), and reference ("You have the brain of a four-year old and I bet he was glad to get rid of it"). This strikes me as much more relevant to Rabelais's humor than Bergson's puppetlike Molière characters, or Freud's two old men in the train to Kraków.

If I had to espouse one general theory of the comic, I would turn not to a philosopher or a psychologist, but to a professional comedian; as Favre points out (14), "un praticien du rire, qu'il s'appelle Coluche ou Guy Bedos, n'est peut-être pas moins instructif que les philosophes et les professeurs" ("a working comedian, whether his name is Coluche or Guy Bedos, is perhaps just as instructive as the philosophers and the professors"). My favorite comedian is Steve Allen, a genuinely funny man whose definition is this: "Laughter is produced out of a sort of minor explosion in the brain, a kind of short-circuit spark in that portion of our 'computer' that automatically attempts to deal logically with incoming information" (Allen 1987, 14). Notice that he makes no attempt to define what causes this spark, inasmuch as obviously the cause will differ for different people, or even for the same person at different moments. Elsewhere he describes comedy as not a science but an art, and concludes, "Laughter, then, seems a simple gift of the gods" (10). And he has this marvelous description, again of Groucho Marx, which applies perfectly to both Aristophanes and Rabelais: "To his sort of mind words are not just what they are to everyone else. They are rubbery, many-sided globs of thought that can be knocked about like plastic into all sorts of shapes" (1956, 246).

The incompatibility between what A and B find laughable is not our only problem. Any discussion of humor must use specific terminology, and most do so in the apparent conviction that readers will agree on the meaning of the terms. Swabey defines and distinguishes, to her own satisfaction, among the comic, humor, and wit, which not all readers will perceive as distinct. There are also serious translation problems; how do we render Freud's *Witz* or the Italian *barzelletta*? Is Baudelaire's opposition between absolute and referential comic really equivalent to Freud's between innocent and tendentious comic, as Flieger claims? Such problems seem to me to exist even in English, at least in this postmodern era; when Beckett says that "nothing is funnier than suffering," or Flieger asserts that the comic and the postmodern are synonymous, they have lost me—I seem to be adrift in a universe where words no longer mean anything.

Even if we could all agree, in 1998, on what is laughable, we should often find ourselves baffled by much that amused the Renaissance. The clearest illustration of this in Rabelais is in the episodes of violent death and dismemberment (frere Jean saving the vineyard or killing an enemy soldier, the drowning of Dindenault, the terrible death of Tappecoue) which were certainly considered to be funny in an age mentally much tougher than ours. An even more striking example of the Renaissance's sometimes brutal sense of humor can be found in no. 96 of Luscinius's *Ioci ac sales mire festivi* (1524): a traveling salesman is condemned to death by the Emperor Gallienus, to whose wife he had tried to sell fake jewels. He is led out into the arena expecting to die, but the Emperor had secretly arranged to have him castrated instead. The audience, to a modern reader's astonishment, finds this punishment laughable: "populus ad tam ridiculum Poenam plurima caperetur admiratione." The sixteenth century, like the third century, where this story presumably originated, was a time of more violence, barbarity and suffering than most inhabitants of the United States can even imagine today, and perhaps a ferocious sense of humor helps to fortify the spirit against war, bandits, torture, and operations without benefit of anesthetic.[5]

There is one further problem, much less obvious and much more insidious: is laughter fundamentally good or bad? The author of this book agrees with Erasmus and Rabelais that laughter is not only good—it is essential, therapeutic and life-affirming. But at least since the early days of Christianity there has been a contrary view: that laughter is sinful, even demonic, and that the truly pious Christian never laughs. This view was impressively articulated by Bossuet, in the seventeenth century, and was the basis of Baudelaire's theory in the nineteenth. (A group of modern psychologists, probably not influenced by the Christian view, even concluded in 1976 that a sense of humor is a "myopic illusion" [Chapman-Foot #4]). That laughter was an essential attribute of the intellectual, a necessary relaxation for tired brains, a means of disarming hostility—these and related principles were very dear, as we shall see below, to most Renaissance humanists—

to most, but not to all. It seems odd that some Christians have always been convinced of the essential wrongness of laughter—or was this attitude originally a reaction against Jewish thought? (If, as Lionel Blue claims, "the most typical weapon of Jewish spirituality is humor") (Eckardt 131).

These problems are all fascinating, and in my opinion they are all insoluble. Fortunately, they are seldom relevant to the purpose of this book, which is to explore what the Renaissance meant by the laughable, and why Rabelais's intended readers laughed at his text. But before examining those questions in detail, it may be helpful to look at some literary laughter before Rabelais.

French Literary Laughter

The history of laughter in French literature has yet to be written. When it is written it will need to begin with the *Chanson de Roland*, where Roland shows his scorn for Ganelon by laughing at him: ("si cumençat a rire," laisse 21). Ganelon understands this so well that he is at once beside himself with fury: "A ben petit quë il ne pert le sens," laisse 22). Scornful laughter is quite common in medieval literature, and can sometimes be actively malevolent; when the wicked lord of Marie de France's "Laüstic" is plotting to kill the nightingale in order to punish his wife, the author tells us that "De ire et maltalent en rist" (line 92). This is very similar to Panurge laughing at the gross humiliation of the "haulte dame de Paris" (P 22), or at the fall of the "gros enflé de Conseiller" (P 17); note that in the latter case Panurge adds "Mais je me rys encores dadvantage" (But I laugh even harder) when he thinks of the page who will be whipped for cutting the stirrup—very unkind laughter indeed.

Eustache Deschamps has a charming anticlerical ballad (SATF V, no. 843) that is quite relevant to our subject:

Sur les differentes manières de rire
Avoir ne puis trop grant merencolie
Des ris que font au jour d'ui mainte gent:
L'un rit des yeux et en riant colie
Et l'autre rit qui ne passe le dent;
Li autres rit si tresorriblement   5
Qu'il semble folz, tant li siet son ris mal

. . . .

Que se semble le ris d'un cardinal.

Aucuns si font un riz d'hypocrisie,
Combien qu'il n'ont de rire nul talent;   10
Et l'autre rit, qui ne se moque mie,
Du bon du cuer, pour quelque esbatement;
Aucuns y a qui rient francement,
Et l'autre rit qui a joye du mal;
Des oreilles rit aucuns tellement   15
Que se semble le ris d'un cardinal.

Senz cause rit aucuns par sa folie,
Qui de rire n'a certain mouvement;
L'autre est joyeux qui a plaine voix crie
Et qui le fait sans mauvaiz pensement;   20
Et l'autre rit maiz traïteusement,
Car son ris vient de parfont et d'aval;
Pour ce en tel cas dit on communement
Que ce semble le ris d'un cardinal.

2

I can't be overly melancholy (i.e., can't help being amused)
About the laughter of many people today:
One laughs with his eyes, and while laughing he gets mad
And another laughs behind clenched teeth;

Another laughs so horrendously
That he looks like a madman, so poorly does laughter suit
    him
. . . .
That it seems like the laughter of a cardinal.
Some laugh hypocritically,
Although they don't really want to laugh;
And another laughs, not mockingly,
But heartily, because he's happy;
There are certain people who laugh frankly,
And another laughs in delight at someone else's misfor-
    tune;
Some laugh so much with their ears (?)
That it seems like the laughter of a cardinal.
One man laughs for no reason, in his folly,
Who has no clear cause to laugh (?)
Another is joyful and shouts aloud
Which he does without evil thought;
And another laughs, but treacherously,
For his laughter comes up from the depths;
For this reason in such a case people say
That it seems like the laughter of a cardinal.

As one would expect from a satirist, nearly all the laughter evoked here is bad laughter: artificial (3–4), hypocritical (9–10), vengeful (14), mad (17–18), and treacherous (21–22). The frank (12–13) and joyful (19–20) laughter are hardly noticed in this company, and Deschamps thus unintentionally provides an apt summary of the subject in French medieval literature.

    The best medieval illustration of evil laughter I know is Antoine de La Sale's *Jehan de Saintré* of the late fifteenth century, in which *rire*, surprisingly, is a key word. Madame and her women initial-ly laugh mockingly at the young Saintré's clumsiness at court, but later Madame laughs at him to disguise her growing love for him; she also dissimulates her love by laughing with her attendants. She laughs—again as a disguise—while asking a favor for Saintré from the Queen. Much later, Saintré laughs with his companions to hide his sadness at Madame's anger, and finally and most shockingly Madame laughs heartily on seeing Saintré defeated and humiliated by her new lover, l'Abbé. Just about all the laughter in this "novel" is what Deschamps would call evil laughter.

Renaissance literature is also full of laughter *at* someone's folly or misfortune. Guillemette, in *Maître Pierre Pathelin*, laughs uproariously at the successful duping of the *drappier* (l. 764); in *Maître Pierre Faifeu* all the children laugh when Faifeu shits in the face of the master who is beating him (II); and to climb higher in the social scale, all Marguerite de Navarre's princes and aristocrats, including the elderly and pious Oisille, laugh at the depiction of the poor lady stuck on the latrine, who emerges covered with excrement (lle Nouvelle). The aristocracy of the time apparently had a more earthy sense of humor than their modern counterparts.

All of this laughter, like Panurge's quoted above, is more or less nasty. But there is also plenty of good laughter in Renaissance literature, even apart from the humanist *festivitas* which will be discussed below. Jean Bouchet takes pleasure in the "innocens ris" of babies (1530 *Triomphes*, Livre I f. 2), as does Jean Lemaire de Belges in a smiling countryside (*Concorde des deux langages*, 67). Noël du Fail's nostalgic portrait of the Good Old Days, in the *Propos Rustiques*, has peasants dressing simply, living frugally—and "rians à pleine gorge" (II).

Bonaventure Des Périers may be the most enthusiastic apologist for laughter, at least in French literature of this period. In the "Première nouvelle en forme de préambule" to the *Nouvelles Récréations et Joyeux Devis* (1558), he affirms: "Le plus gentil enseignement pour la vie, c'est *Bene vivere et laetari.* . . . Ventre d'ung petit poysson! rions. Et dequoy? De la bouche, du nez, du menton, de la gorge, et de tous noz cinq sens de nature. Mais ce n'est rien qui ne rit du coeur" (The noblest lesson for life is *Live well and rejoice.* . . . Odds boddikins! let's laugh! And with what? With our mouths, noses, chins, throats, and all our five natural senses. But that's not enough if we don't laugh with our hearts).

Des Périers's *Nouvelles Récréations* are quite similar to the numerous other *conte* collections of the period, but he is the only short story author to stress in this way the crucial importance of laughter.

Literary laughter, then, can be mocking, cruel, vengeful, or fundamentally good, none of which is surprising. But there is one quite surprising literary use of laughter, and that is in connection with sex. Already in Marie de France's "Yonec" we find "unt ris e jüé" (193) for "they made love"; several of Martial d'Auvergne's *Arrêts d'amour* allege "parler et rire ensemble" as a sign of sexual complicity; and Villon's "gras chanoine" spends his time with Dame Sidoine (T 1473–1506):

> Boire ypocras, à jour et à nuytee,
> Rire, jouer, mignonner et baisier,
> Et nu à nu, pour mieulx des corps s'aisier.

> ❦
> Drinking hippocras, all day and all night,
> Laughing, playing, petting and kissing,[6]
> Both naked, to be more at their ease.

Lemaire de Belges's *Concorde des deux langages* frequently associates Venus and her companions with smiles and laughter, and in the *Illustrations de Gaule* (I.28) Bacchus and his companions at the wedding of Peleus and Thetis are described as "rians

et vociferans par grand lasciuité" (laughing and shouting very
lasciviously). Des Périers's 95th *nouvelle* is about a superstitious
doctor who refused to "rire et prendre le deduit avecques sa
femme en temps sec" (laugh and sport with his wife in dry weather); the story's title says simply: "D'un superstitieux medecin qui
ne vouloit rire avec sa femme sinon quand il plouvoit" (About
a superstitious doctor who only wanted to laugh with his wife
when it was raining). Is this association perhaps one reason for
the disapproval of laughter by some Christians? At least one
Renaissance theoretician equated the sadness which follows laughter with post-coital *tristitia* (Ménager 1995, 27).

I have deliberately quoted medieval alongside Renaissance
examples of literary laughter (and could of course have quoted
many more), because I see no perceptible change in attitude
between them. From the twelfth to the sixteenth century, we can
find examples in literature of laughter which is derisive, aggressive, innocent, heartily good, or sexual. To conclude this brief
overview, let us take a look at two works Rabelais knew well, and
first, the chronicles where he found the name and some of the
exploits of Gargantua.

Probably the earliest of these chronicles is the *Grandes et inestimables Cronicques du grant et enorme geant Gargantua*, printed
in 1532 and perhaps earlier, which Rabelais praises extravagant-
ly in the Prologue to his first book. Some critics believe Rabelais
had a hand in some of the chapbook versions of the Gargantua
story (Huchon, Demerson), but I think this unlikely. The word
rire occurs only twice in the twenty chapters of this chronicle.
In chapter 5 Merlin completes his creation of a male and a female
giant, "et adonc ledict homme va regarder la femme disant
'que faictz tu là, Galemelle;' dist la femme 'je attens Grant Gosier
mon amy.' Adonc Merlin se print à rire, et leur dist que ses parolles
estoyent belles, et que il vouloit que ilz eussent ainsi nom"
("and then the said man looked at the woman, saying 'What

are you doing here, Galemelle?' The woman said, 'I'm waiting, friend Big Mouth.' Then Merlin began to laugh, and told them that these were fine words, and he wanted them to take them as names"). Why does Merlin laugh? In surprise? At the incongruity of the names? But "Grant Gosier" is in fact quite appropriate. Is Merlin simply delighted because the beings he has created (out of whale bones, Lancelot's blood, and Guinevere's nail parings) are endowed with speech?

The only other laughter in this brief story is Gargantua's in chapter 12. The young giant has just been dressed, by order of King Arthur, in his new finery (described in detail), when Merlin asks him how he's doing. "Et Gargantua qui estoit gay respond que tresbien se portoit, et sur ce il se print à rire si tresfort et de si grant affection: pour la gentilesse de sa personne et de l'amour que il avoit à Merlin et au roy Artus que on l'entendoit rire de sept lieues et demye" ("And Gargantua who was merry replied that he was very well, and at once began to laugh so loudly and enthusiastically, because of the elegance of his appearance and the love he had for Merlin and King Arthur, that he could be heard laughing seven and a half leagues away").

Intriguingly, the later, more elaborate versions of the story add a good deal of laughter. In the *Croniques admirables* there are six such additions. In chapter 12 Gargantua swallows down an incredible quantity of wine given him by the monks of Saint-Maur, "dont les moines se prindrent si fort à rire qu'ilz en cuidèrent tous mourir" ("which made the monks begin to laugh so hard that they thought they would die"); in chapter 15 the tailor sewing Gargantua's enormous *brayette* (codpiece) laughs, to Gargantua's annoyance; in chapter 16 the Guerrandoys laugh when Gargantua asks (facetiously) if they don't have a woman for him; in chapter 25, where Gargantua gets diarrhea from drinking English *godalle*, and "dora toutes les murailles de la ville de Londres" ("gilded all the walls of the city of London"), King Arthur and his knights "se prindrent tous à rire si tresfort qu'ilz en eurent les passions plus de sept jours" ("all began to laugh so heartily that they were sick for more than a week"); in chapter 31 Arthur gives Gargantua a solid gold windmill with silver sails, "dont Gargantua se print fort à rire et dist au Roy qu'il vouloit devenir musnier" ("at which Gargantua began to laugh heartily and told the King that he wanted to become a miller"); and in chapter 36 "la belle Gribouille" is audibly delighted at Gallimassue's victory over Galaffre, "car de la grant joye qu'elle en avoit on l'eust bien entendue rire de dixsept lieues loing" ("for because of the great joy she had of it you could have heard her laughing from seventeen leagues away"). Appropriately in this giant chronicle, the emphasis is usually on the volume and length of the laughter, whether it be caused by scatology, incongruity, or simple delight.

There is much more laughter in one of the most popular *conte* collections of the period, the *Cent Nouvelles Nouvelles* (1462). Most frequently, the whole company laughs at a story of feminine sexual *naïveté*, as at the end of 20, where "Il n'y eut celuy de la table après ces motz a pou qui se tenist de rire" ("There was no one at the table who after these words could refrain from laughing"; cf. also 25, 48 and 80). Laughter can also be satirical, at a monk's greed (83), a bishop's hypocrisy (100) or a husband's adultery (59); hypocritical, in 30; used to disguise discomfiture (60); conspiratorial (83); used to dissipate anger (73) or to further a plot (27—but in 76 the plotter must refrain from giving himself away by laughing); or simply as a sign of good humor and amiability of character: "Le cyrurgien, qui estoit le plus gentil compaignon et des aultres le meilleur homme, commença a rire, et firent la paix" ("The surgeon, who was the finest companion and the best man in the world, began to laugh, and they made peace," 81).

I am not attempting to claim either the *Grandes Chronicques* or the *Cent Nouvelles Nouvelles* as typical of works Rabelais's readers had probably read, but merely as interesting examples. Many other examples could of course be adduced, and all would be different, although all probably use what seem to be the basic techniques of medieval and Renaissance literary laughter: laughter at scatology, sexual exploits, and cruel tricks; mockery of folly, hypocrisy, and naïveté; and laughter as evidence of healthy good humor. Supporters of superiority, surprise, and incongruity theories would find plenty of material in literature of this period, and laughter is undoubtedly a key element in many *conte* collections (although in the *Cent Nouvelles Nouvelles*, as in Rabelais, the word *joyeux* occurs more frequently than the word *rire*).

Even such a brief sampling of literary humor must raise the question of what theoreticians of the time had to say about why people laugh, so to this question I now turn.

Rire est le propre de l'homme

As we saw above, twentieth-century humor theorists are likely to be philosophers, psychologists, anthropologists, or linguists. The last three of these disciplines did not exist in Rabelais's time, but humor theory did begin, as far as we know, with a philosopher. When Rabelais asserts, in the liminary poem to *Gargantua*, that "rire est le propre de l'homme" ("laughter is proper to man"), he is using a philosophical tag, traceable back to Aristotle and much used in the Middle Ages, with a straightforward technical meaning. *Risus proprium hominis* simply states that laughter is a characteristic specific to man, as for instance neighing is to horses. As Chauliac succinctly expresses it (tr. Canappe, 1552), "la diffinition essentiale de lhomme, cest animant raisonnable" ("the essential definition of man is rational animal"); "la diffinition accidentale de lhomme, cest animant risible, ou né à rire" ("the accidental definition of man is risible animal, or animal born to laugh," 25). He also gives, as his explanation of the fourth meaning of the technical term *propre*: "Estre risible, cest a dire estre né, & apte à rire, conuient à tout homme, & au seul homme, & en tout temps" ("to be capable of laughter means to be born to laugh and prone to laugh, [a definition that] is appropriate to all men, and to man alone, and at all times," 35). Man is an *animal risibile*, meaning not "laughable" but "capable of laughter"; Montaigne still uses it in this sense in the last line of "De Democritus et Heraclitus" (I.50). This does not imply that laughter is a necessary characteristic of man; Helen Adolf quotes Thomas Aquinas: "Non omne, quod est proprium alicui, pertinet ad essentiam eius, sicut risibile homini" ("Not everything, which is proper to something, pertains to its essence, as 'capable of laughing' does to man").

It is not true, as claimed by Daniel Ménager (1995, 16) that all Renaissance authors tended to see laughter as a defining property of man, but certainly many humanists affirm the principle that laughter is proper to man. Petrarch enumerates thus God's gifts to man: "Dedit rationem dedit orationem dedit lachrymas dedit risus" ("He gave us reason, speech, tears and laughter," *De rem.* II.93); Benedetto Morandi tells us that according to the *dialectici* man can be defined "et risibile et felicitabile animal" (Trinkaus), and Manetti's denial that laughter is an essential attribute of man is a reply to Valla, who had affirmed that it is (cf. also Screech and Calder).

Closer in time to Rabelais, we can find plenty of examples of this cliché. Pontano mentions almost in passing that "homo risibile animal est dictus" (*De sermone* III.7). Heinrich Bebel, in the *Epistola* to the second book of his *Facetiae*, defines himself thus: "homo sum, rideo aliquando." More surprisingly, Paolo Cortesi's little-known treatise *De cardinalatu* (1510) contains a brief section on the *facetie et ioci* suitable for the Cardinal's use, in which he claims: "nihil est. n. tam humanae naturae cognatum quam aspersus dicendi urbanitas sal, nihilque tam proprium hominis quam facetiarum dicacitate delectari" ("Nothing is as closely related to human nature as wit sprinkled with elegance in speaking, and nothing is so much proper to man as to delight in the wit of jokes" [*facetiae*]). Later, Fischart's liminary poem to the *Geschichtklitterung* states confidently:

> lachen in all kraft
> Ist dess Menschens recht eigenschaft

> 𝔔

> full-throated laughter
> Is the true distinguishing characteristic of Man,

and as late as the 1620s, in Middleton's *The Changeling*, Lollio will say to Antonio: "Good boy, hold up your head. He can laugh; I perceive by that he is no beast" (I.2).

Whether or not Rabelais was familiar with any of these authors, we need have no doubt about his stance in the humanist debates on laughter, inasmuch as its importance was constantly stressed by two of his heroes, Thomas More and Erasmus. For both, *festivitas* is a key word, and while definitions of this term remain maddeningly elusive (Bowen, "Festive Humanism"), readers of both humanists are soon convinced that for them it meant something like "a joking approach to life." Thomas More can truly be said to have lived this principle, right up to the joke he made on the scaffold moments before his execution (Lipking).

Erasmus's *Praise of Folly* is one of the century's great comic works; his letters are full of examples of, and appreciation for, laughter and wit; and his ability to use laughter as a satiric weapon will hardly be equaled until Voltaire. The long essays in the *Adages* are usually very serious, but can be enlivened with delightful touches of wit, like the enumeration of a prince's attributes in "Aut fatuum aut regem nasci oportere" ("Kings and fools are born, not made"):

"He is young"; that would recommend him as a bridegroom to a bride, not as a prince to the state. "He is good-looking"; that is the right praise for a woman. . . . "He has no equal in drinking"—for former princes actually delighted in this commendation! It would be fitter praise for a sponge. "He is tall, and stands head and shoulders above the rest"; that's splendid, if one wants to reach something down from a high place. (Phillips 37–38)

Some of the most serious of Erasmus's *Colloquies* use this same technique of witty touches in passing: the horse in the funeral procession with his head tied down so that he appears to be looking along the ground for his absent master ("Funus"), or the passenger on the storm-tossed ship who makes an extravagant vow to a saint and tells his neighbor that of course he has no intention of honoring it—whispering so that the saint cannot hear him ("Naufragium"). Perhaps the best example of hilarious satire is "Abbatis et eruditae" (the Abbot and the Learned Lady), which ends with the peals of laughter of the intelligent, witty bluestocking who has just outargued the crass, ignorant abbot.

More will be said about humanism in chapter 3, but humanists were not the only Renaissance writers interested in laughter. The nonexistence of psychology, anthropology, and linguistics as discrete intellectual domains did not deter ancient and early modern specialists from formulating interesting theories of the comic, which are usually connected with one of two domains that may surprise us: medicine and rhetoric.

Although they agree that laughter is a *proprium hominis*, medical authorities since Aristotle had been unable to decide why we laugh, or what happens inside our bodies when we do. The sixteenth century was one of lively debate on the nature of laughter (is it a "passion de l'âme?" is it connected to "la joie," or not?), and on its physiological origin (the brain? the heart? the spleen?

the diaphragm?). These questions will be discussed in more detail in chapter 5, but we can already see that Renaissance attitudes to the problem of laughter were very different from ours.

Closely related to medical theory is the debated question of therapeutic laughter, which interestingly is being raised again in the 1990s. Can laughter actually promote healing? Is Dr. Rabelais presenting his books to us as a cure-by-means-of-laughter? As we shall see in Chapter 5, these questions have been little studied, and the connection between Rabelais and the only laughter theorist of the time writing in French, Laurent Joubert, has been (in my opinion) exaggerated.

The second domain, rhetoric, appears at first sight to be far removed from medicine. The principles of Ciceronian oratory, which will be analyzed in detail in chapter 4, have nothing to do with the principles of medicine. They deal with laughter as relaxation, as a weapon against anger, and as a means of persuading a judge, an adversary, or a reader. It is thanks to rhetoric that the Ideal Prince, from the Emperor Augustus to Alfonso of Aragon and Castiglione's Courtier, must have wit as part of his character, so that he can take a joke as well as make one. How curious, then, that many sixteenth-century medical authorities, including Joubert, were apparently unable to discuss the physiology of laughter except in the context of rhetoric; obviously, no other general context was available to them.

Although many Renaissance intellectuals shared the conviction of many of their modern counterparts that laughter is indeed a *proprium hominis*, their frame of reference for discussing the question was so different from ours that we need a great deal of information in order to appreciate it (which is why I hope that this book may make a useful contribution to Rabelais studies). But before tackling in detail the technical domains of humanism, rhetoric, and medicine, we need to ask ourselves precisely who laughs, and why, in Rabelais's fictional world.

Laughing Rabelais

"Un éclat de rire énorme" was the judgment on Rabelais of Victor Hugo, whose ex cathedra statements tend to mean less the more one studies them. This one is actively misleading, if it implies that characters in Rabelais laugh constantly. The impression that they do is still current today: "Ses sages imaginaires, Gargantua et Pantagruel, rient beaucoup," asserted Baraz in 1983 (143), while Roland Antonioli thought that for Rabelais "la sagesse ne lui semble [pas] concevable sans le rire" ("wisdom without laughter is inconceivable to him") (362).

Are these generalizations supported by the text? Not precisely. In the four books Grandgousier laughs once (G 7), Gargantua twice (P 3 and G 11), Pantagruel twice in the first book (26 and probably 15), never in the *Tiers Livre*, and once at the end of the *Quart Livre* (67; but in 9 he "cuyda perdre contenance" ["nearly burst out laughing"]). Frere Jean, that superbly comic character, laughs only once ("Et frere Jean de rigoller!" G 39). Panurge laughs (nastily) in P 16 and 17, and never laughs again until the end of the *Quart Livre* (67, probably).

Statistical research on this subject is hampered by Rabelais's use of "Ho!" and "Ha!" in a variety of circumstances, not all of which necessarily imply laughter. Grandgousier's "Ho! ho! ho! ho! ho!" in the middle of his impassioned prayer about Picrochole's invasion (G 28) must surely be an expression of grief, not of hilarity; whereas Gargantua's "Ho, ho, ho, ho! que suis ayse" at the birth of Pantagruel clearly does indicate laughter. And there are other doubtful cases, like Lasdaller's "Hin, hen!" in G 45. But even if we confine our attention to unequivocal laughter words, the results are, I think, unexpected.

If Rabelais's major characters laugh very little, a good many other characters do laugh. Many of them are anonymous: "les assistans" (P 14), "chambrieres" (P 22), the peasants of Touraine

(G 4), the domestics of three visiting nobles (G 12), shepherds (G 25), "les dames" who have played a trick on the "seigneur de Guyercharois" (QL 10), "chascun" in Basché's household (QL 14), or Homenaz's "filles" (QL 52). A number of others are episodic characters, mentioned only once: Epictetes (P 30), Tielman Picquet (TL 40), the Olympian gods (QL Prologue), Breton Villandry (QL 11), Philomenes and Zeuxis who died of laughing (QL 17), and "Messere Pantolfe" (QL 67). Even the giants' merry companions seldom laugh or smile: Epistemon "commencza soubrire" in P 27, and in TL 34 recounts his laughter at the "morale comoedie de celluy qui avoit espousé une femme mute" (Moral Comedy of the Man who had Married a Dumb Wife). Carpalim laughs at the Hans Carvel story in TL 33; Eudemon and Ponocrates roar with laughter at Janotus de Bragmardo's speech, as does Janotus himself (G 20).

So any impression of "un éclat de rire énorme" proves to be wide of the mark. Critics also tend to assume that all laughter in Rabelais is good—an indication of good health, good humor and a sound moral outlook. This is again misleading; of the explicit laughter in the four books, some is frivolous, some healthy, and some (Panurge's in particular) so unkind as to indicate a disagreeable character. Homenaz's unpleasant laughter in QL 53 is deliberately put in a context of physical effluvia: "Icy commença Homenaz rocter, peter, rire, baver et suer" ("Here Homenaz began to hiccup, fart, laugh, dribble and sweat"). This, as we shall see later, is what doctors called *immodicum risus* (De Rocher), and a far cry from the benevolent laughter of the giants.

Many readers have noticed that laughter is commoner in Rabelais's earlier books than in the later ones. In P 26 "le bon Pantagruel ryoit à tout;" in TL 19 he refuses to laugh at the very funny story of Soeur Fessue. We are reassured, at the very end of the *Quart Livre*, to discover that he can still laugh (67). But in any case, *rire* is certainly not a key word for Rabelais.

Why, then, this general conviction, from Rabelais's own time to ours, that the four books are full of laughter? Most obviously because they are so funny that they make us laugh—and, as I hope this book will demonstrate, they were even funnier to their intended sixteenth-century readers than they are to us. Less obviously, as we will see in chapter 4, Rabelais is an accomplished rhetorician, and as all readers of Quintilian (*Inst. or.* VI.3.26) know, the good orator will make his audience laugh more effectively if he keeps a straight face himself. And lastly, readers have jumped to the conclusion that a true Rabelaisian key word necessarily implies laughter.

That word is *joyeux*, and words like *joie*, *joyeux*, *resjouir*, *esbaudir* and *guayeté* are three times more frequent, in Rabelais's text, than *rire*, *rigoller*, *ricasser* and *soubrire*. *Joie* is part of three definitions of *Pantagruélisme* (P 34, TL 51, and QL Prologue), and an essential element of the giants' attitude to life. It can, of course, also be bad rather than good, especially when Panurge or Homenaz are *joyeux*, but most often it comes close to the Christian ideal of joyful confidence in God and His Gospel. Laughter may very well accompany this joy, but it need not do so.

Rabelais's characters may not laugh as much as has been assumed, but Rabelais's readers have always laughed, and we can hope that they will always do so. This book is intended to provide still more reasons for them to laugh, and will, it is hoped, help to refute some tenacious misunderstandings about *Gargantua and Pantagruel*. Perhaps the most difficult of these to combat is the typically modern conviction that in any given passage Rabelais is *either* serious *or* humorous. Milan Kundera takes it for granted that "religion and humor are incompatible" ("The Day Panurge No Longer Makes People Laugh," in *Testaments Betrayed*), and as recently as 1987, as sound a critic as Paul Smith can state, "dans le cas de Rabelais, il reste toujours difficile de séparer le sérieux du comique" ("in Rabelais's case, it is always difficult to separate the serious from the comic," 200). One premise of this book is that we need make no such attempt; Rabelais is very often being simultaneously serious and humorous, and indeed using his wit to reinforce his serious message.

The general conviction that *Gargantua and Pantagruel* is packed with laughter makes it all the more curious that so little attention has been given to the comic by Rabelaisian critics. Only four books are devoted entirely to the subject, and each is fundamentally unsatisfactory. Marcel Tetel's *Etude sur le comique de Rabelais* (1964) is a superficial general discussion, overdependent on Baudelaire and Bergson, which assumes that Rabelais has no deeply held religious convictions, and implies that it is pointless to try to connect humor and serious intent (see the review by Screech in *ER* 6, 64–66). Michel Butor's promisingly titled *Rabelais ou c'était pour rire* (1972) is a lively overview of the main humanist themes in the work, very readable but with nothing illuminating to say on comedy.

In 1979 Gregory de Rocher undertook to relate Rabelais's comedy to contemporary medical theory (*Rabelais's Laughers and Joubert's Traité du Ris*). Although he points to some cogent connections between Rabelais and Joubert (whose treatise was not published until 1579, long after Rabelais's death), De Rocher's book fails to take into account both much other sixteenth-century medical theory (see my chapter 5), and even more importantly the Ciceronian rhetorical tradition that underlies Joubert's theories (see my chapter 4). Nor can I endorse his conclusion, that laughter requires "mixed feelings over something" (140).

Colette Quesnel has recently attempted a general study of laughter in Rabelais: *Mourir de rire d'après et avec Rabelais* (1991). Again, the title sounds more promising than the book turns out to be. The overview of theories of laughter is much too brief; the author assumes that *joie* for Rabelais always implies *rire*, which is not the case; and too much weight is given to a few, sometimes untypical, passages. Daniel Ménager's very interesting *La Renais-sance et le rire* (1995) is not mainly about Rabelais, and in his 1989 *Rabelais en toutes lettres* he devotes only six out of 179 pages to "la vision comique." Not surprisingly, then, Gérard Milhe Poutin-gon's 1995 survey of Rabelais criticism includes only three pages on "le comique."

Nor are there many scholarly articles dealing specifically with Rabelaisian comedy, although naturally the elucidation of intellectual content can lead to a better understanding of that comedy; this often happens with Screech, who has been quite unfairly accused of "taking the laughter out" of Rabelais. But it is not surprising that nearly all the solid scholarly contributions deal primarily with Rabelais's intellectual concerns rather than with his comedy, because it is obvious that to understand and appreciate that comedy, we need to read it in the context of his knowledge—of language, literature, rhetoric, law, and medicine in particular—as well as of his tastes and temperament. To recon-stitute even a small section of this context, at the end of the twen-tieth century, is an impossible task, but as the remaining chapters of this book will try to show, the attempt is in itself rewarding, and I hope may even be modestly illuminating.

CHAPTER 2

"Literary" Laughter

Should you ask me, whence these stories?
Whence these legends and traditions?

HENRY WADSWORTH LONGFELLOW

"Literary" Genres

The previous chapter assumed, for the sake of the argument, that literature is readily distinguishable from what is not literature. In France, this distinction can usually be justified for the Middle Ages, inasmuch as Chrétien de Troyes wrote in the vernacular and Thomas Aquinas and John of Salisbury in Latin. The distinction also works, on the whole (though for different reasons), for the seventeenth, eighteenth, and nineteenth centuries, but not, if I understand correctly, for this postmodern age, in which the problem is not to separate literature from technical writing but to separate it from critical theory. As Patricia Parker explains it, "the relation between the text of something called

29

(for better or for worse) 'literature' and something called (for better or for worse) 'theory' is anything but a *sens unique*" (Parker 7). Fortunately for our purposes, this debate need not (and in my opinion should not) be applied to Rabelais. In the sixteenth century, the problem is simpler: can literature be distinguished from technical writing on philosophy, theology, science, education, and other intellectual topics?

Rabelais was fundamentally a humanist, as we will see in more detail in chapter 3, and the humanists' constant refrain of the revival of Good (meaning Classical) Letters (*bonae literae*; Rabelais's "restitution des bonnes lettres," G 9) refers not only to Ronsard's Pindaric hymns and Alciati's epigrams, but to Petrarch's Ciceronian letters, Erasmus's *Colloquies* and *Adages*, and Paolo Cortesi's treatise on the Cardinal, written entirely in Ciceronian Latin. Sixteenth-century writers of treatises on poetry liked to pretend that Aristotle's categories, or their equivalent, still applied, but they knew as well as we do that large numbers of works of their time cannot be convincingly placed in any literary category.

As modern readers, most of us make a clear distinction between reading for enjoyment and reading to learn. If I sit down after supper with *DOS for Dummies*, that's work; if with an Agatha Christie, that's relaxation. Sixteenth-century intellectuals did not make this distinction; as we shall see later in this book, their after-supper reading might well be Budé's technical treatise on ancient Roman coinage (*De asse*), or Tiraqueau's on the legal niceties of marriage laws (*De legis connubialibus*).

So we need to forget our modern urge to classify written material as *either* literary *or* nonliterary. There is another modern distinction we also need to forget, at least for the purposes of this chapter: that between narrative literature intended to be read on the page, and dramatic literature intended for performance. A moment's thought will suggest that the distinction is necessarily blurred in any age of oral literature; at what point does the *réci-tant* stop "reading" and start "acting"? Hence the critical debates about the thirteenth-century *Courtois d'Arras;* is it a narrative or a little play?

Rabelais was writing less than a century after the invention of printing, when even solitary readers may well have still read aloud. He was also by temperament a writer of dramatic litera-ture, as we shall see below, but that is not the only reason why his narrative style often seems to shade into monologue or dialogue, as in this sentence of breathless *reportage* by Grandgousier's shep-herd about the invasion by Picrochole's troops:

> Un des bergiers qui guardoient les vignes nommé Pillot: se trans-porta devers luy en icelle heure, et raconta entierement les excés et pillaiges que faisoit Picrochole Roy de Lerné en ses terres et dom-maines et comment il avoit pillé, gasté, saccagé tout le pays, excep-té le clous de Seuillé que frere Jean des entommeures avoit saulvé à son honneur, et de present estoit ledict roy en la roche Cler-maud: et là en grande instance se remparoit, luy et ses gens.[7]

𝔔

> One of the shepherds who was guarding the vineyards, named Pil-lot, came before him at that moment and told him in full of the excesses and pillage that Picrochole, king of Lerné, was perpetrat-ing in his lands and domains, and how he had pillaged, devastated, and sacked the entire country, except for the close of Seuillé, which frere Jean des Entommeures had saved, to his honor, and at present the said king was at La Roche Clermauld and was there fortifying himself, he and his men, with great urgency.

We can almost hear the speaker gasping for breath by the end of the sentence.

By far the most common Renaissance "literary" form is the prose dialogue, which is by nature part narrative (it must expound the subject it is treating), and part drama (it presents several persons exchanging points of view). Modern attempts to classify this genre seem to me unsatisfactory (Kushner, Burke). Apart from the interaction of several speakers, it is not easy to see common literary characteristics in Erasmus's *Ciceronianus*, More's *Utopia,* and Castiglione's *Courtier.* The century produced (among many others) dialogues for schoolboys, dialogues on language (Speroni, Valdes, Henri Estienne); dialogues on philosophy (Le Caron, Pontus de Tyard, Spirito de Martino), science (Palissy), love (Leo Hebraeus, Estienne Pasquier), the nature of man (Gelli, Tahureau), and the truths of the Christian religion (Servet, Viret). Erasmus's *Colloquies* include in a single book serious symposia and debates on religion, lessons for women and boys, a joke anthology, and a lighthearted putdown of an abbot by a learned lady.

None of this is surprising, when we reflect that many of the Renaissance's favorite classical and Hellenistic authors wrote dialogues: Plato, Cicero, Lucian, Plutarch, and Macrobius, to name only the most influential. The dialogue was considered suitable for imparting information, for genuine debate, and for satire, and several scenes in *Gargantua and Pantagruel* are printed in dialogue form, like Panurge's conversation (one could hardly call it a debate) with Trouillogan (TL 36) and his bargaining with Dindenault (QL 6).

Even apart from dialogue, it is often difficult to assign Renaissance literary works to a particular genre. Geofroy Tory's *Champfleury,* ostensibly a manual for printers, is also an anthology of mini-essays on all kinds of humanist topics (Bowen 1983). So-called *facetiae* collections (joke-books; see chapter 3) are so diverse as to defy classification, and so are emblem collections, despite the unity implied by their tripartite structure of title, picture and explanation. To what genre could we assign Erasmus's *Adages?* Or Béroalde

de Verville's *Moyen de Parvenir?* Rabelais's own preferences are
clearly for literature which overlaps and muddles genres, hence
the label "Menippean satirist" which has often been applied to
him. His favorite ancient comic writer is Lucian, whose surviv-
ing works encompass dialogues, paradoxical encomia, essays, and
a mock-epic. And we have already noticed that *Gargantua and
Pantagruel* reads sometimes like an epic, and at other times like
a farce, a mirror-of-princes treatise, or a humanist encyclopedia.

To speak, in this chapter, of "Rabelais the narrator" separately
from "Rabelais the dramatist" is to enforce an artificial separation that our author himself would not have made. My justification is that both facets of Rabelais tend to be neglected, perhaps
as seeming too obvious to require further study, and that each
seems to me worth some detailed attention.

Narrative Laughter

EPIC / ROMANCE / CHRONICLE

Our problems are not over, even when we have artificially separated Rabelais's comic narrative from his comic theater. By the
sixteenth century, literary narrative had been flourishing for over
three thousand years (the Epic of Gilgamesh dates to perhaps
2,000 B.C.E.). But although, at least since Aristotle, epic was considered the noblest of the major literary genres, it was not for long
the only expression of narrative. Antiquity already knew historical narrative, late antiquity obviously enjoyed romance, and
the Middle Ages produced epic, chivalric romance, and "historical" chronicle, in verse or prose, in Latin or the vernacular. So
that even without mock-epic, which arrived relatively late to
muddy the waters still further, "narrative" covered a broad field.

Epic, again at least since Gilgamesh, has always been concerned on one level with telling a story, and the "story" element

of Gilgamesh, the *Odyssey*, the *Aeneid,* and the *Song of Roland* still appeals to students today. As has often been pointed out, the plot of most Western movies and most science-fiction television episodes is no different from the basic epic plot in which a quest is successfully accomplished, virtue triumphs, and wickedness is punished.[8]

Rabelais, too, loves to tell a story, and his giants' adventures have moments of genuine excitement. Will Picrochole be defeated? Will the companions survive the storm at sea? But even while recounting dangers and heroic exploits, the narrator loves to poke fun at the whole epic tradition, be it Homeric (frere Jean hiding cooks in a Great Sow, QL 40), Virgilian (the Sibylle de Panzoust, TL 17) or Arthurian (Gymnaste has a sword called Kiss-my-ass, QL 41).[9] These are obvious "in-jokes," but Rabelais also mocks epic more subtly. A storm at sea is a standard epic motif, and Erasmus's version in "Naufragium" is genuinely suspenseful, even though it is told in recollection by a voyager who, obviously, survived it. Erasmus's ship breaks apart so that everyone is obliged to swim, many drown, and the general panic is nicely offset by the calm of the mother, who with her baby is one of the few saved. By contrast, in Rabelais's storm scene (QL 18–22) nothing terrible happens. The description of wild weather in chapter 18 is straight out of Aristotle; we learn from the dialogue of mountainous waves, broken masts and torn sails, but the ship remains afloat and no one is drowned. As many readers have seen, this lack of action[10] is delightfully comic in an episode whose moral is that man must *act* as "cooperateur" with God (chap. 23). It is Panurge's wild language that creates an effect of exciting action, so that we seem temporarily to have abandoned epic for theater.

There are many other "epic" touches in the four books. Because an epic hero is by definition larger than life, it was a fine comic idea to create heroes who are physically larger than life—especially if, as Stephens claims, these are the first good giants in European literature (but see Demerson 1993). *Pantagruel* and *Gargantua* can be divided into the standard three stages of epic (birth, education, and warlike exploits of hero). Both giants have the standard retinue of faithful attendants, who in Pantagruel's case retain something of the traditional one-attribute-per-person of epic and folklore: Carpalim personifies speed, Eusthenes strength, Epistemon wisdom, and Panurge trickery (P 24). (By the *Tiers Livre* Pantagruel's attendants are so numerous, because he has picked up those of his father in the previous book, that one wonders if they don't get in each other's way).

But where does epic leave off and chivalric romance begin? All we can say, and it has been said many times, is that numerous episodes in Rabelais can be seen as sly digs at epic or chivalric exploits, like the resurrection of Epistemon (P 30), which has been compared to the resurrection of Richard in the *Quatre Fils Aymon* (Febvre). In several chapters of the Picrocholine War, the companions employ standard military procedure and are obviously taking the conduct of the war quite seriously, but in G 36 the giant demolishes an entire castle with a large tree he is using as a stick, and in P 28 his son drowns an enemy camp with a "deluge" of urine—hardly epic feats.

Both epic and chivalric romance are fond of "marvelous" episodes, whether they are using Christian miraculous events (the angel who receives Roland's soul) or folklore motifs (Yvain's ring of invisibility). Narrating the impossible was already being mocked by Lucian in his *True History*, and Rabelais, very like Lucian, loves to insist on the veracity of his incredible story. Modern readers assume a generic difference between fictional narrative on one hand, and historical account, presumed to be objectively factual, on the other. Anything called a chronicle, we think, must be historical, and hence more or less accurate. Rabelais's readers were presumably less gullible; they must have enjoyed his frequent use of the word *chronicque* to refer to his giants' adventures, which, like Olivier de la Marche's *Memoires,* are ostensibly based on reliable ancient sources. Olivier begins his book: "Ie trouue par les anciénes Croniques . . ." (chap. I), and as early as his first Prologue Rabelais swears a horrible oath that every word of his *hystoire* is true, and threatens his readers with disease and the flames of hell "en cas que vous ne croyez fermement tout ce que je vous racompteray en ceste présente *Chronicque!*" ("in case you do not firmly believe all I will relate to you in this present Chronicle!"). Perhaps Thomas Nashe remembered this passage when he ended *The Unfortunate Traveller* with "if herein I have pleased any, it shall animate me to more paynes in this kinde. Otherwise I will sweare upon an English Chronicle, never to bee out-landish Chronicler more while I live."[11]

Now *chronicque* (several different spellings are possible) is a more interesting word than it has been given credit for (but see Céard 1988, and Gray 1994, 42). The extraordinary vogue of the *Grandes Chroniques de France*, which were begun at St-Denis in the twelfth century (Hay 65), showed no signs of abating in the sixteenth. Since 1476 they had been available in print under various titles, including *Les Chroniques de France*, also called the *Croniques de Saint-Denis* (Brunet I. 1867–70). The 1493 Anthoine Vérard edition is in three folio volumes printed in beautiful blackletter and copiously illustrated with (usually quite irrelevant) woodcuts. Although most of the text is devoted to the "history" of France, we are given in chapter 1 of volume I a succinct summary of the Trojan story, from Priam, who ruled in Troy 404 years before the foundation of Rome, to Brutus who conquered Brittany.

The 1517–18 Galliot du Pré edition of this chronicle is titled *Mer des histoires & croniques de France*, which is confusing because there is a separate, often similar work called simply the *Mer des histoires*, which according to Brunet is a translation of a Latin work called *Rudimentum noviciorum*, of about 1475 (IV.1449–50, cf. Céard 1977, 72). The first edition (1488) looks very like the *Chroniques de France*; similar elegant and very readable black-letter, two volumes instead of three, and even more elaborate engravings including numerous illustrated genealogical "chains," especially of kings of France. The author seems uninterested in Trojans, but has an astonishing (to modern eyes) scheme of world history, in six ages. The first age runs from the Creation to Lamech son of Methusalah; the second from Noah to Nembroth; the third from Abraham to the acquisition of the Holy Land; the fourth from David to Sedecias; the fifth from the Destruction of Jerusalem to Christ, and the sixth from Christ to 1483. This scheme dates back at least to Isidore of Seville (Hay 38), and as late as 1587 inspired Nicolas Vignier's chronological list, in his *Bibliothèque historiale*, of all historical events since the Creation (Schiffman 3). One can see, without really being able to imagine, that such a view of history springs from (or helps to form?) an intellectual outlook very different from our own.

But the blending of "history" into fiction is not confined to the overlapping of *Chroniques de France* and *Mer des histoires*. Bibliographers have often had problems with the classification of chronicles; Alain Bouchard's *Grandes Croniques de Bretaigne*, according to Brunet (I.1146–49), was classified by Lenglet Du Fresnoy as a novel, and by another author as chivalric romance (Bouchard is also a partisan of Trojan origins, and has the same six historical "ages" as the *Mer des Histoires*). Such confusion is understandable, if we look at a popular chivalric romance, twice edited just before the publication of *Pantagruel*: *La Treselegante Delicieuse Melliflue et tresplaisante hystoire du tresnoble victorieux excellentissime Roy Perceforest/ Roy de la grant Bretaiane* (sic)/ *fundateur du franc palais/ et du Temple du Souuerain dieu* (Paris, 1531).

This enormous work, which Rabelais may well have looked at though surely not read (although we do meet Perceforest "pissant

contre une muraille" in Epistemon's hell [P 30]) is the most extraordinary amalgam of pseudohistorical chronicle and chivalric
romance, which has been called a "véritable encyclopédie
chevaleresque" (Ménager 1989, 32, quoting Giraud-Jung 1972,
50). Its prologue, addressed "Aux tresexcellents/ belliqueulx/
inuictissimes & insuperables heroes françoys," is intended for
"tous bons esperitz amateurs de vertueux gestes," and somewhat
overworks the modesty *topos*: "ie ne vouldroye faillir a demon-
strer enuers vos excellences le bon desir que ay tousiours eu de
illustrer/ recommander/ et extoller le perpetuel renom de vos cel-
situdes . . ." ("I would not wish to fail to demonstrate towards
your Excellencies the good desire I have always had to illustrate,
recommend and praise to the skies the perpetual fame of your
Highnesses"). We know what fun Rabelais had with this kind of
fulsome phrase, but the author also salutes a number of humanists, several of whom (Gaguin and Bouchet) wrote chronicles.
    Perceforest and his brother Gadiffer, we learn in the Prologue,
were appointed kings of England and Scotland respectively by
Alexander the Great, and the very long story continues to juxtapose chivalric characters reminiscent of Chrétien de Troyes (Flori-
das, Gloriande, and so on) with historical or pseudohistorical
people (Julius Caesar, Brutus, Pontius Pilate, and the Emperor
Claudius). The plot, briefly summarized in the prologue, is packed
with adventures, battles, villains, lady-loves, enchanters, visions,
prophecies, "cheualereuses doctrines," and "grandes merueilles"
(a key phrase); and yet most volumes begin with a title like "Le
tiers volume des anciennes Cronicques Dangleterre/ faictz et
gestes du . . . roy Perceforest," and later volumes are full of sentences beginning "LAncienne hystoire racompte que . . ." or "LIs-
toire qui est ancienne et vraye nous fait ici mention que. . . ."
    Epic, romance, and chronicle are so closely intertwined that
to treat them as separable genres is misleading, however tempting it may be. Even Jean Céard, in three dense and fascinating

articles on Rabelais's debt to chivalric romance (1980, 1982, 1988), persists in trying to maintain a distinction which seems to me untenable. For instance, to which genre should we assign Jean Lemaire de Belges's *Illustrations de Gaule et Singularitez de Troie*, generally acknowledged as an important precursor of Rabelais? Céard (1980) has brilliantly deduced, from an apparently casual remark by the narrator in P 29 about "les fables de Turpin," that Rabelais is here making an important historiographical statement. He is rejecting the fictional elements of the traditional chronicle like Lemaire's, and its sources like the *Pseudo-Turpin*, in favor of the newer, humanist approach to history. Acceptance of this point does not mean, however, that we need go as far as Gilman and Keller, who see Lemaire and his chronicle as the unique butt of a series of episodes, and Rabelais's book as striker of the blow that killed the "chronicle" genre (see Lewis).

In fact, this last view shows considerable ignorance of the literary climate of the 1530s. Both chronicle and romance continued to be popular throughout the century. *Fierabras*, which Rabelais mentions, had twenty-six editions between 1478 and 1588 (Ménager 1989, 32, quoting Giraud-Jung 1972, 48). *Perceforest* was published at least twice in the 1570s (Servet 46), and in 1560 appeared the extraordinary romance/chronicle *Alector* by Barthélemy Aneau, now available in a magnificent critical edition by Marie Madeleine Fontaine. As already mentioned, marvels had been a staple of so-called factual narrative since long before Lemaire; in the fourteenth century "Sir John Mandeville" (whoever he was; presumably Rabelais's Montevieille in the Prologue to *Pantagruel*) happily puts green and yellow people, thirty-foot eels, and a lake formed by the tears of Adam and Eve, alongside factual descriptions of Constantinople and Bethlehem. And closer in time to Rabelais, Lemaire is far from the only exponent of such gems as that Gaul is one of four European kingdoms founded by Noah, who is the same person as Janus (as for instance Shem is the same person as Zoroaster), and that Hercules's wife Araxa was half woman and half snake.

Lemaire's most important, and perhaps to Rabelais most ridiculous, contention is of course that the French monarchy is directly descended from Trojan heroes. This belief, which inspired Ronsard's *Franciade* among many other works, was founded on sources at least as unreliable as the "fables de Turpin," like the spurious Annius of Viterbo (Stephens). Its rose-colored view of France's glorious past (and by implication, present) was anathema to humanists with a sense of historical perspective.

We can probably assume, then, that the *Grandes Chronicques* and their family of crude pseudo-Arthurian chapbooks were all part of an early sixteenth-century enthusiasm for romantic chronicles. The format, brevity and lack of rhetorical elaboration of the chapbooks suggest a reading public which was literate, but not humanistically educated, but who wrote them? Did Rabelais himself have a hand in some of them, as Huchon and Demerson believe? That might explain curious touches like the statement in chapter 11 of the *Grandes Chronicques* that Gargantua dined "legierement non pas comme font ung tas de gallans, mais en escoutant les belles parolles et honnestes jeulx et devises du Roy et des princes qui la assistoient" ("lightly, not like a lot of gallants, but while listening to the fine words and honorable games and devices of the King and princes who were there").

Rabelais's debt to the *Grandes Chronicques* has often been discussed, from its exordium, "Tous bons chevaliers et gentilz hommes vous debvez sçavoir que . . ." ("All you good knights and noble men need to know that . . .") through the enormous *jument* ("mare") made by Merlin for Gargantua, to the stealing of the bells of Notre Dame. The humor concentrates on size, sex, and extravagant topography, and is usually a little too crude for modern tastes: Gargantua puts enemy soldiers in "le fons de ses chausses" ("the bottom of his pants," 16); Grant Gosier, on noticing

Galemelle's "playe de nature" ("natural wound"), tells her "que il estoit barbier, et que de son membre feroit esprouvette pour sçavoir si la playe estoit parfonde" ("that he was a barber-surgeon, and that with his member he would make a test to find out if her wound was very deep," 6); Grant Gosier dumps a rock into the sea and creates the Mont Saint-Michel (8). Rabelais's appropriation of motifs and stylistic tricks, like the comic precision of huge numbers, would be humorous even if the sources themselves were not comic.

Given this proliferation of "chronicles" around the time Rabelais was writing *Pantagruel*, it is not surprising that his first two books are much preoccupied with the term. The word is used four times in the Prologue to *Pantagruel*, which is an extended paradoxical encomium of the *Grandes Chronicques*. By presenting his own book as "un peu plus equitable et digne de foy que n'estoit l'aultre" ("just a little more equitable and reliable than the other one"), Rabelais pokes fun at both the chapbook and his own work, and by implication at all other so-called chronicles. *Pantagruel* casts many a passing glance at chronicles: the "Cronicques" of "tous bons hystoriographes" (1); the "chronicques" of Pantagruel's ancestors, which tell the story of Geoffroy de Lusignan (5); the ridiculous title *Gestes des Roys de Canarre* by the ridiculous author Marotus du Lac, monachus (23); and numerous passing references such as "dit l'histoire que . . ." and "ceste histoire tant veridique," the already mentioned "fables de Turpin" (29), "ces tant veritables contes" (32), and "l'Histoire horrificque" (34). *Gargantua*, although its Prologue refers us back to the previous "joyeuses et nouvelles chroniques" and its first chapter to the "chronique Pantagrueline", has fewer such references: "les histoires antiques" (10), a comparison to the "gestes" of the Four Sons of Aymon (27), and the charming title *Supplementum Supplementi Chronicorum* (37). Once the war really gets under way, the epithets for our heroes are more chivalric than historical:

"nobles champions" (42), "nobles chevaliers" (54), and "chevaliers tant preux" (57).

The two later books seem to have abandoned the pastiche of chronicles, perhaps because the chronicles themselves were no longer so popular. We still find a few references to chroniclers, including the one to Enguerrant de Monstrelet's "fascheux compte" (TL 24) so illuminatingly discussed by Duval (1993). But Rabelais's terms for his books and their episodes are now as likely to remind us of *conte*, Virgilian epic, or theater as of chronicle. Throughout the four books, in fact, Rabelais's insouciant interchanging of chronicle, short story, epic, history, romance, and theater to characterize his "novel" is itself evidence that we cannot apply to him our modern need to distinguish carefully among all these genres. It is impossible, in any case, to decide in any given Rabelaisian sentence whether he is poking fun at epic, romance, or chronicle. To begin a chapter (G 42) with "Or s'en vont les nobles champions à leur adventure" ("Now the valiant champions are off to their adventure"), which would be a serious statement in, say, *Perceforest*, is hilarious when applied to a carousing and swearing monk whose next "adventure" will be getting hung up in a tree by his helmet. Frere Jean was apparently conceived from the beginning as (among other things) an anti-epic and romance hero, judging by the first description we have of him (G 27): "jeune, guallant, frisque, de hayt, bien à dextre, hardy, adventureux . . ." ("young, gallant, frisky, cheerful, very deft, bold, adventurous . . ."). All these adjectives would be more suited to Yvain or Perceforest than to a "moine claustrier"; a good monk, we feel, is definitely neither "guallant," "frisque," nor "adventureux," and why would he need to be "bien à dextre"? The enumeration continues, of course, with epithets which are comic for other reasons, but our first impression of frere Jean is that however improbably he is a chivalric hero.

I would like to end this section by quoting another work, related to both chronicle and romance, which is often cited for its influence on Rabelais, the *Disciple de Pantagruel* of 1538, from which Rabelais took numerous elements of the *Quart Livre* voyage: Bringuenarilles, the Andouilles, a monstrous whale, and (inevitably) a storm. The *Disciple* is considerably more "literary" than the *Grandes Chroniques*, and also much more fantastic; it is heavily indebted to Lucian's *True History*, and its elaboration of surrealist detail makes Rabelais's voyage appear pedestrian by comparison. It is also presented as a comic work; the running title of the 1538 edition is: "LE VOYAGE & Navigation que fist Panurge, Disciple de Pantagruel aux Isles incongneues & estranges, & de plusieurs choses merveilleuses difficiles à croyre qu'il dict avoir veues, dont il faict Narration en ce present Volume, & plusieurs aultres Joyeusetés pour inciter les lecteurs & auditeurs à Rire" ("THE VOYAGE and Navigation made by Panurge, Disciple of Pantagruel, to unknown and strange [or foreign] islands, and of many things marvelously difficult to believe which he says he saw, and which he narrates in this present Volume, and many other Jollities to incite readers and listeners to Laugh").

So we already have a lively melting-pot of adventure narratives for Rabelais to stir around: epic, chivalric romance, "chronicle," and chapbook. But however frequent his references to them, I do not believe that any was as important an influence on his own "chronicles" as yet another narrative genre: the mock-epic. This was apparently less congenial to the French, before the seventeenth century at least, than to the Italians, of whom Rabelais certainly knew two, Pulci and Folengo.

PULCI

The *Morgante,* often called the *Morgante Maggiore*, of Luigi Pulci, in its most complete version (1484) is an enormous poem in twenty-eight cantos that manages to be both a genuine epic and a witty burlesque. Like its distant ancestor, the *Song of Roland*, it is overtly Christian; it begins:

> In principio era il Verbo appresso a Dio

> In the beginning was the Word close to God,

and ends with a fervent hymn to the Virgin Mary. As in the later epics by Boiardo and Ariosto, every canto is packed with heroic adventures, perils, and battles, and there are many heroes and heroines besides Orlando, Rinaldo, and the giant Morgante, who is converted by Orlando in canto I.

Critics have long been aware of numerous details Rabelais may have taken from the *Morgante*: the monks helping the hero to slaughter pagans (III.73); the voice from heaven encouraging the hero (IV.12); the monstrous horse with wings (XIII.51); the storm during which Morgante holds the sail open as Pantagruel will brace the mast (XX.44); the whale killed by Morgante, which turns upside down when dead (XX.48); Marsilio's dream of conquest, which may have helped to inspire Picrochole's (XXV.193–95); the frequent encounters with wicked giants; and the standard epic use of hyperbole (Rinaldo and Ricciardetto, with the help of Baiardo, slaughter thirty thousand pagans at the battle of Roncisvalle, XXVII.76).

It is also obvious that the single most comic character in this wild and woolly story is an ancestor of Panurge. In canto XVIII Morgante meets Margutte, who when asked if he is a Christian or a pagan replies that he believes only in "la gola e'l culo e'l dado" ("the gullet, sex, and dice," 132), and that committing sins is his specialty. He has burglar's tools, robs churches (and in XIX.130 has pockets full of nefarious implements), but he has never been guilty of treachery (142).

Rather surprisingly, the virtuous Morgante accepts this disreputable character as companion, and a good part of cantos XVIII and XIX is devoted to their comic exploits, which include wrecking an inn, eating a unicorn, a giant tortoise, a monster, and an elephant, and playing assorted tricks on each other. They also, to be fair, rescue a young lady from a ravening lion and some giants, and restore her to her parents. But the emphasis is decidedly on the comedy, and many readers are disappointed when, as suddenly as he had appeared, Margutte dies (of laughing, XIX.149). Had Pulci perhaps been reproached with giving too coarsely comic a tone to his epic?

Many other witty touches enliven this action-filled story of virtuous Christians triumphing over treacherous infidels. At one point (XVI.59) Orlando reproaches Ulivier with behaving like the abbess who got up in a hurry in the night and put on her lover's underpants instead of her headdress (a well-known *fabliau* and farce plot). But the work as a whole cannot be called "Rabelaisian," in any of the senses of that term; its style is too even and consistent, and the frequently concrete vocabulary is not used for shock effect as it is by Rabelais.

FOLENGO

Much more difficult to discuss is the macaronic verse mock-epic *Baldus*, by the Italian humanist monk Teofilo Folengo. The difficulty lies not only in Folengo's language: more or less hexameters in a mixture of Latin and (often dialectal) Italian, but also in bibliographic problems I have discussed elsewhere (Bowen 1993 and 1995). Briefly: there is no extant MS of the *Baldus*, but there are four very different printed editions, the Paganini (1517), the Toscolana (1521), the Cipadense (1539?), and the Vigaso Cocaio (1552), published after Folengo's death in 1544. Obviously, this last edition could not have influenced Rabelais; unfortunately it is the only version easily accessible in modern editions. Even more unfortunately, it was the basis for the "translation" (adaptation, rather) called the *Histoire maccaronique de Merlin Coccaie* of 1606, which seems always to be quoted by French critics of Rabelais (Tetel 1988, Jeanneret 1987) with very misleading results. All this confusion could have been avoided, for in 1904 Thuasne devoted to Rabelais and Folengo a hundred pages full of sensible information and valid *rapprochements* (159–265). In any case no critic, to my knowledge, has seen quite how close Rabelais often is to Folengo, although Thuasne's "Tout le roman de Rabelais se ressent du poème de Folengo" ("Rabelais's entire novel shows the influence of Folengo's poem," 176–77) is much closer to the mark than Bakhtin's "A certain influence of Folengo on Rabelais cannot be denied, but it concerns superficial elements and, generally speaking, is not essential" (299–300). Essential, I believe, is exactly what it is.

A detailed analysis of this extraordinary work would fill a chapter, but perhaps a brief summary will be helpful. The Toscolana version (I am quoting a 1522 blackletter edition in the Rare Book Room at the University of Illinois) is divided into twenty-five cantos or *Macaronicae*. After a comic invocation to the Muses of Macaronic art, who live on a mountain larger than Mount Olympus, with a lake of milk, shores of butter, and cauldrons of perpetually cooking pasta, the story begins at Montauban in France. With a courtly tournament as background, the hero Guido, a descendant of the famous Rinaldus of Montauban, falls in love with Baldovina, daughter of the French king. They marry and flee to Italy, where Baldus is born, Baldovina dies, and Guido goes off to become a hermit, leaving his son to be brought up by peasants. The next nine cantos take place in Cipada and recount Baldus's youthful hooliganism, his friendship with the rogue Cingar, the giant Fracassus and the dog-man Falchettus, and their cruel tormenting of Baldus's "brother" Zambellus. Baldus is imprisoned, and cantos V through VIII detail tricks by Cingar which do nothing to advance the plot (for instance, disguising a pot of shit as a pot of honey), but tell us a good deal about Folengo's scorn for peasants, Jews, and monks. Eventually Cingar's trickery gets Baldus out of prison, and after an epic battle in the inn Baldus and Cingar escape from Cipada with a new companion, the noble Leonardus.

From this point the adventures follow each other so closely that a summary would be both inordinately long and probably confusing. Alongside the often-discussed episodes of the whale, the sheep-drowning and the storm at sea, which are obvious sources for Rabelais, there are adventures on land, on sea, and in the underworld that involve a huge cast of secondary characters, including a centaur, a wild man, mythological beings like the Furies and the god Aeolus, sorcerers and witches, devils, a personified Manto (the founder of Mantua), thirteen hundred pirates and assorted "real" people from all walks of life. Some of these adventures are fairly realistic, but most are completely fantastic. The companions find a cave containing a marvelous machine, which is a working model of the universe (canto XII); Leonardus is killed by two bears on order of the sorceress Muselina (XVI); a dragon turns into a beautiful woman holding a book (XX); tricks are played with stones of invisibility, and Cingar's nose grows to an incredible length (XXI); the companions float through the air to the house of Phantasia, which is held up by crickets (XXV). Some narrative coincidences are worthy of Voltaire; among the numerous "lost" characters miraculously rediscovered are Baldus's father Guido, who tells his story and immediately dies (XVII), and Baldus's two sons, Cingarinus and Marcellinus, whom Cingar stumbles on in the underworld (XXIII). These wildly unlikely events are interrupted from time to time by apparently extraneous material: a eulogy of Mantua and the Gonzaga (XII); a meeting with the helpful magician Merlinus Coccaius (Folengo's pseudonym), who tells part of the story in the first person (XX); a list of contemporary composers (XXI); the council-meeting of Ambition on the Guelfs and Ghibellines (XXIV–XXV). Fantasy and magic become ever more pervasive as the companions descend into a partly mythological underworld, but the story (in this version) has no conclusion; it merely ends in a pumpkin (*zucca*) where feigning poets have to have a tooth extracted for every lie they tell.

The tone of this farrago is constantly changing; courtly/chivalric in canto I, it is grittily realistic in II–X, erudite in XIII–XIV, and in the final cantos sometimes solemn and sometimes playful. Characters also change. Baldus the stone-throwing young delinquent evolves into Baldus the Christian warrior attacking the forces of darkness, whereas Cingar at different moments is a gratuitous practical joker, a courageous warrior, a sniveling coward, and a learned authority on astrology. Sometimes we seem to be reading a pseudo-epic, at other times a genuine epic, or a humanist treatise. The reader must constantly change intellectual gears, just like Rabelais's reader.

The general tone of the *Baldus*, however, is not as close to Rabelais as this summary might suggest. Folengo's battles are much more violent, often involving severed limbs flying through the air:

> Tu nisi per celsum palazzi monca solarum
> Brachia cernebas testas gambasque volare (X.cxiiij)

You would have seen nothing else flying high in the palace but severed arms and heads and legs.

Enemies are thrown out of windows or over buildings, tortured, or burnt to death (Muselina and Gilbecchus in XVIII). There is much more scatology, for which Folengo occasionally apologizes:

Ante foras Berte [Zambellus and Lena] pleno cum ventre cagabant
(Parce rogo lector mea si nunc musa puzabit) (V.lxxv)

On Berte's doorstep Zambellus and Lena defecated with full stomachs [Beg pardon, reader, if now my muse stinks]

This scatology is more often taken for granted:

[Cingar] totum se merdam reperit esse:
Nam cagarola solet procedere sepe spauentu (XXXIII.ccxxiiiv)

Cingar found himself covered with shit:
For shitting customarily accompanies fear.

Critics like Saintsbury who describe Rabelais's work as a "dunghill"
(see Chapter 1) have not read the *Baldus*. More interestingly, laughter is much commoner in Folengo than in Rabelais; lines like

Omnes astantes risu schioppare videntur (IV.lxiv)

All the bystanders were seen to burst out laughing

are frequent, and all the characters laugh from time to time:

De risu baldus schioppat: crepatque lonardus
Ac mercatores omnes strepitose cachinnant (XI.cxxv)

Baldus bursts out laughing; Leonardus hoots;
And all the merchants giggle noisily.

Even the fish laugh when the dead whale turns upside down (XIX.clxxxvi).

But if Rabelais's mock-epic is less fantastic than Folengo's, less action-packed and violent, less scatological and less overtly comic, it is still a very obvious descendant of the *Baldus*. Most obviously in the often-discussed similarity between the early Panurge of the first book and Cingar, who is introduced in II as descended from Margutte, "Accortus: ladro: semper truffare paratus" (Nimble; a thief; always ready to trick someone, lxixv), and with pockets full of *sgaraboldellis* used in his nefarious exploits. Like Panurge, Cingar is a chameleon of a character; a wily and sometimes vicious trickster, a courageous warrior when he and Baldus are besieged in the inn by the entire population of Cipada, a weeping bundle of fear on the ship during the storm, an erudite expounder of astronomy and astrology. In IV, when he sends Fracassus and Falchettus off to Turkey to enlist the Turks' aid to destroy Cipada, he says nonchalantly that of course if necessary they will all deny Christ and become Muslims (lxiij); in XX he confesses his sins devoutly to Merlinus Coccaius with the rest of the companions.

The gradual evolution, in the *Baldus*, from light-hearted adventure story to serious crusade, is not unlike the changing tone of Rabelais's four books. The Pantagruel who laughs at Panurge's obscene suggestion for building the walls of Paris (P 15) becomes the Christian hero devoutly praising the Eucharist (QL 65).

But no character or individual episode can account for the reader's impression that Folengo and Rabelais have produced the same kind of mock-epic. This impression is created in part by constant shifting of tone and perspective, but above all by the style. Writing in very different languages (but each is a personal, individually created language), they share a lively irreverence for the Great Books of Classical and Medieval Europe, which reminds us of Wodehouse ("It's like Shakespeare. Sounds well but doesn't mean anything," *Joy in the Morning*, chap. 16). Folengo loves to parody tags from Virgil, as in: "Arma: viri: tabuleque: et plurima gaza per undas" ("Arms, men, planks, and so many treasures into the water") or "Omnia vincit amor, tamen ipsa [hunger] superchiat amorem" ("Love conquers all things, yet hunger overcomes love") (XVI.clviv). The last part of the *Baldus* is an extended parody of Aeneas's descent into the underworld (as is Panurge's in the CL), and Virgil and Dante specialists would undoubtedly find many more verbal echoes than I can.

Despite the different languages, there are definite verbal parallels between the two authors. Rabelais's "que le cancre puisse te venir aux moustaches" ("may cancer get your mustache," QL 21) reminds us of numerous curses in Folengo: "veniat tibi cancar in occhis" ("may cancer attack your eyes," VII.lxxxviv), "cancar te mangiet" ("may cancer eat you up," XIX.clxxxviv), and so on. A number of characters are compared to frogs, and several are thrown down, or thrown over a building "veluti ranam" ("like a frog," X.cxiiv), as Loup-Garou will be thrown "comme une grenouille" ("like a frog") into the main square of the town (P 29). Similarly, Janotus de Bragmardo's escort of "troys vedeaulx" (pun on *veaux* [calves] and *bedeaulx* [beadles], G 18) recalls Tognazzus dragging Zambellus along "more vedelli" (IV.lxiiiv), and two incidents of the dying calling on saints (X.cxvi and XV.clii) make us think of the soldiers massacred by frere Jean in the vineyard.

Folengo's use of *fantaisie verbale* (see Bowen, "Rabelais and Folengo") is understated compared to Rabelais's (though both are essentially poets, in my view), but there are more close resemblances in their use of comic motifs, and in the author's attitude to his reader. Apostrophes to the reader are common in both, and for a brief period Merlinus Coccaius is the same kind of unreliable first-person narrator as Alcofribas.

References to tripe and *budelle*, as indeed to food in general, are frequent in both, although the extravagant food passages dear to Jeanneret are in the Vigaso Cocaio version, not the Toscolana; Falchettus runs like the wind to catch game for dinner (XV), as does Carpalim in P 26; there is a phony "resurrection" in VIII, and a forcible undressing (of Tognazzus in V) like Panurge's undressing of a monk in P 16. The much-discussed reaction of Pantagruel, at his first sight of Panurge, "Nature l'a produict de riche et noble lignee" ("Nature brought him forth from some rich and noble line," P 9), which is unconfirmed by anything we subsequently learn about Panurge, recalls the first description of "Leonardus nobilissimus" in IX: "valentus . . . clare Sanguine progenitus . . . virtuti deditus omni" ("valiant . . . born of noble stock . . . dedicated to all virtue," cviiijv). Two cantos later Baldus learns more about this noble origin, and swears eternal friendship with Leonardus (cxviij).

Such examples could be multiplied, but even beyond their frequency the kind of youthful zest each author brings to the recounting of outrageous adventures has a definite family resemblance. Each loves incident and anecdote for its own sake; Cingar's ruse for getting Baldus out of prison (IX) could have been employed at the end of IV; cantos V–VIII are exclusively occupied with Cingar's tricks, which (like Panurge's in P 16) have no bearing whatever on the plot. These cantos also allow Folengo to elaborate his scorn for gullible peasants, rapacious Jews, and monks who live like pigs, and give us a vivid picture of day-to-day country life in Italy.

I think the *Baldus*, either in the Toscolana or Cipadense versions, was often in Rabelais's mind as he wrote, and colored his presentation of giant heroes and their companions, Panurge's character and exploits, and individual adventures like the storm scene. It also encouraged him to produce a book quite unlike any previous French narrative fiction: what Pangloss might have called a satirico-philosophico-comico-humanist encyclopedia.

If I have given more space here to the *Baldus* than to epic, chronicle, or *chronique*, it is because Folengo and Rabelais seem to me to be kindred spirits, however odd that may sound. Did the fact that both were monks with Reformation sympathies (Lutheran sympathies, in Folengo's case) have anything to do with this? More probably, it is sheer coincidence that both had the same kind of enthusiasm for liberal causes, intellectual trivia, and sending up the swashbuckling adventure story that has always enchanted readers from the time of Homer to that of Umberto Eco.

There is, clearly, no way to characterize with any precision Rabelais's own narrative style by comparison with these related but very different narrative genres. His intended readers must have relished his disparagement of fantastically unreliable chronicles and wildly inventive romances, and his frequent passing references to epic, chapbook, and pseudo-epic. Whether the earlier literature to which he makes constant glancing references was entirely serious, like Lemaire de Belges and the *Mer des histoires*, or already parodic, like the chapbooks, the *Disciple de Pantagruel*, Pulci, and Folengo, does not seem to matter; all were grist to the mill of Rabelais the master of witty narrative.

Laughter on Stage

Whether or not Rabelais actually said on his deathbed: "Tirez le rideau, la farce est jouée" ("Draw the curtain, the farce is over"), there can be no doubt that his four books are profoundly theatrical. Numerous chapters consist only of direct speech; as already noted, the action (such as it is) of the storm scene is conveyed in exclamation and apostrophe, not in narrative; and most of Rabelais's vivid episodic characters, from the *écolier limousin*

through Janotus de Bragmardo, Her Trippa and Bridoye to Dindenault and Homenaz, come alive through their speech rather
than through description of their appearance or actions; the
exceptions are the Sibylle de Panzoust, who is described at some
length, Nazdecabre the deaf-mute, and Thaumaste, who keeps
silence through nearly all of his long scene with Panurge.

Orality does not inevitably imply theater—it can imply rhetoric,
as we will see in chapter 4. But critics have long agreed that
"Rabelais et le théâtre" is a fruitful topic. Floyd Gray rightly stresses the ties of the *Pantagruel* prologue to the tradition of the classical *histrio* or *prologus* (Gray 1986, 15), and Rabelais's frequent
emphasis on the sense of sight (Gray 1974, 32). It is obvious that
Rabelais *sees* gestures, like a stage director: the Sybil throwing up
her skirts to moon the companions; Couillatris with his face turned
up to heaven, bareheaded, arms raised, fingers spread out (QL,
Prologue); even Panurge imagined by Pantagruel in TL 10, blind-
folded, bowing his head and kissing the earth. The first book is
already packed with lively dramatic scenes, including Gargantua's pro–contra monologue (3), the nonsense debate between
Baisecul and Humevesne (11–13), the sign debate with Thaumaste (19), and all Panurge's other *mises en scène*. Panurge is presented from his first appearance, like Cingar before him, as a
farceur specializing in multiple roles: erudite polyglot (9), dash-
ing adventurer (14), gratuitous practical joker (16, where we learn
that he is a former snake-oil salesman), phony courtly lover (21),
military strategist (25), satirical poet (27), *conteur* (29), gifted heal-
er (30), and theater director (of Anarche's destiny and marriage, 31).

Gargantua has a more sober and less farcical tone, but also
contains some dramatic gems: the *propos des bien-yvres* (5), Janotus de Bragmardo's extraordinary speech, punctuated by cough-
ing and spitting (19), Picrochole's council meeting (33, superbly
staged by Jean-Louis Barrault and before him by a group of Sor-

bonne students in 1967 or '68), and frere Jean's hilarious monologue at supper (39). Passing references to the comic theater include
the comparison of Janotus to Pathelin (20), Gargantua's obser-
vation of *bateleurs* (carnival entertainers) on days too wet for physical activity (24), and Gymnaste's performance as *bateleur* to impress
the enemy soldiers (35).

The *Tiers liure des faictz et dicts Heroïques du noble Pantagruel* (Third Book of the Heroic Deeds and Sayings of the Good Pantagruel) contains no *faictz*, heroic or otherwise; it is the only "novel"
before *Tristram Shandy* consisting entirely of talk. Nevertheless,
and despite the prevalence of Pantagruel's enormous (and very
undramatic) monologues, the book is full of delightful conver-
sations that frequently would go over rather better on stage
than the often stilted dialogue of Jodelle's *Eugène* or Grévin's *La
Trésorière*. The rhyming dialogue between Panurge and Pantagruel (chap. 9) is potentially good theater, as is the Trouillogan-
Panurge "debate" (36) and a number of *contes*, including Soeur
Fessue (19), Hans Carvel (28), and Seigny Joan (37). An instructive comparison may be made with an English version of Hans
Carvel's ring (*Tales and Quicke Answeres*, 1532?) which runs as follows (Bowen 78)[12]:

> A man that was ryght iolous on his wyfe, dreamed on a nyght as he
> laye a bed with her & slepte, that the dyuell aperd vnto him and
> sayede: woldest thou nat be gladde, that I shulde put the in suretie
> of thy wyfe? yes sayde he. Holde sayde the dyuell, as longe as thou
> hast this rynge vpon thy fynger, no man shall make the kockolde.
> The man was gladde thereof, And whan he awaked, he founde
> his fynger in his wiues ars.

This might be called a "bare-bones" version; it gives only the facts
necessary to render the denouement comprehensible. By contrast, Rabelais's version (an entire page in the Huchon edition)

is a torrent of verbiage. We learn first what kind of person Hans Carvel is, both physically ("ventru quelque peu, branslant de teste, et aulcunement malaisé de sa persone" ["a wee bit paunchy, nodding his head, and rather awkward in his person"]) and psychologically ("docte, expert, studieux, home de bien, de bon sens, de bon jugement, debonnaire, charitable, aulmonsnier, philosophe: joyeulx au reste, bon compaignon et raillart, si oncques en feut" ["a learned, expert, studious man, a worthy man, with good sense and good judgment, genial, charitable, giving alms, philosophical, moreover blithe, a good companion, and a joker if ever there was one"]). This is lively narrative, but also good stage-setting; we can visualize Hans Carvel the actor at the start of the play. The narrator, frere Jean, tells us less about the wife: she is "jeune, belle, frisque, guallante, advenente, gratieuse par trop . . ." ["young, pretty, frisky, gallant, attractive, much too gracious . . ."], a stereotype, whereas Hans Carvel is a character. Is it a coincidence that this description recalls the first description of frere Jean himself in G 27? The monk then relates Hans's jealousy, and his efforts to convince his wife of the necessity of fidelity, which are a close parallel to the efforts of Molière's Arnolphe.

Then we are told about his dream, and the narrative becomes a dialogue between Hans and the Devil. Hans, the "studieux," knows exactly how to talk to "monsieur le Diable:" "Je renye Mahon, si jamais on me l'oste du doigt" ["I'll deny Mahomet if anyone ever takes it off my finger"]. And the story ends with a description of the wife's convulsive movements to get rid of the finger, which "n'est ce qu'il y fault mettre" ["is not the thing to put there"]. A delightful combination of narrative and theater, typical of the *contes* which have replaced the *chroniques* in Rabelais's last two books.

The *Tiers Livre*, from the *tragicque comedie* of the Prologue through Panurge's three quotations from *Pathelin* (7, 9, 34) to the reference to the *Mystere de St. Martin* in 47, is a highly theatrical book. And so, even more profoundly, is the *Quart Livre,* preceded as it is by the much-discussed dedication "A tresillustre Prince et Reverendissime Mon Seigneur Odet, Cardinal de Chastillon." I will have more to say in chapter 4 about this epistle's presentation of the doctor-as-orator, but it is at the same time portraying the doctor-as-stage-director, a concept going back to Hippocrates, who compared his art to "un combat et farce jouee à trois personnages: le malade, le medecin, la maladie" ("a combat and farce played by three personae: the patient, the doctor, and the illness"). The conflation of farce with combat is interesting; the only other farce besides *Pathelin* which Rabelais quotes by name, the "morale comoedie de celluy qui avoit espousé une femme mute" (TL 34), in which Rabelais himself was an actor (though Epistemon does not make clear how the eight actors listed managed a *patelinage* which has only three roles), may explain why he thought of the basic farce plot as a "combat."

The story of Couillatris (who also quotes Pathelin) in the Prologue is already good theater, as is the Chiquanous episode (Lauvergnat-Gagnière 237) and even more so the Villon story (13), the whole point of which is that Villon and his fellow-actors take revenge on a hater of the theater. The drama staged by Basché and his household is referred to as both a "Tragicque comedie" (12) and a "tragicque farce" (13).[13] Even closer to farce, and announced in advance by Panurge as a dramatic performance ("Il y aura bien beau jeu, si la chorde ne rompt" ["There will be fine sport if the line doesn't break"[14]]), is the Panurge-Dindenault dialogue of chaps. 6–7, the first part of which is printed as though it were a play, and which is reminiscent of a farce called *Le Marchand de pommes,* whose merchant persists in vaunting the qualities of his apples to two housewives who want only to buy eggs.

Other episodes which could easily be little plays include the storm scene, including its reference to "Tous les Diables" who "dansent aux sonnettes"("All the devils are doing a morris dance,"

19), as in a mystery play, the genuinely suspenseful drama of the peasant of Papefiguiere and the little devil (45–47), the banquet in Papimanie (52), and the Carnival procession of Gaster's faithful servants (59). Bakhtin would see almost all the theater references in Rabelais as carnival-related, but this is an overly narrow view; more fruitful is Carol Clark's suggestion that Rabelais's fondness for "litanies" or what Amory calls "hurricane word-formations" may well owe something to the visual effect of carnival processions. In any case, this theatrical atmosphere is again surprising in a book in which once again nothing constructive happens; the companions proceed from island to island and from one surrealist encounter to the next, without coming any closer to their goal, the Oracle of the Dive Bouteille.

Where then, if I am right in seeing so much theater in Rabelais's four books, does it come from? A good deal of critical attention has been focused on French farces and mystery plays, but that is not the whole story by any means. Let us take a look at some other theatrical genres Rabelais knew, or may have known.

OLD COMEDY

The case of Aristophanes is particularly intriguing. Rabelais owned a copy of the *Plutus* (Plattard 175), and quotes from the *Knights*, the *Clouds*, the *Wasps* and the *Ecclesiazusai*. Plattard points out that these quotations could have come at second hand from commonplace books, but *Knights*, in particular, has numerous jokes about tripe and sausages, and it ends with the punishment of Paphlagon (Kleon), who is forced to become a sausage-seller (as Anarche at the end of *Pantagruel* is forced to become a crier of green sauce). Critics have unanimously concluded that there is no discernible influence of the plays on Rabelais, despite the fact that Du Bellay called Rabelais "Celuy qui fait renaitre Aristophane" (*Deffence et Illustration*, II.12). In many ways the two writers seem to me so alike that I chose Aristophanes for my illustrative analogy in chapter 1.

To begin with, both are what today we would call surrealists. Ordinary people from real life (father and son, slaves and women, Panurge and frere Jean) interact with monsters, giants, mythological and historical characters, birds, clouds, Bringuenarilles, Quaresmeprenant, managing in both cases to make the impossibly surreal appear somehow normal and plausible. Secondly, both are ferocious satirists, mercilessly ridiculing tyrants, politicians, scholastics, or the Sorbonne. Imagine how much more merciless Rabelais's satire could have been at a less dangerous moment in history. Among other satirical techniques, Aristophanes could have bequeathed to Rabelais the monomaniac character; Philocleon in the *Wasps* may well be a distant ancestor of Bridoye and Homenaz.

Both also, I think, handle language in the same kind of way. There are no good translations of Aristophanes, even the ones that make him sound like W. S. Gilbert, because every line contains a political allusion and at least one witty word-play. Both form hilarious proper names whose meaning is readily apparent (Philocleon = fanatical supporter of the tyrant Kleon; Picrochole = evil man dominated by his excess of black bile). And both love the throwaway pun-in-passing that simply cannot be conveyed in another language.

Aristophanes also seems to me to share something of Rabelais's essential lightheartedness, even when the abuse under attack is seriously threatening. This lightheartedness can be conveyed in puns and word-play, by the often gratuitous obscenity which both love, and by the rapid changes in tone, from serious to frivolous, so common in both. I should be delighted but not surprised if some day a scholar with much better Greek than mine discovered, after all, that Rabelais had read and thoroughly appreciated his great predecessor.

Plautus is another author who tends to come to mind when the lowborn trickster is outwitting the rich and powerful, and it is interesting that of Rabelais's six explicit citations of Plautus

(Plattard 225–26), one occurs immediately after a reference to Aristophanes (QL 64). This particular juxtaposition probably derives from an adage of Erasmus (III.4.70), but it also suggests that Rabelais may have seen affinities between the two.

The Renaissance, like the Middle Ages, usually preferred Terence to Plautus, but we are not surprised at Rabelais's preference for the latter (Plattard lists two quotations from Terence, but both are Erasmian adages, and such frequent commonplaces that to use them did not imply having Terence in mind). Terence wrote heavily didactic "bourgeois comedy," whereas Plautus created witty, lively, usually amoral, but eminently actable farce. His clever fusing of the sentimental elements of New Comedy with the slapstick and obscenity of popular farce is still highly effective on stage today, and both Erasmus and Rabelais, I believe, had theater in their bones.

Panurge's relationship to Pantagruel is not unlike a Plautine slave's to his master (with overtones of the Roman parasite's restive obsequiousness), and several of Panurge's ruses could be inspired by those in the plays. Panurge, like Strobilus in the *Aulularia* or Palaestrio in the *Miles gloriosus*, has no fundamental moral sense; he simply takes each situation as it arises and deals with it as ingeniously as he can.

But quite apart from questions of character, I would claim that Rabelais, like Plautus and like the farce authors discussed later, had an instinctive "feel" for a scene that would play well. Christiane Lauvergnat-Gagnière refers to the Chiquanous episode as "une bonne farce montée comme au théâtre" (237), and we could say the same of many other episodes just mentioned.

FARCE

I am certainly not claiming the ability to distinguish definitively between Plautine dramatic effects, and those of French farce, in Rabelais. Moreover, as noted above, *Pathelin*, quoted or explicitly referred to by Rabelais a dozen times (Plattard 324–25), may well be more "Plautine" than it has been given credit for, and other farce authors (about whom we still know very little) may have been familiar with Plautus.

So-called French farce is an extremely disparate genre. Its heyday was 1450–1550, but its ancestor was the brief, brutal *Garçon et l'aveugle* of the late thirteenth century, and several farcical interludes in mystery plays date before 1450. Many French humanists disapproved of farce; La Boétie refers disparagingly to "Les théâtres, les jeux, les farces, les spectacles, les gladiateurs . . . et autres telles drogueries" ("Theaters, games, farces, spectacles, gladiators . . . and such-like trash," *Discours de la servitude volontaire*, Garnier-Flammarion edition, 155). Rabelais's close familiarity with *Pathelin* might suggest an enthusiasm for the genre in general, but apart from the "patelinage" mentioned above, about the curing of the dumb wife, he refers to very few other farces. In the Saint-Victor library, "Franctopinus, *De re militari, cum figuris Tevoti*" suggests *Colin fils de Thevot le maire*, a farce of which we have several versions, *Maneries ramonandi fournellos* (see chapter 3) could be a reference to the *Ramonneur de cheminées*, and *L'Invention Saincte Croix* is the name of a real play. It would be as easy, and as purely speculative, to postulate his debt to the contemporary *sottie* as to the farce.

His references to *Pathelin*, however, show a keen appreciation of the witty language characteristic of the play. Only one reference is to the plot, when Janotus de Bragmardo carries off the cloth Gargantua has given him "en tapinois, comme feist Pathelin son drap" ("furtively, as Pathelin did his cloth," G 20). All the other quotations (except the simple mention of Pathelin in the underworld, serving as treasurer to Rhadamanthus and stealing pies from Pope Julius II, P 30) are to key phrases in the farce. In the *parolles gelées* ("frozen words," QL 55–56) episode, at the end of a dazzling series of word-plays on *mot* and *parole*, "Panurge fascha quelque peu frere Jan, et le feist entrer en resverie, car il le vous print au mot sus l'instant qu'il ne s'en doubtoit mie, et frere Jan menassa de l'en faire repentir en pareille mode que se repentit G. Jousseaulme vendent à son mot le drap au noble Patelin" ("Panurge angered frere Jean quite a bit, until he was beside himself, for he took him at his word at the moment when he least expected it, and frere Jean threatened to make him sorry for it the way G. Jousseaulme was sorry he sold the cloth on his word to the noble Patelin"). Pathelin is hardly *noble*, but then Panurge himself apparently has pretensions to nobility, if we may judge by his desire in TL 10 to bequeath his "nom et armes" to his son! Panurge's "il le vous print au mot" summarizes the essential plot of the play; first, Pathelin promises to pay Guillaume for the cloth, and also promises him roast goose, but as the audience knew and as Rabelais makes clear when he has Panurge say in TL 30: "Et si mangerons de l'oye, cor beuf que ma femme ne roustira poinct" ("and we'll have goose to eat, and my wife won't roast it!"), the expression *faire manger de l'oie à quelqu'un* meant "to make a fool of someone." Pathelin and Guillemette, together, do indeed make a fool of Guillaume, but when the shepherd asks Pathelin for help he promises (twice) to pay him "à vostre mot," only to end the play by paying him indeed, not *at* his word, but *with* his word, the "Bée!" Pathelin instructed him to repeat to the judge in order to get his case dismissed.

Among the other Pathelin quotations, several are to phrases so celebrated that they had already passed into current usage by Rabelais's time: "J'entens, par mon serment, de laine" (P 12), "six solz et maille qui ne virent oncq pere ny mere" P 17), and "Retournons à noz moutons" (G 1). I would reject Plattard's last phrase, Janotus's "Nous les faisons comme de cire" (G 19), as being such a common cliché that it need not be referred to *Pathelin*.

I suggest, then, that it was the playing with words, and in particular the playing with clichés, that Rabelais found most attractive in French farce. Taking metaphorical or idiomatic expressions literally is very common indeed in farce, in that a standard characteristic of the farce fool is his (always his!) ignorance of the simple fact that language can be metaphorical. Besides the often-quoted examples of Mahuet Badin, who gives his eggs to a man sharp enough to say to him "My name is Market Price," and Jean who jumps on his mistress's back to "lead" her to market, we have at least one whole play based on this technique. In *La Farce de l'Arbalète* a wife tries to "improve" her husband by dinning certain precepts into him, a project doomed to failure because he takes all her advice literally. "You must ripen (*mûrir*, mature) your head," she says, so he puts on a little straw hat like the ones farmers use to ripen fruit. If she tells him to "macher l'escripture Et gouster le sens" he begins to chew on a Bible; when adjured to "parler a traict" (deliberately, soberly), he starts talking to the arrow on his crossbow, and so on.[15]

This is the same technique, sometimes called "le proverbe en action," often used by Rabelais, especially in the *Quart Livre*. The Bringuenarilles chapter (17) is based entirely on a literal reading of "nous ne trouvasmes que frire" (we found nothing cooking/to cook/to cook with), an idiom meaning simply "we couldn't find a single thing." Similarly with the Ruachians who literally "ne vivent que de vent" ("live on nothing but wind," QL 43), and when Pantagruel "rompoit les andouilles au genoil" ("broke the sausages over his knee,"[16] QL 41) he was acting out a cliché meaning to waste one's time doing something frivolous or futile (Brueghel's equivalent is "beating the water with an eel," in *Flemish Proverbs*).

Rabelais did not, of course, need to read a farce anthology in order to pick up this technique, variants of which already occur in Aristophanes and Lucian, writing in Greek, and Plautus, writing in Latin. But there is one remaining theatrical genre that I suspect he knew very well.

MONOLOGUE

When theater, especially Renaissance theater, is discussed, dramatic monologue tends to get left out (on the grounds that it isn't "real" theater?). Plattard does not even mention the most celebrated monologue of the time, the *Franc-archer de Bagnolet*, which frere Jean quotes once (G 42: "Je ne crains rien fors l'artillerie," ["I'm not afraid of anything except artillery"]), and Panurge twice (QL 23 and 55). The *Franc-archer* belongs to a small group of monologues that are genuinely dramatic. The soldier begins by complacently recounting his military exploits and his non-heroic attitude:

> Par le sang bieu, je ne crains page
> S'il n'a point plus de quatorze ans (12–13),

> Good grief, I don't fear any page—
> As long as he's not older than fourteen,

and

> Je ne craignoye que les dangiers,
> Moy; je n'avoye peur d'aultre chose (99–100)

> Me, I was only afraid of danger;
> I had no fear of anything else.

He uses military imagery ("le coullart") to boast at length of his sexual prowess, and is planning an assault on a henhouse when he suddenly notices a scarecrow, which he mistakes for a soldier; presumably it is wearing a military uniform of some kind. He at first sees a white cross and assumes the soldier is French, but then realizes it has a black cross, the Breton emblem, on the back; his attempts to placate the imagined enemy are hilarious:

> Dea! je suis Breton si vous l'estes:
> Vive sainct Denis ou sainct Yve!
> Ne m'en chault qui, mais que je vive! (209–11)

> Hey! I'm a Breton if you are;
> Long live Saint Denis or Saint Ives!
> I don't care which, as long as I can live!.

Convinced the *gendarme* is going to kill him, he makes a comic confession, and even when the scarecrow falls over, he still thinks it is human, and calls the audience to witness that he has not touched it. Finally, he realizes the truth:

> Par le corps bieu, j'en ay pour une!
> Il n'a pié ne main, il ne hobe;
> Par le corps bieu, c'est une robe (341–43)

> By God's body, I've been taken in!
> He doesn't have foot nor hand, he can't move;
> By God's body, it's just a dress,

and staggers off carrying the scarecrow, with the usual farce *envoi* to the audience.

This monologue is truly a little play, and still an excellent choice for performance today.[17] But Rabelais doubtless had seen and heard many other comic monologues, from specifically Carnival pieces like the *Testament de Carmentrant* (ed. Aubailly) to the frequently obscene *sermons joyeux* with their imaginary saints

(Saint Raisin, Sainte Andouille) and their very explicit vocabulary:

Notable assistence, retenez
Ces motz pleins de devotion.
C'est touchant l'incarnation
De l'ymage de la brayette
Qui entre, corps, aureille et teste,
Au precieulx ventre des dames

𝟐

Noble spectators, keep in mind
These words full of devotion.
It's about the incarnation
Of the image of the codpiece
Which goes, body, ears and head,
Into the precious belly of the ladies.

This introduction to the *Sermon Joyeux de Frere Guillebert* (c. 1505; ed. Koopmans) is typical of the genre; this one also uses kitchen Latin, and a refrain: "*Foullando in callibistris*."

So we need to bear in mind that "comic theater" should include more than just farce. There are even interesting comic passages in some morality plays, most notably the *Condamnation de Bancquet*. The monologue, I believe, is particularly relevant to Rabelais, because it is both narrative and dramatic, and Rabelais was both fundamentally a storyteller and fundamentally a man of the theater. The cowardly, boasting Panurge is of course the latest of a long line of *soldats fanfarons* stretching back to Plautus's Pyrgopolynices, but when we listen to his exaggerated lamentation and outrageous complacency, we could easily be hearing the *franc-archer de Bagnolet*.

This rambling excursus through an assortment of narrative and theatrical genres is naturally not intended to be exhaustive. There is narrative in many other genres besides epic, romance and chronicle, and a number of Renaissance dialogues (especially Erasmus's, and those of German humanists which will be discussed in the next chapter) would make more effective plays than some of those actually written for the stage. All I have tried to do here is to broaden the perspective of literature Rabelais probably knew, and to stress that narrative and theater are often closer, in the sixteenth century, than modern readers would assume.

CHAPTER 3

The Comic Humanist

*What though his head be empty, provided
his commonplace book be full?*

JONATHAN SWIFT

From Humanism to Trivial Pursuit

P. O. Kristeller formulated his now-standard definition of Renaissance humanism in 1945. Since then his views have been developed, occasionally challenged, and nuanced, most recently by Benjamin Kohl (1992) and Erika Rummel (1995), but they have never seriously been undermined. Kristeller, Trinkaus, Baron, Monfasani, and other historians have explored in great detail the intellectual concerns, the political and religious affiliations, and the literary style of Italian, French, English, Dutch, Polish, and Hungarian humanists from Petrarch to Casaubon, so that we now have a much more accurate picture than ever before of what they thought about human nature, true religion, good government, and effective education. Humanists, by this definition, were primarily linguists, thoroughly trained in Greek and Latin language and literature and therefore capable of teaching them in a university or of intelligently editing classical (and in some cases biblical) texts. The humanists most read today are of course those, like Erasmus, Thomas More, and Rabelais, who were also deeply interested in humanity as a subject, but we should not therefore assume that all humanists thought of man as their central subject; many were far more interested in restoring lost iota subscripts, or in explaining anomalous uses of the past perfect subjunctive.

Some humanists, like Poggio, physically recovered lost manuscripts of classical texts; many, greatly aided by the recent invention of printing, produced authoritative critical editions, some of which are still quoted today; and relatively few wrote influential works on the subjects closest to their hearts: education, the Ideal Prince, good government, and Utopia. These subjects are frequently evoked by Rabelais, as they are by Erasmus in his very readable *Adages* and *Colloquies*, as well as in many other works.

Erasmus and Rabelais belong to a particular species, as it were, of humanist. Both are what we today call Evangelical Christians: genuinely religious, outraged by many attitudes, beliefs and practices of Catholicism, but unwilling to leave their Church even when it had become clear that Reformed churches were well established. Both were also able to express serious religious views humorously, which might lead us to assume that humanism and comedy were natural allies; but this is far from the case.

A few Italian humanists actively disapproved of laughter, as some Christians have always done (see chapter 1). Manetti, in the fifteenth century, denied categorically that laughter was proper to man (Trinkaus). Closer in time to Rabelais, Volaterranus (Raffaele Maffei) affirmed that tears were more suitable to the human condition than laughter. They were certainly in the minority;

as we shall see below, many humanists from Petrarch to Pontano collected *facetiae* and affirmed the value of laughter. But Petrarch, generally acknowledged then as now as the first great Renaissance humanist, was not primarily celebrated as a wit; nor were his illustrious successors Salutati, Valla, Bruni, or Alberti. Of the big names of Renaissance humanism, only the maverick Poggio goes down to posterity as a humorous writer. And the best-known French humanists of the sixteenth century: Guillaume Budé, Jean Dorat, Louis Le Roy, Pontus de Tyard, Adrien de Turnèbe, and Etienne Pasquier, were rarely humorous—although Turnèbe did write a commentary on the joke passage in Cicero's *De oratore*, and Pasquier immortalized *La farce de Maistre Pierre Pathelin*. The exception is Henri Estienne, whose *Apologie pour Hérodote* is full of scabrously comic anecdotes—with, naturally, a highly moral purpose. Others of his French works strike a modern reader as often hilarious, but when he claims that French has no need to import the word *poltrone* from Italy, inasmuch as the French are never *poltrons* (cowards; *Deux Dialogues*), or proposes that French and Italian sign a mutual treaty to defend themselves against the claim of Spanish (*Précellence*), I suspect that he is actually quite serious. As he certainly is in his far more numerous works in Latin (although the *Pseudocicero* begins on a playful note, with discussion of the terms *cauillari*, *iocari* and the disputed *facetosi*).

Although we must not assume that all humanists were capable of valuing wit and writing wittily, we know that Erasmus, Rabelais's intellectual mother as he put it himself, certainly was (see Chapter 1), and we know that for him laughter and religion, so far from being incompatible, were inextricably linked: "Vera hilaritas nascitur e pura sinceraque conscientia" ("true hilarity springs from a pure and sincere conscience," "Convivium religiosum"). We also need to beware of another myth about humanists, most influentially stated by Bakhtin, and that is that "humanist culture" was radically divorced from "popular culture." It is true, I think, that humanists in general were intellectual snobs—*odi profanum vulgus* ("I despise the vulgar rabble") might be their collective device—but it was not possible in the sixteenth century, as it is today, for intellectuals to live in an ivory tower and ignore the existence of miners, sailors, and cleaning ladies. Much more than today, all citizens were part of the same community, and that community, whatever its social class or location, was necessarily church-centered. The Church demanded participation, not just in its own rites and ceremonies, but in many kinds of collective activity, whether celebratory or expiatory. Rabelais's adoption of themes and language from marketplace, procession, and carnival is not, *pace* Bakhtin, an isolated expression of solidarity with the downtrodden lower classes against their oppressors.

We need only look at the language of Reformation polemic to be convinced that Rabelais, far from being an isolated instance, is actually typical of his generation of humanists. Luther, well known for his truculence of language, is said to have called Henry VIII *asinus* (donkey), *porcus* (pig), *faeces latrinae* (excrement of the latrine), and *scurra levissimus* (irresponsible buffoon; the epithet "most light" is charming for a man of the king's substance). Thomas More, whose Latin style in the *Utopia* is lively but never obscene, making a complicated joke about Luther's "posterior reasoning" in the *Responsio ad Lutherum* (I.10; play on Aristotle's *Posterior Analytics*), produces this magnificent sentence:

> Quum sibi iam prius fas esse scripserit, coronam regiam conspergere et conspurcare stercoribus: an non nobis fas erit posterius, huius posterioristicae linguam stercoratam, pronunciare dignissimam: ut uel meientis mulae posteriora lingat suis prioribus: donec rectius ex prioribus, didicerit posteriores concludere, propositionibus. (p. 180)[18]

🍐

> Since he [Luther] has written that he already has a prior right to bespatter and besmirch the royal crown with shit, will we not have the posterior right to proclaim the beshitted tongue of this practitioner of posterioristics most fit to lick with his anterior the very posterior of a pissing she-mule until he shall have learned more correctly to infer posterior conclusions from prior premises?

Would today's readers of the *Utopia* ever imagine its author capable of this kind of (very "Rabelaisian") invective?

The general, and very understandable, tendency of modern readers is to concentrate on Renaissance works which interest them, and to ignore those which do not. We read *Utopia*, and not the *Responsio ad Lutherum*; Erasmus's *Praise of Folly*, his essay-like adages, and some of his colloquies, but not his *De copia*, his *Lingua,* or his *Encomium medicinae*. But the last three, respectively a rhetorical manual, a moral sermon, and a rhetorical exercise, may well have been the works a sixteenth-century reader would have cited first. The *De copia* in particular was a bestseller for generations.

Or take the case of the French humanist printer Gilles Corrozet. If you check recent bibliography, you will find a dozen articles on his emblem book, the *Hecatomgraphie*, and two on his *Divers propos memorables des nobles illustres hommes de la Chrestienté*. Yet the emblem book was printed only three times during the sixteenth century, the *Propos memorables* at least nineteen times between 1556 and 1605 (Freeman; Bowen, "Facétie/ *sententia*"). The discrepancy in critical attention is again based on what interests today's readers (emblems), not on what interested Corrozet's contemporaries (strings of quoted moral sayings and anecdotes).

Corrozet's *Propos memorables* and Erasmus's *Lingua* are good illustrations of an aspect of Renaissance humanism which has been little studied, and which I propose to call trivial pursuit. If this term appears too frivolous to apply to the intellectual giants of the Renaissance, think of it as an updating of the perfectly respectable rhetorical concept of *amplificatio*.

Renaissance humanist education, as we are by now amply informed (France, Grendler, Grafton/Jardine), was based on rhetoric, and one of the fundamental mechanisms of rhetoric is appropriating and creating *copia*, or in modern terms information storage and retrieval. Students, and humanist readers in general, were collectors; in their commonplace books, they hoarded information, memorable remarks, moral tags, and purple passages culled from their reading. In *Love's Labour's Lost* (V.1) Holofernes uses the adjective "peregrinate," and Nathaniel, immediately pulling out his "table-book" (commonplace book) says delightedly: "A most singular and choice epithet." In some cases, no doubt, this information storage was an end in itself, the equivalent of today's collecting of antique thimbles or Star Trek memorabilia; but in others it was a means to an end: that of providing illustration and example for the schoolboy essay or the writer's treatise, poem, narrative, or play. Humanists so trained continued this storage process throughout their lives, frequently publishing their collections: of adages, apophthegms, fables, *facetiae*, emblems, historical *exempla*, moral commonplaces, epithets, and so on. Erasmus's *Lingua* is an enumeration of all the known arguments for the excellence of the tongue—and also against its potential for evil; Corrozet's *Propos memorables* is an unstructured anthology of "memorable" remarks by famous people. A rhetorically trained author was a walking dictionary of quotations, as we can see most obviously in any essay by Montaigne.

This emphasis on *copia* was encouraged not only by humanist education, but by the reading of Classical and Hellenistic authors. Ann Moss sees the origin of Renaissance commonplace books in medieval theological works, but we must look much further back. Among the best-loved sources of Renaissance humanism are two second-century works, Plutarch's *Symposia-ca* (*Table-Talk*) and the *Deipnosophists* of Athenaeus, an enormous, rambling dialogue (eight volumes survive) about all aspects of cooking and feasting; and, from the fifth century, the *Saturnalia* of Macrobius. The structural principle of all these works is the same: having mentioned a topic, let us enumerate and examine every conceivable aspect of it before proceeding to the next one.

We need to remember, with regard to information storage, that whereas to us post-Romantics the repetition of well-known tags or anecdotes is a symptom of lack of original thought, to the Renaissance quotation from antiquity, what Schiffman (24) calls "the deeply engrained commonplace reflex," was a form of contact with ancient wisdom; therefore the more quotations (the more clichés from our perspective) the better. Shakespeare's Autolycus describes himself as a snapper-up of unconsidered trifles (*Winter's Tale* IV.2.26), a fair characterization of a sixteenth-century humanist, except that to the latter there is probably no such thing as an unconsidered trifle. King Alfonso's remark that donkeys are better off than princes because they are allowed to dine undisturbed is as "memorable," as worthy of storage and retrieval, as the details of the death of Cicero.

If the acquiring of *copia*, or information storage, was a long and arduous process, information retrieval or the creation of *copia* was a much simpler matter—sometimes, we suspect, so simple as to be virtually unconscious. It takes two main forms: the straightforward list, and the use of recalled material to embroider a *topos* with what seems to us to be irrelevant material.

The first technique, the simple list, is most obviously applied to description. Jean Lemaire de Belges clearly thinks that an enumeration of twenty-five flowers and nine flowering trees suffices to evoke the beauty of Mount Pelion, decked out by Flora for the wedding of Peleus and Thetis (*Illustrations* I.29), and in *Le Tem-*

ple d'Honeur et de Vertus even provides alliterative enumerations
(ed. Hornik, 62):

> Dessoubz Pan sont les vergiers verdoyans,
> Bergiers bruyans, moutons moult honnorez,
> Fromens fort meurs, fruictages fort frians,
> Rosiers rians, fleurs et freses flairans,
> Preaux plaisans, parcz par tout bien parez.

> Under the charge of Pan are the green orchards,
> Noisy shepherds, highly-honored sheep,
> Very ripe wheat, very tasty fruits,
> Laughing rose-bushes, scented flowers and strawberries,
> Pleasant meadows, parks everywhere well adorned.

But the list technique can work in any kind of context. Shakespeare, as Walter Ong informed us years ago, structured his "lust
in action" sonnet on a list of terms he found, in the same order,
in Ravisius Textor's commonplace book.

As late as 1680, in Act III of Thomas Otway's *The Orphan*,
Castalio exclaims with tragic emphasis: "Woman, the fountain
of all human frailty!" This banality seems obvious enough to
require no supporting evidence, but as though it has flipped a
switch marked "Woman, frailty of" on his filing system, Castalio
at once goes on:

> What mighty ills have not been done by woman?
> Who was't betrayed the Capitol? A woman.
> Who lost Mark Anthony the world? A woman.
> Who was the cause of a long ten years' war,
> And laid at last Old Troy in ashes? A woman.
> Destructive, damnable, deceitful woman.

And so on for eight more lines. I found this reference by following up a quotation in P. G. Wodehouse, himself no mean practitioner of trivial pursuit, and a regular user of Bartlett's *Familiar Quotations*. Shakespeare's Holofernes might say of Lemaire and Castalio, as well as of many Wodehouse characters, "He draweth out the thread of his verbosity finer than the staple of his argument" (*Love's Labour's Lost* V.1).

The second technique is more subtle, but by modern standards just as "trivial." Suppose that you were a Classical archaeologist and that a publisher asked you for a treatise on ancient Roman coinage. You would probably list the relevant sources of information, which are not many; enumerate the different names for Roman coins together with what we know about their changing value over time, and estimate their equivalents in U.S. dollars. Shall we say about fifty pages? You would not, almost certainly, eventually produce 819 pages of impassioned argument about Roman coinage but also about etymology, rhetoric, names of plants, the restoration of pure Latin, the glories of France, the evils of wealth and tyranny, the neglect of the liberal arts, the banquets of Anthony and Cleopatra, the boundaries of the Roman Empire, French bread, the measurements of the earth, Hercules as a figure for Christ, or the dearth of owls in Crete. But all this, and much, much more, results from Guillaume Budé's trivial pursuit of Roman coinage in the *De asse* (the *as* was a small Roman coin). Can a two-letter word ever have generated *copia* on so grand a scale?

The *De asse* is even less read today than Erasmus's *Lingua*, not only because of its heavily pedantic Latin and numerous quotations in Greek, but because of its total lack of structure. I am unconvinced by the efforts of La Garanderie and Margolin to impose an order on it; it is, simply, an unstructured compilation of information (as Erasmus's *Adages* explicitly are). The work was several times revised by its author, always with an increase in page numbers, was frequently reprinted, and almost as frequently epitomized and anthologized; humanist Europe obviously loved it.

If we had to assign the book to a literary genre, it might well be to what the French called a *blason*. *Blason* is an interesting word, with a heraldic derivation and a variety of meanings. In the sixteenth century it can imply either praise or denigration. To literary critics, it is best known in connection with an early sixteenth-century French poetic fad for lyrical description of parts of a woman's body: a *blason* of the lady's eye, hair, bosom, or less often mentioned body parts; what Shakespeare called "the blazon of sweet beauty's best, /Of hand, of foot, of lip, of eye, of brow" (Sonnet 106). In this case the basic meaning is praise, but there is also a trivial-pursuit implication of "everything I can think of to say about this *topos*." And in this wider sense, many other literary works could be called *blasons*, including some of Ronsard's hymns; the *Hymne des Daimons*, for example, is a straightforward enumeration of everything the poet has ever read or heard about demons, fairies, dryads, and mythological enchanters.

I believe it is very important to recognize that our humanists, alongside and not always overlapping with their lofty intellectual concerns, were devoted practitioners of trivial pursuit. Budé is not the only one whose collection grew over the years, as we can see from these examples. Erasmus's *Adages*: 818 in 1500 and 4,251 in 1536 (Balavoine 1984); Alciati's emblems: 105 in 1532 and 212 in 1621; Domenichi's *Facezie e motti*: 492 in 1548 and 981 in 1574; or compare the earliest and latest published versions of Montaigne's *Essays*. Many of these published anthologies became sources of *copia* for later writers: Alciati developed adages from Erasmus into his emblems, later emblematists elaborated on Alciati, Montaigne illustrated his essays from Corrozet's *Propos memorables*, and so on and on. After Budé, Montaigne may provide the most striking illustration of trivial pursuit, in the thirty-eight pages (Jourda edition) of examples of animal behavior in the *Apologie de Raymond Sebond*.

The examples just given of both trivial pursuit techniques are all quite serious, though Lemaire's alliterations and the *blasons* may cause today's reader to smile. Only Rabelais, apparently, exploited the comic possibilities of trivial pursuit, to such an extent that I would claim this technique as fundamental to *Gargantua and Pantagruel*. Most obviously, Rabelais loves lists, often in the form Frederic Amory calls "hurricane word-formations": 217 children's games in G 22, 63 verbs of violent motion in the *Tiers Livre* Prologue, 170 adjectives for tired testicles in TL 28; there are many other examples. A mention of snakes, in QL 64, prompts Eusthenes to recite a list (from a recently edited work by Aristotle) of twenty-eight reptiles in alphabetical order (most commonly Rabelais's lists have no order).

More subtle are the lists whose origin only a fellow humanist would recognize, like the reptiles just mentioned, or the meteoric phenomena at the beginning of the storm at sea (QL 18), also taken from Aristotle: "categides, thielles, lelapes, presteres . . . psoloentes" and so forth, or like the enumeration of strange and improbable deaths, à propos of the death of Bringuenarilles in QL 17, taken from Ravisius Textor's thirty-eight successive chapters on this subject.

All these lists, and their numerous relatives, are intended to be comic; but Rabelais can do serious trivial pursuit as well as Budé when he wants to. The *Tiers Livre* has been called the most "encyclopedic" of the four books, and it frequently supplies more detailed information than we really needed about methods of divination, dreams, or whatever else is under discussion. But the most striking example of serious trivial pursuit in Rabelais is perhaps the detailed description of the Abbey of Thelema (G 52–57). To well-informed humanists, the meaning of this episode was unambiguous: the moral and intellectual élite can do what they will to do (FAY CE QUE VOULDRAS) because their will coincides with God's will (*thelema*). And is this not a wonderful dream, of an ideal community combining the nobility, elegance and culture of Castiglione's courtiers with the pure religion of early Christianity, to the exclusion of all ignorance, wickedness, hypocrisy, and deformity? In order to understand this message, do we really need to know about the roof "couvert d'Ardoize fine: avec l'endousseure de plomb à figures de petitz manequins et animaulx bien assortiz et dorez" ("covered with lead backing with figurines of little animals well garnished and gilded"), or the marvelous staircase, "de laquelle l'entrée estoit par le dehors du logis en un arceau large de six toizes. Icelle estoit faicte en telle symmetrie et capacité, que six hommes d'armes la lance sus la cuisse povoient de front ensemble monter jusques au dessus de tout le bastiment" ("whose entryway was from outside the building symmetrically made six fathoms wide and accommodating six men-at-arms, who, with lance on thigh, could ride up together abreast all the way up on top of the entire building"), or the ladies' gowns "de toille d'or à frizure d'argent, de satin rouge couvert de canetille d'or, de tafetas blanc, bleu, noir, tanné, sarge de soye, camelot de soye, velours, drap d'argent, toille d'argent, or traict, velours ou satin porfilé d'or en diverses protraictures" ("of cloth of gold with silver fringe, of red satin covered with gold purl, of white, blue, black, or tawny taffeta, silk serge, silk camblet, velvet, silver broadcloth or cambrick, gold tissue, or purfled with gold in various portraits")? Not a single one of these details helps to convey the Evangelical message. Once launched on his *blason* of the perfect anti-abbey, Rabelais has simply given his imagination (and a few reference works, probably) a free rein to pursue all the possible details which could pertain to it.

Many other Rabelaisian episodes grow out of the "let's run with this idea" approach to writing. The war with the Andouilles, in the *Quart Livre*, is (among other things) a list of all possible and imaginable sausage jokes; etymological, proverbial, linguistic, Erasmian, and of course phallic. These jokes are comic, at the same time that their context has something serious to say about Carnival and Lent (even if Samuel Kinser and I disagree about the precise message in this case). An even more interesting example is the *Quart Livre* storm, whose import, like that of Thelema, is quite clear. Rabelais has cleverly woven into a coherent episode several varieties of trivial pursuit: the enumeration of exotic naval terminology, in French and other languages and dialects; the list of meteorological phenomena already mentioned; the accumulation of hoary storm-at-sea jokes like calling for salt meat because we are shortly going to get plenty to drink; and the careful demonstration by Panurge of as many sins against Evangelical Christianity as possible: he is superstitious, calls on saints and the Virgin Mary, refuses to swear, demands confession, makes a vow, proposes paying someone (whom?) to go on a pilgrimage, and weeps and throws up instead of working and trusting to God.

The subject of trivial pursuit needs more detailed treatment than I can give it here. The few critics who have tackled it—without using my term, of which they would no doubt disapprove (Genette, Schor, and Moss, for example), have usually done so from a specific perspective. Most recently, critical interest seems to be focusing on the encyclopedia (e.g., Kenny), and concepts of organizing disparate material; but the whole point about trivial pursuit is that it has no order.

In this chapter I shall consider three more applications of trivial pursuit: humanist *facetiae,* Reformation satire, and Rabelais's Library of Saint-Victor, and chapter 4 will have more to say about the rhetorical basis of this and other techniques. Let us first consider a form of trivial pursuit that many humanists obviously found very congenial.

Humanist *facetiae*

As we have noted, humanists loved to collect things they considered "memorable," and among these they numbered *facetiae,* for which I shall use the general term "jokes." As I have explained elsewhere, there are problems in defining joke collections as a genre; but then there are problems of definition in all Renaissance genres. I have, however, not seen any objections to my claim that it is possible to distinguish the verbal joke, *rencontre* or *motto*, from the short story, at least in the period before Rabelais.

Cicero, in the *De oratore*, makes two distinctions whose influence was to be surprisingly long-lived: between *cavillatio,* or humor infused throughout a speech, and *dicacitas,* or witty one-liners; and between joking *in re* (humorous subject-matter) and *in verbo* (verbal wit). The Renaissance quite often made one or both of these distinctions, in collections entitled *Facezie e motti*, *Tales and Quicke Answeres*, or Des Périers's *Nouvelles récréations et joyeux devis*; the stories of Boccaccio's Sixth Day all concern a *leggiadro motto* or a *pronta risposta*.

But this is not the only definition problem. We should like to think of a *facetia* as necessarily comic, but this is far from the case. Poggio's *Facetiae* include ghost stories, many of the *Mensa philosophica* anecdotes are serious hagiography, and in other collections a *facetia* can be a maxim, a fable, or a riddle. In my gloomier moments, I have sometimes thought that the only honest definition of *facetia* would be "a remark or story which the compiler decided, for some impenetrable reason, to collect." The reputation of the *facetia* for consistent wit probably derives from Domenichi, whose enormous collection was one of the most influential of the fifteenth century, and which does contain almost exclusively anecdotes intended to be funny.

Cicero's jokes, and their development in Quintilian and Macrobius, seem to have fallen by the wayside during the Middle Ages (though Gervase of Tilbury is credited with a *Liber facetiarum*, now lost, which he produced for the son of Henry II Plantagenet), but were revived for the Renaissance, like so much else, by Petrarch (*Rerum memorandarum libri*, II.37–91). From

Petrarch to Castiglione's *Libro del Cortegiano*, I count twenty-one joke-collections (*RQ* 39, 1986), in Latin, Italian, "German," and English, of extraordinarily varied content and purpose. After the samples of humanist invective given above, it should come as no surprise that obscenity is a frequent element in humanist jokes. Poggio's *Facetiae* are the best-known example, and his specialty is the suggestive metaphor, like that of the wife who says she cannot send a message to her absent husband because he has taken away her pen and left her inkwell empty. Even Erasmus, who strongly disapproved of obscenity in general and of Poggio in particular, included in his mini-joke collection, the "Convivium fabulosum," an anecdote proving that the bottom is the most honorable part of human anatomy.

In this domain, as in so many others, modern perceptions have been shaped by the literature traditionally considered (often quite arbitrarily) to "represent" the sixteenth century. Even so, it is possible to deduce from that literature that our cherished separation between the "intellectual" and the "popular," or the "refined" and the "rude," did not exist with nearly as much force in the Renaissance. Consider the story told by an aristocratic young woman, in Marguerite de Navarre's *Heptaméron*, of the lady who fell in the privy and emerged covered with excrement. The entire company, including the venerable and very religious Oisille, laugh at this story (Bowen 1984).

The most complete edition of Domenichi's *Facetie, motti & burle* (1574) contains 981 jokes, a surprising number of which concern lovemaking, adultery, prostitutes, incest, masturbation, farting, urinating, excrement, or syphilis. Sometimes these anecdotes use metaphors, like the woman washing clothes in the river Arno in winter, who, when asked if she isn't cold, replies "Messer no, che io hò il fuoco sotto" ("No sir, because I have a fire under me"); her (male) interlocutor retorts: "accendetemi di grati questo moccolo" ("please light this candle for me," I.47); or the elderly Bernardo Vitale, who in bed puts his reading-glasses on his wife's nose so that his *mercantia* will seem bigger to her (II.16). But many of them use precise anatomical terms, of which *culo* is by far the most frequent.

Domenichi's compilation draws on a number of earlier antholo-gies of *facetiae*, nearly all of which were by humanists. He takes material from Poggio, Panormita's *De dictis et factis Alphonsi* (1455), the anonymous *Detti piacevoli,* probably written in the 1470s (Bowen 1994), Heinrich Bebel's *Facetiae* (1508–12), Cas-tiglione's *Cortegiano* (1528), and either Luscinius (1524) or Gast (1541), or both. Of these collections, only Panormita's and Cas-tiglione's contain no sexually explicit or scatological material, and the one non-humanist work he quotes, the *Motti e facezie del Pio-vano Arlotto* (1480?), a kind of hagiography of an idealized priest, includes several obscene anecdotes.

The compiler's own attitude to obscenity, in the collections which have prefaces, varies a good deal. Bebel prefaces each of his three books of *facetiae* with a different dedicatory epistle, none of which addresses the quite obtrusive obscene and scatological content of the book. He stresses the necessity of *ioci* for relaxation, twice referring to them as *pabulum*. In the epistle to Vitus de Furst that prefaces the third book, he does defend himself against two charges: of depicting so many stupid and immoral reli-gious (but they should make their deeds as virtuous as their words); and of using inelegant Latin (but it is very difficult to translate vernacular German into good Latin). However, he must have been reproached about the large number of *ioci* that are obscene (the man playing Christ in a Passion play in church who has to be removed because looking at the woman playing Mary Mag-dalene gives him an erection, II.130), or scatological (a priest defe-cates in church during a baptism, III.13). Bebel answered these reproaches in a very short address *Ad lectorem* at the beginning of the third and last book (105–6). His *facetiae* have been accused

of appearing "nimium lascive spurceque" ("too lascivious and
dirty"), but he claims to have heard all of them "a gravibus viris
in conviviis recitari . . . et maiori ex parte apud matronas"
("told by serious men at banquets . . . and most of them when
ladies were present"). If this is true, convivial table-talk in Rabelais
seems pale beside that of German society in the early sixteenth
century.

A few years later Joachim Gast, who used a good deal of material from Bebel, gave the first edition (1541) of his joke collection
a title that appears to state his position quite clearly: *Convivalium
sermonum liber, meris iocis, ac salibus non impudicis, neque lascivis,
sed utilibus et seriis refertus. Nonnunquam etiam admixtae sunt iucun-
dae, & verae narrationes, eaque omnia ex variis cum veterum, tum
recentium monumentis decerpta* ("A book of table-talk, crammed
with simple jokes, and witticisms neither immodest nor lascivious, but useful and serious. Mixed in with them are some joyful
and true narratives, and all of them taken from various books,
both of the ancients and of the moderns"). The dedicatory epistle reinforces this impression; after enumerating the standard
topoi proving that relaxation is necessary to human life: Scipio
and Laelius playing on the beach with shells and stones, Socrates
playing with children, and so forth (St. Augustine is also quoted), Gast states firmly that he has collected "iocos et convivales
sermones" from ancient and modern writers, and has included
"nihil impudicum, aut turpe, quemadmodum plerique soliti sunt,
sed pia omnia, sancta, plausibilia, et nihil a Christianae profes-
sionis nomine abhorrens" ("nothing immodest, or offensive, as
many people do, but all are pious, holy, plausible, and there is
nothing abhorrent to the name of the Christian faith," A3r).

However, as so often with Renaissance books, the content does
not always correspond to these good intentions, and Gast tells a
number of stories about adultery, farting, and defecation. Like
Bebel, he was perhaps reproached with this inconsistency, for

later editions carry, instead of the 1541 dedication, an Epistle to the Reader more or less apologizing for the *obscoena* included. Nobody, claims the author self-righteously, delights in obscene words or deeds; his are included only in an attempt to correct corrupt *mores*, and even Popes and Cardinals could not object to them (!). Gast considerably expanded his book through a number of editions, but never removed the stories which strike a modern reader as obscene. Reformation Germany may have simply had a more robust sense of humor than ours.

Perhaps the most important author for the context of obscene jokes is Gioviano Pontano, whose 1502 *De sermone* is actually a treatise on joking, and the only work of the period which is both theoretical treatise and joke anthology. His theory is an interesting combination of Aristotle and Cicero; wit, for him, is an Aristotelian virtue (to which he gives a new name, *facetudo*), and is the mean between the extremes of *agrestitas* and *scurrilitas*. Despite his emphasis on relaxation, and conversation as opposed to formal discourse, he is constantly engaged in definition and categorization. The interrelationship of his key terms, *urbanitas*, *festivitas*, and *facetudo*, occupies several chapters, and he is often concerned to categorize a joke both rhetorically and morally. One of the period's most frequently repeated jokes is about the traveler on horseback with a very protuberant stomach, leaving by the city gate, who when mocked by the bystanders for carrying his luggage in front of him, replies: "It's the sensible thing to do when you're surrounded by thieves" (IV.3, 129–30; Bowen 56).[19] Pontano gives as the foundations of this joke *a corporis habitu*, and *a morum turpitudine*. As with so many of Cicero's and Quintilian's categories, the reader is tempted to ask: is all bodily deformity, and all moral turpitude, laughable?

Pontano mentions obscenity quite often. His official stance is disapproving: obscene jokers are *lascivi* (I.16); joking should not be *lascive* or *contumeliosa* (V.3); *scurrilitas* must be avoided

(VI.1); the best jokes are ones without *oscenitas* (VI.2). However, he also devotes an entire chapter (IV.2) to showing that some of the best jokes consist of expressing obscene subject matter *nec turpiter nec oscene* ("neither offensively nor obscenely"): "sic faceti homines, arte adhibita ac translationibus usi, rem naturaliter turpem dictis honestant et . . . ipsum per se oscenum est in lepidum vertunt ac facetum" ("thus witty men, using applied art and metaphors, by their words make honorable something naturally offensive and . . . turn something in itself obscene into something pleasant and witty," 125). He gives a number of examples throughout the book, most often of how to use metaphor for this purpose, as in the celebrated Classical joke by Julia, daughter of the Emperor Augustus and notorious for her dissolute lifestyle. When asked why all her children resembled her husband, she replied: "I only take a pilot on board when the ship is already loaded" (185; Bowen 44).

But once again, practice, in the *De sermone*, corresponds only imperfectly to theory. Even if most of the numerous examples of metaphor and periphrasis to convey obscene content, like the Julia joke and like the story of Vitalis putting his eyeglasses on his wife ("Quid aut festivius aut in re licentiore venustius?" ["What could be more witty, or more pleasant on a licentious subject?"], 168), do not use anatomical terms, their meaning is perfectly clear. And while cruder anecdotes are sometimes reproved for being too obscene, they can be applauded. A parasite at the dinner table, when a sow's womb (*vulva*, considered a culinary delicacy) was placed before him, hauled out his *pudibunda* and placed them alongside it. When his fellow-diners protested, he said that he supposed such meat would require such a knife. "Quod quidem actu foedum, oscenum responsu, ac relatu, pro loco tamen atque auditoribus, non iniucundum" ("Which although it was grossly done and obscenely replied and narrated, still for the time and the hearers, it was not disagreeable," 192).

Pontano's anthology is one of the funniest of the period, partly because it has so many obscene jokes, and it is regrettable that it has never been translated. He used material from antiquity (especially Plautus, Cicero, and Macrobius), from recent humanist works (Poggio and Panormita), and from stories told him by contemporaries, including members of his own family. In a period when most compilers of *facetiae* merely took in each other's washing, as it were, Pontano's originality of approach is refreshing, and he is one of the best illustrations of the by now obvious fact that humanist comedy was not always "refined."

We might expect Rabelais the comic humanist to make extensive use of this *facetia* tradition, but curiously, he does not (Demerson 1994, Bowen 1986). Traditionally, rhetorical jokes had a variety of functions. They could be used as weapons in the orator's persuasive armory; might not a one-liner or two have helped Ulrich Gallet to soften up Picrochole (G 31), or improved Gargantua's address to the vanquished (G 50)? Joking, and the ability to take jokes made against oneself, had been since the Emperor Augustus and his fifteenth-century imitator Alfonso of Aragon part of the persona of the Ideal Prince; Gargantua and Pantagruel do not resemble them in this respect. The next chapter will have more to say about comic rhetoric, and chapter 5 will explore the question of therapeutic laughter, but my point here is simply that the few humanist *facetiae* Rabelais does use occur in surprising contexts. Julia and her loaded ship, for instance, are quoted not as a joke but as support for a learned legal and medical argument about eleven-month pregnancies (G 3); the fool's judgment about paying for the smell of the roast meat (TL 37) is intended to encourage Panurge to solve his dilemma by consulting a fool, as frere Jean's version of Hans Carvel's ring (TL 28) is supposed to persuade him that it is futile to take precautions against cuckoldry. No one laughs at any of these *facetiae*, and most strikingly of all, when Panurge retells the hilarious old chestnut about

Soeur Fessue's reasons for not disclosing her rape by Roydimmet (TL 19), Pantagruel's reaction is: "Vous . . . jà ne m'en ferez rire. Je sçay assez que toute moinerie moins crainct les commandemens de Dieu transgresser, que leurs statutz provinciaulx" ("You'll never make me laugh at that. I know well enough that all monkery is less afraid to transgress God's commandments than their provincial statutes").

Only a few other *facetiae* appear in *Gargantua and Pantagruel*, sometimes half-submerged like Panurge's *boutade* at the beginning of the storm (QL 18): "Maigor dome hau, mon amy, mon pere, mon oncle, produisez un peu de sallé. Nous ne boirons tantoust que trop, à ce que je voy" ("Steward, ho! my friend, my father, my uncle, bring out something salty; we'll soon have only too much to drink, from what I see!"). But the expected ship-in-storm joke, about the passenger adjured to throw overboard his heaviest belongings to lighten the ship and who throws his wife, never materializes.

So Rabelais's fondness for trivial pursuit does not lead him to make the expected use of "les facecieuses et joyeuses responses de Ciceron" (QL 39), nor of Poggio, Bebel, or Pontano. Nevertheless, study of humanist *facetiae* can help to put Rabelais's own comedy into perspective—and also to show us how relatively mild Rabelais's sense of humor is for the time. This last fact will be even more conclusively demonstrated in the next section.

Reformation Satire

If it is very difficult to come up with a generally valid definition of the comic in the so-called *facetiae* that humanists thought worth collecting, there is nothing subtle or ambiguous about my next example of humanist comedy. Reformation Germany produced some superb anti-Catholic satire, both visual and literary. Its most famous literary satire (though more often quoted

than read) is the *Epistles of Obscure Men*, which I shall be ana-
lyzing shortly, but I should first like to consider another example of the genre which is seldom mentioned by critics, despite its
availability in English translation (Best): the anonymous *Eccius
dedolaltus* of 1520. This little gem, which should probably be attributed to Willibald Pirckheimer, may not quite deserve its trans-
lator's label "the greatest of Reformation satires" (13), but it should
be required reading for anyone still convinced that "humanist
wit" and "carnival wit" come in separable categories.

The Eccius or Eckius of the title (to whom Rabelais will attribute
a volume titled *Maneries ramonandi fournellos*, which is bad Latin
for 'How to Sweep Chimneys'), was at the time one of Luther's
most celebrated opponents, especially after their Leipzig dispu-
tation of 1519, during which Eck provoked Luther into expressing support for some of the doctrines of the Hussite heresy. Eck's
theological qualifications are amply demonstrated by Irena Backus's
account of the disputations of Baden and Berne (1993). The details
of the pamphlet wars between Eck and his supporters and the
Lutherans need not concern us. The essential point is that Eck
was the archconservative theologian the Reformers loved to hate,
and Johannes Rubeus one of his warmest supporters.

Eccius dedolatus is in the form of a play, a series of brief scenes
set in Eck's house, the house of the witch Canidia, the air above
Leipzig (where Canidia is traveling on her goat), Rubeus's house
in Leipzig, and the meeting-room of the Leipzig theological faculty. We first see Eck, in a very funny parody of Classical laments,
bemoaning his illness and suffering; he sends a letter to Leipzig
by Canidia; she returns with, also on the goat, Rubeus and a surgeon; after a burlesque confession Eck is beaten in order to smooth
his rough edges (*dedolatus*), shaved, purged, cut open, operated
on, and finally castrated; after which he is cured.

The incidental comedy of this satire is about equal parts erudite and vulgar. There are Classical quotations and reminiscences on every page, from Seneca, Aristophanes, Lucian, Homer,

Virgil, and Plautus, together with jokes about Eck's own writings and those of his supporters and adversaries. Erasmus, Luther, and many other contemporaries are named, usually in diatribes against them by Eck. The implied reader is a classically educated intellectual of strong Reforming sympathies, who shares the author's conviction that Eck is not only a menace, but also a hypocrite; his animus against Luther springs not from conviction but from a desire for profit—"we fight for gain, not truth" (62).

How interesting, then, that this is also one of the most scatological satires ever penned. On the return trip from Leipzig, Canidia sits on the goat's head and Rubeus on his back, while the poor surgeon dangles below them, hanging on to the goat's tail. Once airborne (by virtue of Canidia's three magic words, which are Tungerus, Hochstrat, and Pfeferkoren spelled backwards), the surgeon laments a horrible stench, which he assumes is the goat breaking wind. But no, says Rubeus, "I eased my bowels" (49); even Canidia complains of the smell. Once in the house, the surgeon examines Eck's urine ("Ugh! how it smells!"), and gives him a purge that causes him to throw up poorly digested scholastic commentaries, Greek letters, and a red beret, and to defecate Hochstraten's indulgences and assorted coins ("Intolerable reek! So bad, you have to hold your nose!"). The author obviously revels in all this excrement, and assumes that his readers will also; no question that here at least affairs of the intellect and of the "bodily lower stratum" coexist in perfect harmony. James Mehl (1994) has stressed the work's many borrowings from the *Epistles of Obscure Men*, and also its ties to the Fastnachtspiel and the *depositio beani*, an initiation rite for young boys, during which they were soundly beaten.

The *Epistles of Obscure Men* (Latin title *Epistolae obscurorum virorum*, hence the usual abbreviation EOV) has been celebrated from its time to ours as one of the Reformation's great literary satires. It has also, until quite recently, been gravely misinterpreted; the research of Overfield, Nauert, and Mehl has shown that the book was in a sense too successful for its own good. The basic issue between Reuchlin and the allies of Pfefferkorn was not humanism versus obscurantism, but a concern for justice versus antisemitism; and Ortwin, the recipient of the fictional letters, was a perfectly respectable, though undoubtedly conservative, humanist, and by no means the ignorant, immoral and gross booby portrayed by his correspondents. In fact, his portrayal is so wildly caricatural that he may well have been able to laugh at it himself; but uninformed contemporaries (including Rabelais), and future generations, all assumed that the portrait was lifelike.

Unfortunately, non-Latinists are unable to appreciate the full comedy of the EOV. The only English translation was done by Francis Stokes in 1925 and will strike most readers as disconcertingly old-fashioned British English. It is also regrettably prudish, toning down the earthy language of the original until it is almost unrecognizable. For instance, would you guess that the following sentence: "Then was I sore afraid, and fell into such a pickle that I savored ill in the nostrils of those who stood by" (II.63) is a translation of: "Tunc fui ita perterritus quod perminxi et permerdavi me, quod omnes nasum praetenebant" ("Then I was so terrified that I pissed and shitted all over myself, so that they all held their noses")?

There is less excrement in the EOV than in *Eccius dedolatus*, but much more preoccupation with sex. The letter-writers, who nearly all have absurd pseudo-German names like Lyra Buntschuchmacherius and Eitelnarrabianus von Pesseneck, are often concerned with their love lives; boasting of a mass rape (I.4),excusing lovemaking as good against melancholy (I.13, with innuendos about Ortwin's intimacy with Pfefferkorn's wife), describing their lady-loves (I.21 and II.39), confessing enslavement to a woman (I.33), suggesting sharing a mistress (I.45), hinting at Arnold von Tongern's homosexuality (II.25) or Pfefferkorn's wife's frivolity

(II.37), or describing a magical charm to compel a woman's love (II.42). The medieval *topos* of the immorality of the clergy is cleverly brought up to date.

So Rabelais could have found plenty of comic scatology and obscenity in the EOV. And the Obscure Men are comic in many other ways. Their stupidity is perhaps the most hilarious element. They are quite sure that logic is the science of sciences (I.11), and that Greek is irrelevant to the study of Scripture (II.10). Letter I.28 includes an ecstatic encomium of the *Ovide moralisé*, thought by the writer Conrad Dollenkopf to be inspired by the Holy Spirit. Diana and Semele both signify the Virgin Mary; Cadmus, Bacchus and Pyramus are all figures of Christ; Thisbe is the soul of man, and so on. And their stupidity is often accompanied by fatuous self-satisfaction and self-congratulation on their intellectual superiority, to Reuchlin and his supporters in particular. The very first letter is a lengthy discussion of the kind of intellectual issue that engages their passionate attention, especially when they have had plenty to drink: is the correct title for a theological degree candidate *Magister nostrandus* or *Noster magistrandus?* Rabelais will remember this in the book title Chault couillons *de magistro nostrandorum magistro nostratorumque beuuetis* lib. octo gualantissimi ("Hotballs, *On the guzzling-bouts of doctoral candidates and doctors*, eight highly lively books," P 7). They frequently show their self-satisfaction by laughing: "Ha ha ha! oportet me ridere!" ("Ho, ho, ho! I can't help laughing!" I.43) exclaims a correspondent explaining to Ortwin that of course he works hard—all that drinking is very tiring; "ego risi ita quod statim perminxissem me" ("I laughed so hard that I pissed all over myself"), states another frankly (I.4).

This coexistence of crude humor and ferocious satire was certainly very congenial to Rabelais, and produced, as well as numerous passing references to *Magistri nostri*, two episodes that must have been favorites of the sixteenth-century reader: Janotus de

Bragmardo and the Library of Saint-Victor. Rabelais must also have reveled in the constant mingling of different Latin styles, which no translation can reproduce. The writers are by turns precious, pompous, pedestrian, and abruptly colloquial ("ego bene merdarem in vestram poetriam" ["I would like to shit on your poetry"], I.3). One complete letter consists of variations on the theme of "I can't think why you haven't written to me": "Si estis inimicus meus quod non vultis mihi amplius scribere, tunc scribatis mihi tamen quare non vultis mihi amplius scribere, ut sciam quare mihi non scribitis, cum ego semper scribo vobis, sicut etiam nunc scribo vobis, quamvis scio quod non eritis mihi rescribere" ("If you are my enemy because you don't want to write to me any more, then still write me why you don't want to write to me any more, so that I may know why you don't write to me, when I always write to you, just as even now I am writing to you, although I know that you are not going to write back to me," I.15). Any Latin 103 student would find this hilarious. These educated boobies are also ignorant of the most basic rules of Latin prosody and versification, and congratulate each other fulsomely on reams of atrocious doggerel. No wonder much of humanist Europe roared with laughter over the EOV.

Although not all humanists were humorists, many were, and Rabelais was certainly familiar with humanist *facetiae* and with some German Reformation satire.[20] Like Erasmus and many others, he also was particularly fond of Classical and Hellenistic comic writers: most obviously Lucian, less obviously Plautus and the satirists Martial and Juvenal. As we saw in chapter 2, there is one overtly humanist work among the Italian mock-epics he loves to recall: Folengo's *Baldus*. But my point in stressing the *Eccius dedolatus* and the EOV has been that humanist comedy, so far from being in anthithesis to "popular" or "carnival" humor, could coexist quite happily with it, as a glance at the humanist Machiavelli's pornographic comedy *Mandragola* will confirm.

We surely do Rabelais a disservice by artificially separating "humanist" from "comic" episodes in the four books. It is simply not true, as too many critics have tried to claim, that jokes have nothing to do with serious humanist preoccupations. Certainly there are passages in Rabelais that we might describe as "straightforward" humanism: the letter on education, for instance (P 8); Pantagruel's Evangelical prayer before the battle with Loupgarou (P 29); Gargantua's sermon to the pilgrims (G 40); *Tiers Livre* disquisitions on lots (10), dreams (13), language (19), Evangelical marriage (30) or Pantagruelion (49–52). Certainly, too, there are purely comic anecdotes and episodes, more often in the first two books than in the last two. But recent research has warned us that we do well to exercise caution, even here. Who would have guessed that the grotesque "description" of Quaresmeprenant (QL 29–32) contains satire of current medical terminology (Fontaine; see Chapter 5), that there are specific references to Christian *caritas* in the stones and metals of the child Gargantua's ring (Weinberg 1984), that Panurge's recounting of Mother Goose tales to Loupgarou's troops (P 29) shows Rabelais taking a humanist position about historiography (Céard 1980; see chapter 2), or that a passing reference to a pointless episode in Enguerrant de Monstrelet (TL 24) throws light on the structure of the entire *Tiers Livre* (Duval 1993)? If a future researcher discovers humanist significance in frere Jean's riddle about why a lady's thighs are always cool (G 39), I shall be pleased but not surprised.

Later chapters will discuss specific aspects of Rabelais's humanism: rhetoric (chapter 4), medicine (5), and law (6). I would like to conclude the present chapter with an analysis of an episode that in my view provides an ideal illustration both of trivial pursuit and of comic humanism, and that has been surprisingly little discussed by previous critics.

The Library of Saint-Victor

The list of 139 books in the Library of Saint-Victor (P 7) must surely have been the most hilarious chapter of Rabelais's first book, for the initiated, and the least interesting, for the uninitiated. It is Rabelais's first virtuoso display of trivial pursuit; it has no function in the narrative, nothing prepares us for it, and it will never be referred to again. But Rabelais himself obviously loved it, inasmuch as the definitive list of 139 items grew out of the 1532 version, which has only forty-two. The early chapters of this first book contain little humanist material: some comic satire on bad etymology (2), logical *pro et contra* argument (3), and medieval law (5), and the barbarous Latinized French of the scholar from Limoges (6). In chapter 7, suddenly, we are in an exclusively humanist world, where our laughter depends on our familiarity with Latin, Greek, theology, law, and medicine. This is showing-off raised to the level of art.

The library of the Abbaye de Saint-Victor existed, and a good deal is known about it (Franklin). Rabelais's catalogue is his own creation, and as has been pointed out, some of its implications are obvious (Moreau): no books of the Bible are listed, and there is a clear bias against church practices and Scholastic commentary. The 1532 catalogue begins with four short titles in Latin: *Bigua salutis* ("The Cart of Salvation"), *Bregueta iuris* ("The Codpiece of the Law," with an implied joke on the French word *droit*, which can mean right-hand, law, or upright or erect), *Pantofla decretorum* ("The Slipper of the Decrees") and *Malogranatum vitiorum* ("The Pomegranate of Vices"), followed by four in French on the same "The Something of Something" pattern, suggesting that the stimulus for the list was the numerous medieval theological titles in this form. Of the final 139 items, 119 will have this form, though sometimes more elaborately: "Reuerendi patris fratris

Lubini provincialis Bauardie *de croquendis lardonibus* libri tres"
("Reverend Father Friar Gulligut Smellsock, Provincial of Prat-
tleborough, On the Nibbling of Bacon Snacks, Three Books").
The first eight titles also use another comic procedure that will
be common throughout: the juxtaposition of concrete and abstract,
which was already a standard feature of devotional works (Lacroix)
and which Rabelais gleefully exaggerates: "La savate de humil-
ité" ("The Gym Shoe of Humility"), "Les entraves de religion"
("The Shackles of Life in Orders"), *Cacatorium medicorum* ("The
Commode-pot of the Medics"), and so on.

The first title, *Bigua salutis*, is an authentic one (the sermons
of Michael of Hungary, published in 1498), and at least six
other titles will be those of real books, but that is a very small proportion. More characteristic is the way the second title was suggested by the first: *Bregueta iuris* looks at first sight like a legal
parallel to its theological predecessor. A number of collections of
legal commonplaces were called *Brocardia juris* (see Chapter 6),
and the deformation of a real word into an obscene double-entendre will be a common device in the rest of the list. There are other
examples of one title suggesting the next: "L'aguillon de vin"
("The Goad to Wine," i.e., cheese) followed by "L'esperon de fro-
maige" ("The Spur of Cheese," i.e., wine—perhaps with a glance
at the *Esperon de discipline* by Rabelais's friend Antoine du Saix),
or "Le chiabrena des pucelles" ("The Shitter-shatter of the Maid-
ens") followed by "Le culpelé des vesves" ("The Shaven Tail of
the Widows," I think with a suggestion of merry widows, in that
prostitutes shaved their pubic hair regularly).

The modern reader's immediate reaction to a list of 139 items
is that there must be a structural principle at work somewhere,
but I do not see any attempt at structuring this catalogue. We can
see that there are ninety French titles and only forty-nine in Latin
(whereas the real library of Saint-Victor certainly had mostly
Latin titles); that at least thirty items joke with defecation ("La

martingalle des fianteurs" ["The Martingale of the Crappers"]),
sexual activity (*Cullebutatorium confratriarum* ["The Tumbleto-
rium of the Confrairies"]) or syphilis ("Almanach perpetuel pour
les gouteux et verollez" ["Perpetual Almanac for Gouties and
Poxies"]), whereas twenty-three have to do with food (usually
lower-class food), eating, or fat stomachs.

At first glance we have here a simple exercise in trivial pursuit, whose main butt is old-fashioned scholastic theology. But,
as so often with Rabelais, much more is going on in this list,
and to analyze the clever comedy in every title could fill a book.
(There is one book on the catalogue, by Paul Lacroix, but his main
concern was to find a real book being satirized behind each one
of Rabelais's titles, which frequently results in far-fetched conclusions). Let us take a few examples.

The *Maneries ramonandi fournellos* attributed to Johann Eck
and mentioned above is a good case in point. None of these three
Latin words, meaning "How to Sweep Chimneys," will be found
in a dictionary of Classical Latin; theologians speak and write
barbarous pseudo-Latin. A French reader is reminded of a farce
called *Le ramoneur de cheminées* (Tissier vol. 4) which is an extended obscene double-entendre: the elderly chimney-sweep laments
that he can no longer sweep a number of chimneys in one day,
because his equipment is worn out; theologians have their minds
more on "sweeping chimneys" than on practicing and propagat-
ing the faith. Chimneys suggest fire and burning; theologians are
more interested in burning heretics than in the truths of Christianity. Note that none of this brilliant satire can be conveyed in
translation.

Sometimes a title looks like sheer nonsense: *Antipericata-
metanaparbeugedamphicribrationes merdicantium*. The second
word, "of the shitters," is an obvious pun on *mendicantium*, "of
the mendicant orders of friars." The first word is a succession
of Latin and Greek prepositions (with the exception of *beuged*,

which makes no sense to me nor to the classicists I consulted[21]),
followed by *cribrationes*, "siftings" or "discussions." I think the
implication is that works by, or about, members of the religious
orders always deal with matters extraneous to (in front of, on the
edge of, round about) genuine religion. The monk Rabelais probably knows what he is talking about . . .

There is no indication that Rabelais had read the *Eccius dedolatus*, but there is plenty of evidence of his familiarity with the EOV.
Already in 1532 we find near the beginning of the list *Ars honeste
pettandi in societate* per M. Ortuinum ("The Art of Farting Decorously in Society, by Master Hardouin"). Rabelais must have felt
strongly about the Reuchlin affair to risk this; most of his seven
other references (listed in my 1991 article) to the EOV were added
in later editions. The charming idea that one can fart "honor-
ably" or "decorously" in society is similar in form to titles like
"Tartaretus *de modo cacandi*" (Pierre Tateret was a theology professor at the Sorbonne, and *tarter* meant "to shit"), or "Beda *de
optimitate triparum*" ("Beda, on the Optimity of Tripes"; Noël
Béda was the *syndic* of the Sorbonne, perhaps the French repre-
sentative of oppression most hated by the humanists; he had a fat
paunch [*tripes*], and if he also ate tripe, that would betray his lower-
class origins).

Although conservative theology is the most frequent butt of
these titles, there are also references to politics (*L'entrée de anthoine
de Leive es terres du Bresil*[22] ["The Entry of Antonio de Leiva into
the Territory of Brazil"]), literature ("Merlinus Coccaius *de patria
diabolorum*" ["Merlin Coccai On the Fatherland of the Devils[23]"]),
Roman and Canon Law ("Preclarissimi iuris utriusque doctoris
Maistre Pilloti Racquedenari *de bobelinandis glosse Accursiane
baguenaudis repetitio enucidiluculidissima*" ["The Most Illustrious
Doctor of Both Branches of the Law, Master Pilferus Scrapepenny, On Coping with the Idiocies of the Glosses of Accursius, a
Most Lucidly Unraveled Treatise"[24]]) and medicine (*Campi clysteri-*

orum per § C ["Fields of Enemas, by Paragraph C"][25]). But theology inspired the title I find the funniest of the whole list, and
which I make no apology for presenting once again: *Questio sub-
tilissima, Utrum Chimera in vacuo bombinans possit comedere secun-
das intentiones? et fuit debatuta per decem hebdomadas in concilio
Constantiensi* ("A Most Subtle Question, Whether a Chimera,
bombinating in the void, can devour second intentions, and it was
debated for ten days at the Council of Constance"). Lacroix and
the EC assume that the main point of this is an attack on the Council of Constance (1414–18), but I think this is incidental. Most
obviously, it is a pastiche of nominalist abstract speculation of the
"How-many-angels-can-stand-on-the-head-of-a-pin" type. *Quaes-
tio* suggests a section heading in, most famously, Thomas Aquinas's
Summa (which Rabelais calls the *Somme angelicque* in a later title);
Subtilis Doctor was the sobriquet of Duns Scotus, who turns up
again in *Barbouilamenta Scoti* ("The Jumblebotches of Scotus").

So the most important context for this title is not the Council of Constance, but late medieval scholastic philosophy, and nom-
inalism in particular. Like so many other titles in the catalogue,
but much more cleverly, this one plays with the juxtaposition of
concrete and abstract. A chimera, according to Classical mythol-
ogy, was an imaginary monster, variously represented. In the mar-
ginal doodles (by Holbein?) to the Myconius copy of Erasmus's
Praise of Folly (Q4v), there is a chimera with a woman's head, lion's
paws, eagle's wings, and a fish's tail, while Barthélemy Aneau's
version in his 1552 *Picta Poesis* (40) has a lion's head, cow's body,
tail like a serpent's, and four different animals' and birds' feet.
The verb "bombinating" suggests an insect's buzz, but a chimera,
if it did exist, would be an animal, not an insect. Nor could it, even
if it were an insect, buzz in a vacuum, which, according to most
scientists since Aristotle, does not exist, and which we know
Rabelais repudiated: "vacuité (laquelle n'est tolerée en Nature)"
("a vacuum [which is not tolerated in Nature]," QL 62). Because

it is imaginary, we should also not expect it to eat, still less to eat (concrete) second intentions (abstract at two removes). In nominalist terminology a first intention is a term denoting an abstraction, for example, "genus"; a second intention denotes a first intention, for example, "the idea of genus."

So we have here an interplay of concrete verbs, bombinating and eating, with mythical or abstract nouns, chimera, vacuum, second intentions. The Council of Constance, grappling with the schism in the Church and the Hussite heresy, had better things to do with its time than to debate this "most subtle question" for ten weeks.

It will be clear from the foregoing that I cannot agree with the analysis of this chapter by Floyd Gray (1994, 83–105). Far from expressing "inlassablement la même absurdité" (90), the list contains numerous, and varied, examples of humanist satire; far from aiming not to inform us but merely to make us laugh (102), it manages to inform us while making us laugh; and Lefranc's notes, far from containing all necessary information (104), are sometimes mistaken and often incomplete or misleading; much more relevant information certainly remains to be unearthed. Rabelais's humanist satire is a good deal more subtle than that of Luther, Thomas More, the *Eccius dedolatus* or the EOV; the times had become much more dangerous. It also seems lighthearted by comparison with Erasmus's more ferocious attack on the formalities, quiddities, and ecceities of medieval philosophers in the *Praise of Folly*. But even if lighthearted, it nails the adversary to the wall as effectively as do the other humanist works discussed here, and the chapter as a whole is surely a demonstration of humanist comedy unequaled in the rest of Rabelais's work.

This chapter has made no claim to cover every aspect of Rabelais the comic humanist; a few other aspects will be the focus of the following chapters. My aim here has been to make a case for the frequently earthy quality of much humanist wit, and for the coexistence of wit with serious intent. Viewed against this background, Rabelais's four books are in many ways typically humanist.

The previous discussion, in particular of the Library of Saint-Victor, was also intended to show that the more minutely humanist comedy is examined, the funnier it is. At regular intervals, some critic of the comic drags out the old proposition that to try to explain humor is necessarily to spoil it. This, *pace* Henry Appia and the *TLS* reviewer of Screech's *Rabelais*, is nonsense; the better we understand these library titles and many other abstruse Rabelaisian jokes, the more we relish the comic in his writing.

CHAPTER 4

The Comic Orator

*Why should I goe gadding and fisgigging after
firking falantado amfibologies? Wit is wit
and good will is good will.*

THOMAS NASHE

Rabelais and Rhetoric

To separate the humanist from the orator is, of course, merely critical strategy, in that most humanists were in a sense by definition orators, as will become clear shortly. The previous chapter focused mainly on nonrhetorical aspects of humanism, with the exception of Trivial Pursuit, which as we noted is an elaboration of the *amplificatio* required for rhetorical *copia*. In order to discuss more specifically the rhetorical component of Rabelais's humor, some readers may appreciate a general introduction to the subject of Renaissance rhetoric.

Like "humanism," the term "rhetoric" carries quite different connotations in different time periods. This chapter will be concerned, not with the many modern uses of the term, from I. A. Richards to Kritzman via Genette, but with what our Renaissance humanists understood by rhetoric; that is, very much what Cicero (especially in the *De oratore*) understood by it. Rhetoric, in this sense, has five parts: *inventio* ("finding" one's subject and arguments), *dispositio* (organization), *elocutio* (style), *memoria*, and *pronuntiatio* (delivery). Renaissance humanists, and most famously Ramus, in the middle of the sixteenth century, tended to assign invention and disposition to logic and the other three to rhetoric, which explains why so many contemporary rhetorics deal only with style. The orator's aims are to teach, persuade and delight; discourse is classified as demonstrative (praise or dispraise of a person, thing or action, in the present, according to Thomas Wilson), deliberative (persuasion, dissuasion, "exhorte or dehort," with reference to the future), or judicial (debate, with accusation and defense, about the past; Aristotle's terms were epideictic, deliberative, and forensic); every discourse has clearly defined parts—Fabri lists them as: 1) *salutation, exorde, prohesme,* or *commencement,* 2) *narration,* 3) *diuision* or *particion,* 4) *confirmation,* 5) *confutation* and 6) *conclusion* (38–39); there are three kinds of style: grand, middle and low. These are the generally accepted basic tenets of Ciceronian rhetoric (France, Grendler).

Renaissance humanism, we now know, was based on rhetoric, to an extent difficult for modern readers to comprehend; we are so accustomed to regarding rhetoric as artificial and therefore as inferior to "plain," "sincere," or "authentic" speech and writing. "That's mere rhetoric," we say, implying that the most genuine utterance will dispense with rhetoric altogether; an attitude which Aristotle, Cicero, and most Renaissance writers would have thought eccentric. Only "ignorans," according to Fabri, maintain "que il n'est point de rhethorique aultre que la naturelle acoustumance, et l'en doit parler en francoys ainsi comme il vient à la bouche, sans y garder ordre" ("that there is no rhetoric other than natural usage, and one should speak French as it comes to the mouth, without worrying about order," 8). Rhetoric has, indeed, always had its detractors as well as its partisans; they include such heavyweight authorities as Socrates (according to Plato), who in the *Gorgias* scornfully compared rhetoric to cookery and cosmetics; Cornelius Agrippa, who called it "the art of fauninge flatterie" (43); and Montaigne, who found it no different from "le babil de vostre chambriere" ("the babble of your chambermaid,: I.51). François I, according to his sister, didn't want stories told by "ceux qui avoient estudié et estoient gens de lettres" ("those who had studied and were literary men and women"), fearing that "la beauté de la rethorique feit tort en quelque partye à la verité de l'histoire" ("the beauty of the rhetoric would in some way detract from the truth of the story," *Heptaméron*, Prologue). But these, however prestigious, are minority opinions, and certainly for most Renaissance humanists rhetoric was the foundation both of good education and good writing, as it would continue to be for centuries.[26] Peter France notes that "rhetorique" was dropped from the French school curriculum only in 1902.

We badly need a study of Cicero's orator in the Renaissance; as a model of the broadly educated, philosophically inclined, invincibly moral polymath, he inspired followers in domains that may surprise us. Alberti's ideal painter is a Ciceronian orator; so are Cortesi's ideal cardinal (1510), Castiglione's ideal courtier (1528), Blaise de Vigenère's ideal secretary (Maillard), and Ascham's ideal archer (Wilson).

A superficial reading of Rabelais might suggest that he either ignores or actively despises rhetoric. Frere Jean answers, to Ponocrates's mock disapproval of his swearing: "Ce n'est . . . que pour orner mon langaige. Ce sont couleurs de rhetorique Ciceroniane" ("That's only to decorate my speech. Those are colors of Ciceronian rhetoric," G 39), implying that rhetoric consists only of stylistic elaboration (*colores*), while for Carpalim (TL 34) "couleur de Rhetoricque" refers only to discourse used to seduce ladies. The hilarious *coq-à-l'âne* (nonsense) speeches of Baisecul and Humevesne (P 10–13) look like a parody of judicial rhetoric, as does Janotus de Bragmardo's plea (G 19) for the return of the bells (which is also a satire on scholastic logic). Frere Jean, the only Rabelaisian hero who never changes, is essentially a doer, not a speaker; we first see him turning his back on his fellow monks' purely verbal reaction to crisis, to rush out and attack the enemy singlehanded. Is Rabelais making the traditional "deeds are more efficacious than words" distinction of rhetoric's opponents?

In fact, as Cave, Screech, and others have forcefully demonstrated, rhetoric becomes increasingly central to Rabelais's comic universe. Paul Smith sees the Prologue to *Pantagruel* as already fundamentally indebted to rhetorical precepts (Smith 1984, 162), and the famous letter on education (P 8) replaces the scholastic emphasis on grammar and logic as the foundation of liberal studies by stressing languages and style (Duval 1986). The uselessness of Gargantua's "old" education is dramatically demonstrated to Grandgousier by the young page Eudémon's rhetorical encomium (Brault), and the good "new" humanist education includes the reading of Scripture "avec prononciation competente à la matiere," and the recitation of *sententiae* from the day's reading, "eloquentement" (G 23). The last three books are full of Ciceronian oratory in the form of letters or speeches; Panurge's misuse of rhetoric may be the basic premise of the *Tiers Livre* (see below); and in the *Quart Livre* he takes revenge for Dindenault's irrelevant rhetoric about his sheep by watching merchant, shepherds, and sheep drown, haranguing them the while "par lieux de rhetoricque" about "les miseres de ce monde" and "le bien et l'heur de l'autre vie" (QL 8).

The epistle to Odet de Châtillon, which introduces the *Quart Livre,* develops the old Hippocratic *topos* of the doctor as actor "en quelque insigne comoedie" (see chapters 2 and 5). He is not quite a laughing doctor, but his expression should ideally be "joyeuse, seraine, gratieuse, ouverte, plaisante" ("joyful, serene, gracious, open, agreeable"[27]), which comes close. His aim is to "resjouir" (rejoice, cheer up) his patient, "et ne le contrister en façon quelconques" ("not to sadden him in any way whatever"). This whole pasage is a detailed development of Ciceronian *pronuntiatio*, which encompasses not just the orator's intonation and dramatic expression but his clothing, gestures, and entire manner, and which illustrates once again "the quasi-theatrical character of Latin oratory" (Cave 132).

I find it odd that Rabelais's humanist-giant heroes do not conform to this "joyful actor" model. As we saw in the previous chapter, Rabelais quite strikingly fails to use humanist *facetiae* in rhetorical contexts. Pantagruel and Gargantua do laugh, though much less than inattentive readers have assumed, but they are quite unlike the Renaissance princes modeled on the Emperor Augustus, who both make jokes and laugh at jokes made against them: Alfonso of Aragon, Cosimo and Lorenzo de' Medici, and Louis XI of France, to name the most celebrated (Bowen 1984). But we should not therefore conclude that Rabelais's use of rhetoric is always, or even usually, serious.

If, instead of thinking of rhetoric only in the context of public oratory, we concentrate on rhetoric as the basis of literary genres, we immediately become aware of Rabelais's four books as extended *exercices de style*. Alongside obvious examples of formal oratory (G 15, 31, 50; TL 43), we find Ciceronian letters (P 8, G 29, QL 3 and 4); a sermon (G 45), two laments (G 3 and 28); paradoxical encomia (TL 3–4, 49–52); enigmas (G 2 and 58); a *coq-à-l'âne* (P 10–13); an *explication de texte* (G 38); a facetious ecphrasis (QL 2), and numerous *blasons* (see Chapter 2): of women's genitalia (P 15), the underworld (P 30), the colors blue and white (G 9–10), Gargantua's *torchecul* (G 13), the abbey of Thélème (G

51–57), testicles (TL 26), fools (TL 38), Dindenault's sheep (QL 6–7), and the frozen words (QL 55–56). As already noted, Rabelais's fondness for *amplificatio* or trivial pursuit leads him on to tell us much more than we needed to know about all these subjects, as well as about tripe, ladies' dress and *coiffure*, methods of divination, or sausages. His *blason* technique varies from the simple list (Gargantua's games, G 22, or Eusthenes's venomous beasts, QL 64) to the elaboration of Thélème, but is always comic; as Screech pointed out long ago, when Rabelais is serious, he is also terse. In fact, nearly all of these rhetorical set-pieces are comic; the only exceptions are the hortatory orations, the letters, Grandgousier's second lament (G 28) and his brief sermon to the pilgrims (G 45), and Pantagruel's speech on the death of Pan (QL 28).

To try to separate Rabelais the comic orator from Rabelais the comic linguist would be to impose a modern distinction on a century which would not have made it (H. Gray). More and more, as his books keep appearing, we have the impression that Rabelais's earlier preoccupation with things (walls, battles, bells, *fouaces,* and an ideal abbey) is giving way to a fascination with language. And, as Demerson has noted, "Quant aux personnages du roman, on peut dire que c'est leur type d'éloquence qui leur tient lieu de personnalité" ("As for the novel's characters, we can say that it is their type of eloquence which constitutes their personality," Demerson 1984, 10).

Of the four books, it is the *Tiers Livre* that can be fairly said to be most largely preoccupied with rhetoric. It begins and ends with a paradoxical encomium, of debts and the herb Pantagruelion respectively, and its central figure, Panurge, is the walking antithesis, not just of the good Stoic and the good Evangelical Christian, but of the good orator, as Screech first showed us years ago. I think, however, that the importance of rhetoric for this book has still not been fully appreciated.

Let us first consider the ostensible subject of the *Tiers Livre*: Panurge's marriage dilemma, which is actually a double dilemma: should he get married? and if he does get married, will his wife be unfaithful? There are a number of reasons why Rabelais might have chosen to construct an entire book around the question of marriage. It was an immediately comic subject for a "celibate" monk to treat. It encouraged sarcastic forays into the battles of the *Querelle des femmes* and the retelling of hoary old chestnuts about the sexual insatiability and the curiosity of women. It was closely related to medical topics of reproduction and the production of sperm, on which Dr. Rabelais had views to express (see Chapter 5). It permitted a firm Evangelical statement, in chapter 30, that marriage is "*much* better" (and not just "better," as St. Paul had said), than burning with lust. It gave Rabelais an excellent pretext to endorse current royal policy in opposition to the Church on the matter of marriages of children without parental consent; and, last but not least, any educated reader would at once have recognized it as a traditional rhetorical *topos*. According to Thomas Wilson's *Arte of Rhetorique* (1553), rhetoric deals with two sorts of "questions": "infinite" (meaning general; his example is "Is it better to marry or not?"), and "definite" (meaning specific; example: is it better for a priest to marry, or not?). Panurge, obviously, is willfully mixing the two; sometimes his question is general: "Is marriage a desirable condition?" whereas at other times he is really asking the specific question: "Should I, Panurge, penniless and getting old, now marry?"

It may seem perverse to quote an English, post-Rabelaisian rhetoric here. But Wilson's *Rhetorique* is closely based both on Cicero's *De oratore*, and on Aphthonius's *Progymnasmata*, which Rabelais probably also knew. Curiously, the Ciceronian rhetorical strain seems to have been much stronger in Italy and in England than in France. This is particularly evident when we look at the fortunes of the *facetiae* section of the *De oratore* (II.54–71), which, besides forming the basis for Castiglione's section on *motti, facezie,* and *burle* in the *Cortegiano* (II.42–93), also figures largely in the rhetorics of Wilson (1553), Cavalcanti (1559), Trissino (1563), and Tomitano (1570). In France, by contrast, there is no comparable *facetia* section in Fichet (1471?), Fabri (1521), or Gratien du Pont (1539), even before Ramus handed over *inventio* and *dispositio* to logic, leaving rhetoric essentially with *elocutio* or style. And after Ramus, there are no *facetiae* in Fouquelin (1555) or Courcelles (1557), nor in any of the century's numerous *Arts poétiques,* to my knowledge. Does this help to explain why Rabelais's characters seldom use *facetiae* as Cicero would have recommended using them? Wilson also seems particularly appropriate to Rabelais, in that one of his lengthy examples of rhetorical exercise is Erasmus's attempt to persuade a young gentleman to get married (54–80).

The transformation of Panurge in the *Tiers Livre* has often been discussed, and sometimes exaggerated. In *Pantagruel* he was already a coward, who in chapter 21 runs away to avoid blows, "lesquelz il craignoit naturellement" ("of which by nature he was afraid"), and already a pseudo-*érudit*: he is apparently familiar with Hebrew grammar in chapter 17, and with Aulus Gellius and Zoroaster in chapter 24. The most radical transformation is that of actions to words: in *Pantagruel* he is a trickster, specializing, like his model Cingar, in ingenious practical devices, whether useful to the plot (25) or entirely gratuitous (16), whereas in the *Tiers Livre* he does nothing but argue, complain, or perorate. Has he then changed completely? I think not; his trickster nature is now simply manifesting itself in words, not deeds; "la prestidigitation est devenue verbale" ("the conjuring has become verbal," Gray 1974, 117–18). Already in the first book, but much more blatantly in the third, he conforms to Wayne Rebhorn's definition of the trickster as *homo rhetoricus* (Rebhorn 1992); Evelyne Berriot-Salvadore goes so far as to call him "un Picrochole de la rhétorique" (38).

There are already indications in the first book that rhetoric and Panurge are not strangers. Our first impression of him, in chapter 9, is Pantagruel's physical description of him (Defaux), but our second impression is purely verbal: his linguistic *tour de force* is a notable rhetorical display by a man so fond of words that he will play with them even when he is urgently in need of physical sustenance. His encounter with Thaumaste can be read as a parody of philosophical oratory, and his mock trophy (27) as a debunking *exercice de style*—he can manipulate not only different languages, but also different kinds of language.

Panurge orator: *The Parisian Lady*

He is most obviously a rhetorician, in this first book, in the much-discussed episode of the "haute dame de Paris" (21–22). Panurge, whose gross sexual advances have been spurned by a Parisian noblewoman, takes a brutal revenge by causing more than 6,014 dogs to piss on her (piss and shit on her, in the first edition), in church. Feminist critics, naturally enough, have been attracted to this episode as an apparently obvious example of Rabelais's antifeminism (Freccero, Glidden), despite the narrator's clear indication that the lady is hardly an admirable character. She is hypocritical: "elle fist semblant de se mettre à la fenestre pour appeller les voisins à la force" ("she made as if to go to the window to call the neighbors for help"); "elle commença à s'escrier, toutesfoys non trop hault" ("she started screaming, however not too loud"), and greedy: "Par la vertus desquelles parolles il luy faisoit venir l'eau à la bouche" ("By virtue of these words he made her mouth water").

The episode is not, I believe, about gender, nor about carnival (Bakhtin) or theology (Rigolot 1994), but about rhetoric. Panurge, having made up his mind to "venir au dessus d'une des

grandes dames de la ville" (meaning both to bed her and to dominate her), opens his campaign in a strangely perverse way by
addressing her as follows: "Ma dame, ce seroit bien fort utile à
toute la republicque, delectable à vous, honneste à vostre lignée
et à moy necessaire, que feussiez couverte de ma race, et le croyez,
car l'experience vous le demonstrera" ("My lady, it would be most
useful for the whole commonwealth, pleasurable for you, honorable to your line, and necessary for me, that you should be covered by my breed; and take my word for it, for experience will
demonstrate it to you"). The opening of this speech is puzzling
(in what way would their union profit the state? how could the
penniless vagabond Panurge contribute to the nobility of the lady's
family?) until we realize that he is simply enumerating the four
topics essential to any set rhetorical theme: *utile, iucundum,
honestum, necessarium* (Clark 128), or, as a contemporary English
jingle put it:

> Four things to praise all topics amply go:
> Virtue and use, pleasure and goodness show
> (Grafton/Jardine 17)

Down to the word "necessaire," the sentence might therefore
sound like the opening of a formal encomium, which will then
go on to explore each of the four topics in detail. Panurge's
ability to manipulate rhetorical techniques is already evident in
his insinuation that while the *necessarium* applies to him, all the
iucundum will be for the lady! He is an obvious example of the
orator so frowned on by Plato, Agrippa, and Montaigne, the one
who can "make the worse appear/ The better reason," like Mil-
ton's Belial (*Paradise Lost* II.113–14). He is also a good illustration of Cave's contention that "*copia* implies the notion of mastery"
(3). Mastery of rhetoric also implies sexual potency, as Cave emphasizes, and throughout the *Tiers Livre* Panurge will be convinced

that he is both sexually inexhaustible *and* able to talk his way out of any dilemma. The apparently serious beginning to this sentence renders all the more comic Panurge's sudden descent, not just into vulgarity but into the impersonality of animal husbandry: *couvrir* is used of horses and dogs, not of human beings. The bathos is reinforced by the end of the sentence, which reverts to a rhetorical context; arguments "from experience" are routinely used in formal debate.

The lady's outraged rejection focuses, not on Panurge's desire, but on its expression: "Meschant fol vous appertient il me tenir telz propos? A qui pensez vous parler?" ("You crazy wretch, have you any right to talk to me that way? Whom do you think you're talking to"), implying that she is offended by the form rather than the content of the proposition. Panurge thereupon changes his *propos*, launching into a declaration whose grossness is reinforced, rather than attenuated, by its dazzling succession of metaphors (some of which Frame was unable to translate) from banqueting ("chere lie"), the pedals of an organ or a weaver's loom ("manequins à basses marches"), music ("sonneroit une *antiquaille*"), law ("alibitz forains"), medicine ("poullains grenez"), rat-catching ("ratouere"), and housekeeping ("espousseter"). The last two, particularly homely, metaphors remind us that Panurge's mind is more on practical action than on high-flown words.

The lady's next rejection is much less strongly worded: "Allez meschant allez, si vous me *dictes* encores un *mot*, je appelleray le monde" ("Be off, you wretch, be off. If you say one more word to me, I'll call my men"), emphasizing once again that she is fixated on the *words* Panurge is using. So, ever the versatile orator, Panurge embarks on a series of hyperboles, presumably more the kind of neo-Petrarchan *mots* the lady expects. Her beauty and elegance are such that the whole order of nature would have to be subverted before they could include one drop of malice; her beauty was destined by nature to be a model for all others; she is all honey, sugar, and manna; Paris should have awarded her the apple, because she outdoes Juno in magnificence, Minerva in prudence, and Venus in elegance.

So far, so good; although the Judgment of Paris reference reminds us that medieval and Renaissance moralists saw this *topos* as a condemnation of Paris, who in preferring Venus made the wrong choice—which is why, in Cranach's version of the *topos*, the little Cupid firing at Paris has donkey's ears. Might this not imply to an erudite reader that the "haute dame" would be an even worse choice? But Panurge apparently now tires of his hyperboles, or perhaps feels that he has amply demonstrated his rhetorical ability, and thereby proved that if he doesn't talk like this all the time it's because he doesn't want to, not because he is unable to. His next sentence reverts to the bathos technique: "O dieux et deesses celestes, que heureux sera celluy à qui ferez celle grace de ceste cy accoller, de la baiser"[28] ("O celestial gods and goddesses, how happy will be the man to whom you grant that boon to embrace this lady, to kiss her")—fine so far, but now comes the plunge into bathos—"et de frotter son lart avecques elle" ("and to rub his bacon with her")—a sentence that always reminds me of Jeeves telling Bertie Wooster that full many a glorious morning had he seen flatter the mountaintops with sovereign eye, and then turn into a rather nasty afternoon (*The Code of the Woosters*, chapter 4). This is one of the few sentences Rabelais later changed; the first edition reads "vous" instead of "elle." In the last sentence of the speech, he also changed "Doncques, pour gaigner temps, faisons" ("So, to save time, let's do it") to "Doncques . . . boutte poussen-jambions" ("So . . . let's push-thrust-straddle"), suggesting an intent to heighten the vulgarity of tone.

Shortly after this, Panurge leaves, "sans grandement se soucier du reffus qu'il avoit eu" ("without worrying very much about the refusal he had had"). During the next day's encounter in church, Panurge continues to proffer obscenities (the *équivoque* on "A

Beaumont le Viconte" and on his *cousteau* [knife], the appellation "Jan Chouart" for his penis), but also offers an imaginary rosary and imaginary costly cloth and jewels. When the lady still refuses, his conclusion is "Bren pour vous . . . je vous feray chevaucher aux chiens" ("Shit on you . . . I'll have you ridden by the dogs"). All this surely suggests that the episode is much more concerned with rhetoric than with the war between the sexes, and that so far from being the disappointed and frustrated suitor he has been imagined, Panurge knew from the start that without the right kind of rhetoric his courtship had no hope of succeeding. He surely gets much more pleasure, in chapter 22, from the lady's humiliation than he would have from sleeping with her. If any spectators had objected to the harshness of his revenge—note, however, that none does—he could have claimed to be reminding her of what lies behind the love rhetoric of Petrarchan poets: a simple bodily function, corporeally closely related to the pissing (and in the first edition, shitting) of the dogs. We don't even need modern Freudians to point out the close connections between oral emission and genital and anal emission (Cave 149); Plutarch had already drawn attention, in the *De garrulitate*, to a connection between garrulousness and barren seed (cf. Bowen 1979 and Cave 166 n. 10).

Panurge orator: *The Praise of Debts*

It should not be a dramatic surprise, then, that the Panurge of the *Tiers Livre* is a dishonest orator, as well as neither a good Christian nor a good Stoic. In the definition traditional since Quintilian, the orator is a *vir bonus ac dicendi peritus*[29] ("a good man skilled in speaking"), and as many rhetoricians, including Fabri, point out, if the man is not good his skill in speaking makes him not just despicable but also dangerous. The entire series of marriage consultations shows Panurge making "the worse appear the better reason," in, as Duval has recently shown (1993), a perpetual "chanson de ricochet" (TL 10). If Pantagruel concludes from the oracle that Panurge will be beaten, cuckolded and robbed by his wife, Panurge produces a rhetorical set-piece proving the contrary, "au rebours." If the oracle renders an individual judgement (Hippothadee, Rondibilis, Trouillogan), Panurge descends from his rhetorical platform to dismiss the advice in down-to-earth, even earthy, terms. So fundamentally is he a rhetorician that he even explains his dilemma to the fool Triboullet "en parolles rhetoriques et eleguantes" (45).

The *Tiers Livre* has been called a humanist encyclopedia, and it certainly provides astonishingly varied and detailed information on lots, dice, dreams, oracles, medicine, law, botany, and folly, as well as on more specific topics like the proper treatment of conquered peoples (1), green sauce (2), Hebrew marriage customs (6), "natural" language (19), Pauline theology (30), and royal policy on marriages without parental consent (48). It is an encyclopedia, not in the modern sense (an ignorant person can retrieve information from it), but in the Renaissance sense: an erudite reader can pick up on an entire way of thinking that underlies apparently casual remarks like "l'opinion erronee de certains espritz tyrannicques" ("as certain tyrannical spirits have opined," 1), or "C'est abus dire que ayons languaige naturel" ("It's a misstatement to say that we have a natural language," 19). Rabelais is writing for, and to, like-minded intellectuals who agree with him that Machiavelli's views are an "opinion erronee," and that the story purporting to prove that Phrygian was the original language is not to be taken seriously.

In cases like this, Rabelais can be terse, because he knows that his readers are familiar with the intellectual controversies to which he is alluding. He does not need to quote Machiavelli (or Calcagnini or Ammonius) to bolster his point, which is quite clear. But many chapters of the *Tiers Livre* could be called exercises in Trivial Pursuit; at the end of chapter 13 many readers feel that they have learned rather more than they needed to know about dream interpretation, the proper frame of mind for dreamers, the most suitable diet for them, and the two gates of sleep in Homer and Virgil. And surely only a professional botanist (like Rabelais) could remain fascinated throughout the four chapters of minute description of the plant called Pantagruelion (49–52).

This kind of *copia* must have been very congenial to Rabelais's intended reader, whether he knew it all already or was learning as he read. Panurge's *copia*, by contrast, is either misleading or wrongly applied, like Folly's Classical references in the *Praise of Folly*. Perhaps the most striking example of misapplied *copia* occurs in chapter 33. Rondibilis has completed his Galenic picture of the insatiable female at the mercy of her "animal intestine," and has assured Panurge that yes, he does know a remedy against cuckoldry. He begins an anecdote, adapted from Aesop and Plutarch and presumably familiar to most readers, but has not finished his first sentence when Panurge rudely butts in with a story of his own, relevant only in that it also concerns annual feast days. Rondibilis simply waits till he has finished, and then picks up again, continuing his sentence where it was broken off, except that he repeats the subject, "Jupiter," which his listeners might have forgotten in the meantime. This is a Panurge, reminiscent of his earlier incarnation in P 9, so fond of the sound of his own voice that he cannot help speaking, even when his discourse is deferring the revelation of the remedy for which he is so eager.

At the beginning of the book, after a parenthesis designed to refute Machiavelli and support Guillaume Du Bellay (1), we are immediately confronted with the new, purely verbal Panurge, the specialist in what Floyd Gray calls "la subversion du langage" (Gray 1974, 134). His reaction to Pantagruel's gentle remonstrance about his debts is a long speech (over two pages in the Huchon edition) which is the perfect introduction to his "self-justifying rhetoric" (Cave 192) in the rest of the book. He begins by opposing to Pantagruel's expressed anxiety about his ever becoming rich an imperative of his own: "Pensez vivre joyeulx" ("Just put your mind to living joyously"). If you, my master, are "joyeulx, guaillard, dehayt," says this model servant-companion, I shall be more than sufficiently rich. This sounds like a generous reaction, matching solicitude with solicitude, but unfortunately for Panurge the narrator has just told us, only a few lines previously, that Pantagruel *is* always *joyeulx*; like a good Stoic, he is never upset by external accidents like Panurge's outrageous behavior. On the contrary: "Toutes choses prenoit en bonne partie, tout acte interpretoit à bien. Jamais ne se tourmentoit, jamais ne se scandalizoit" ("All things he took in good part, all actions he interpreted for the good; never did he torment himself, never did he take offense"). Panurge's admonition seems to serve mainly to show his complete ignorance of Pantagruel's real nature—a foreshadowing of his ignorance in many other domains.

Panurge then says, rather petulantly, "everybody fusses about economizing, but people often talk about it when they don't even know what it is"—as though he, naturally, does know what it is. He produces a *sententia* that neatly encapsulates the whole series of consultations to follow: "C'est de moy que fault conseil prendre" ("I don't need your advice, I just need to make up my own mind"[30]). This is, of course, precisely what Pantagruel (10 and 29), Raminagrobis (21), and Trouillogan (36) will tell him, and what he is temperamentally incapable of doing.

Like the orator he is, Panurge now adduces an *exemplum* to show that his prodigality cannot possibly be a vice, inasmuch as he has acted in imitation of the "Université et Parlement de Paris," living models of "Pantheologie" and justice. How impressive! But Rabelais's readers know quite well that he deeply despises both these institutions, and Panurge's stress on the extravagance

of the banquets required for the installation of a new bishop iron-
ically adds a further dimension to the satire; the reader understands that the university and the parliament, as well as incarnating
the opposite of true theology and true justice, are disgraceful
examples of conspicuous consumption. Panurge's *exemplum*, as
so often in following chapters, proves the exact opposite of his
intention, at the same time as it highlights his total unaware-
ness of everything that the humanist Pantagruel stands for.

Panurge's argument in the rest of chapter 2 that prodigality
is a demonstration of the cardinal virtues must have delighted
his readers, especially those familiar with the *Praise of Folly*. It
is difficult for us today to grasp the sophomoric character of
Panurge's reasoning—so difficult that otherwise perceptive critics have been beguiled into sympathizing with him (Saulnier
1957). Every schoolboy knew by heart the four cardinal virtues:
wisdom or prudence, justice, fortitude and temperance, and their
meaning and relationship according to Classical and later moralists. Such a schoolboy would not need Screech's notes to his
critical edition; he would immediately perceive, and laugh at,
Panurge's outrageous definitions. For this wastrel, wisdom or
prudence consists in throwing money away because no one can
be certain of the future, and it would therefore be foolish to provide for it. Justice is divided, according to Aristotle, into two kinds:
commutative (referring to the laws of exchange, rents, and so on)
and distributive (payment according to merit, for example wages;
Tournon [1995] sees a reference here to contemporary economic
theory). Here begin Panurge's hilarious misinterpretations of
Classical *exempla* (familiar, once again, to every schoolboy).

Certainly Cato said that the wise head of the household (*pater-
familias*) should be a seller, not a buyer; meaning that he should
sell what the household does not need in order to save for the
future. Panurge pretends to assume that this means he should
buy dear and sell cheap, which is the opposite of Cato's meaning.

Panurge has demonstrated distributive justice by "distributing" his wealth to hungry companions and generous young women, who have taken to heart the axiom that we are born not for ourselves but for our family and friends. These women are thus entitled to be called "platonicques et ciceronianes." As Jourda and Screech point out, this erudition can all be found in Erasmus's *Adages* and *Apophthegms*, standard fare in the classroom, as well as in their Classical sources.

Fortitude, of course, means moral courage, not the brute strength required to cut down old-growth trees. Panurge pretends to approve deforestation on the grounds that forests harbor dangerous beasts, brigands, murderers, counterfeiters (which seems unlikely), and heretics (a frequent preoccupation of his, as we saw earlier in the chapter). Transforming forests into clearings can be called "jouant des haulx boys" (a musical metaphor for what bankrupt nobles do as a last resort), and will provide *sieges* (tree-stumps) suitable for Judgment Day (but shall we all be sitting down on Judgment Day?).

Everyone knows the meaning of temperance; only Panurge could justify "mangeant son bled en herbe," a popular idiom for "wastefully consuming his patrimony" (Cotgrave), or as we might say today, selling wheat futures, on the (literal) grounds that a) by eating grass he is living temperately, like a hermit; b) by preventing the wheat from maturing he is saving the energies of weeders, reapers, gleaners, threshers (with Virgilian reference thrown in), millers, and bakers; c) he is also saving the damage caused to the crop by mice and other beasts; d) (changing register) from *bled en herbe* you can make green sauce, which is good for the digestion, state of mind, eyes, appetite, taste buds, heart, tongue (!), complexion, muscles, blood, diaphragm, liver, spleen, kidneys, vertebrae, bladder, and genitals: "vous faict bon ventre, bien rotter, vessir, peder, fianter, uriner, esternuer, sangloutir, toussir, cracher, vomiter, baisler, mouscher, haleiner, inspirer, respirer,

ronfler, suer, dresser le virolet, et mille autres rares adventaiges"
("makes you do things well: belch, fizzle, fart, shit, urinate, sneeze,
sob, cough, spit, vomit, yawn, blow your nose, puff, inhale, breathe,
snore, sweat, get your pecker up, and myriad other rare advan-
tages"). As Screech (ed. TL 35 n. 130) puts it, "And all this in
the name of temperance!"

This four-part oration is on one hand obviously rhetorical,
and on the other hand obviously a perversion of rhetoric. The
last and longest section begins by taking an idiomatic expression
literally—one of Rabelais's favorite devices—and then trivially
pursuing it wherever it wants to lead him. Never mind that "bled
en herbe" ("wheat in the blade") is not the same thing as "sallades
et racines" ("salads and roots"), that the "saving" of workmen
involved with the wheat harvest means putting them out of work
or that starving people would presumably rather have mice-nib-
bled grain than no grain at all. Never mind that green sauce is
not a medicine, but a very popular condiment for cooked meat;
I have seen at least half a dozen different recipes for it, usually
spinach-based or basil-based. And never mind that not everyone
is anxious to hiccup, fart, sob, cough, spit, throw up, and yawn.
Panurge's concluding flight of sheer fantasy about this miraculous cure-all may remind us that he had "aultresfoys crié le the-
riacle" ("hawked quack medicine," P 16); it certainly expresses
the opposite of temperance, both in the copious bodily functions evoked and in the sheer exuberance of the language. Even
if we had never met the speaker before, we could still laugh heartily at this masterly demonstration of how to make the worse appear
the better case. Pantagruel does not laugh; he sees through the
rhetoric to the subject—an indefensible defense of wasteful spend-
ing—and calls it *haeresie*, not of course using that word to
mean what Panurge means by it.

This verbal *tour de force*, which would have sufficed on its
own to introduce both the new Panurge and the central theme

of the *Tiers Livre*, turns out to be merely the overture to the main *opus*: the praise of *debteurs et emprunteurs* (debtors and creditors) in the next two chapters—nearly seventy-nine pages in the Huchon edition. A detailed *explication* of these pages could fill a book. Panurge begins in a low key, with a very practical reason for remaining perpetually in debt: creditors are necessarily anxious for the continued good health of the debtor, like servants who know they must die when their master does (learned excursus on ancient Gaul). Pantagruel does not counter this one, and we know that his silence, in the *Tiers Livre*, always indicates disapproval (Screech).

Panurge now abandons practicality and launches himself into higher spheres. It is typical of his fatuous self-satisfaction that the first rhetorical argument to occur to him is to compare himself to God; he has created creditors *ex nihilo* (out of nothing), and creditors are "creatures belles et bonnes." His learned reference to Plutarch does not actually prove that the "perfection" of debtors is in proportion to the number of their creditors, but no matter. He is more interested in his own comfort ("Cuidez-vous que je suis aise?" ["Will you believe how happy I am?"]) than in intellectual abstractions, and he revels in the solicitude of his creditors, who make him feel like the actor playing God in the Passion play, accompanied by his attendant angels. His creditors "sont mes candidatz, mes parasites, mes salüeurs, mes diseurs de bons jours, mes orateurs perpetuelz" ("are my candidates, my parasites, my glad-handers, my good-day-sayers, my perpetual speechmakers"[31]).

This is already a quite impressive flight of fancy, but Panurge has only just started. We learn next that he thinks debts are the modern equivalent of the mountain of Virtue described by Hesiod—judging by the fervor with which "au jourdhuy tout le monde" ("today everyone") aspires and strives to be in debt. But (nice little rhetorical parenthesis, to vary the tone) not everyone can attain the "félicité soubeline" ("sable-smooth felicity") of the bankrupt state (two rhetorical questions, which Pantagruel does not answer).

We have now reached the main course of this rhetorical feast: a paradoxical encomium of debts as the essential "soul" that holds everything in the universe, macrocosm and microcosm, together. It is a superb pastiche, not just of Ficino's claims for love as the universal bond, but of assorted Renaissance depictions of harmony as *discordia concors* (in Erasmus's "Festina lente," for example). Rabelais's readers know perfectly well that debts are evil, according to all Classical and Christian moralists, and also that Panurge's whole stance is dishonest because he is fixated on borrowing—there is no mention, and certainly no likelihood, of his ever lending anyone anything.

As is often the case with Lucian's paradoxical encomia, the more indefensible the *topos* the more admirable the skill of the rhetorician. In the preliminary flourish of chapter 2, Panurge had already shown himself a theologian, a dialectician, a physiologist and an historian. In chapters 3 and 4, he incarnates all these again, at more length and in each case using enough technical terminology to convince the listener of his expertise ("connexion et colligence," "digere et chylifie," "mouvemens diastolicques et systolicques," and so on). Panurge is just like Plato's Gorgias, who maintains that the rhetorician can speak convincingly on any subject without knowing much about it.

There are several levels of wit in these two chapters. Most obviously, the reader enjoys Panurge's manipulation of the techniques of satirical eulogy current since Lucian (Tomarken): exclamations, rhetorical questions, hyperbole, periphrasis, "learned" digressions (he even knows Greek!), and so on. We are still at the beginning of this third book, and the new, tediously erudite Panurge is still a surprise to the reader. Is it really the *blasonneur* of women's genitalia and the *conteur* of obscene fables (P 15) who is now talking about "le nombre des syllabes resultantes au couplement de toutes les consonantes avecques les vocales" ("the number of syllables resulting from coupling all the consonants with all the vowels"), or "L'appetit en l'orifice de l'estomach moyenant un peu de melancholie aigrette" ("the appetite, in the orifice of the stomach, with the help of a little bitter melancholy")?

Panurge's use of the technical vocabularies of theology, philosophy and medicine (none of which are by definition laughable) is thus comic in its context, and also by its contrast to idiomatic or slangy expressions like "je me donne à sainct Babolin le bon sainct" ("I give myself to Saint Babolin the good saint"), "O le beau mot" ("O what a lovely statement"), or "Vertus guoy" ("Goshamighty!"). This contrasting-style technique, which will be used to such effect by La Fontaine, is hardly perceptible, alas, to most of today's readers.

But Panurge's encomium is also comic because in the course of it, he cannot help revealing his (reprehensible) character and attitudes. As already noted, his egoism leads him to begin by imagining himself as God, but he also betrays opinions diametrically opposed to Pantagruel's. During his dramatically somber picture of the debtless macrocosm, in which nothing functions, he appears to toss off a charming pun: "Venus ne sera venerée" ("Venus will not be venerated"). This turns out, however, not to be gratuitous wit, for a few lines later he says "les Astres ne y feront influence bonne" ("the stars will exert no good influence there"). So he believes in the positive influence of the stars, which Pantagruel (and Rabelais) emphatically do not.

The passage most revealing of Panurge's character is his *blason* of the Golden Age in chapter 4. It begins: "O quelle harmonie sera parmy les reguliers mouvemens des Cieulz. Il m'est advis que je l'entends aussi bien que feist oncques Platon. Quelle sympathie entre les elemens. O comment Nature se y delectera en ses oeuvres et productions. Cerés chargée de bleds: Bacchus de vins:

Flora de fleurs: Pomona de fruictz: Juno en son aër serain seraine, salubre, plaisante. Je me pers en ceste contemplation" ("O what harmony there will be among the regular movements of the heavens! I think I hear it as well as Plato ever did. What sympathy among the elements! O how Nature will delight in her works and productions! Ceres laden with wheat; Bacchus, with wines; Flora, with flowers; Pomona, with fruits; Juno in her serene air, herself serence, salubrious, pleasant. I'm lost in this contemplation"). A very conventional opening. But now comes one of Rabelais's "which-item-does-not-belong-here?" enumerations, and the real Panurge begins to show through the rhetoric. "Entre les humains Paix, Amour, Dilection [the word Pantagruel will use for *agape* at the beginning of chapter 5], Fidelité, repous" ("Among humans, peace, love, fondness, fidelity, repose"). How delightful! But the next two items are "banquetz" and "festins"— this is the Panurge who "ne feist que troys pas et un sault du lict a table" (it took him only three steps and a hop from bed to table) in P 9, and who will make so much fuss about skipping dinner in TL 15. And this sentence ends: "joye, liesse, or, argent, menue monnoie, chaisnes, bagues, marchandises, troteront de main en main" ("joy, blitheness, gold, silver, small change, chains, rings, merchandise will trot about from hand to hand")—this Panurge cannot keep his attention on peace and harmony for very long, because thoughts of "menue monnoie" and what it can buy are always at the forefront of his mind.

A little later he produces with his usual air of fatuous self-satisfaction some quite horrendous opinions:

Je vous jure le bon Vraybis, que si cestuy monde, beat monde ainsi à chascun prestant, rien ne refusant, eust Pape foizonnant en Cardinaulx, et associé de son sacre colliege, en peu d'années vous y voiriez les sainctz plus druz, plus miraclificques, à plus de leçons, plus de veuz, plus de bastons, et plus de chandelles, que ne sont tous ceulx des neufz eveschez de Bretaigne.

❧

I swear to you by honest-to-goodness that if this world, blessed world, thus lending to each and every one, refusing nothing, had a pope teeming with cardinals and associates of his sacred college, in a few years you would see there saints more clustered, more miracle working, with more readings, more prayers, more batons, and more tapers, than are all those of the nine bishoprics of Brittany.

Splendid! Except that, as was the case with the "Université et Parlement de Paris" in chapter 2, Rabelais's reader knows quite well that all the items mentioned here are anathema to good Evangelical Christians: Pope, Cardinals, saints, miracles, vows, confraternity symbols, and even candles. No wonder Pantagruel seldom needs to condemn Panurge; he condemns himself nearly every time he opens his mouth.

After a quotation from "le noble (!) Patelin," the rest of chapter 4 is occupied by the physiological excursus supporting Plato's contention that blood is the life principle and the creator of semen in the male body. To a knowledgeable reader, and most humanists certainly had at least a smattering of medical knowledge, this is comic both because Panurge has suddenly become a medical specialist, and because he is espousing as obviously correct a theory considered by many in the Renaissance to be rather old-fashioned. It is of course also typical of Panurge that his whole rhetorical development, with its lofty flights of fancy about the peace and harmony of the Golden Age, should come to a crashing finale with a praise of semen. At the beginning of chapter 5, Pantagruel will take only a few words to demolish this house of cards by quoting St. Paul, who said we should owe nothing to one

another except *agape*. Panurge had already, in his Golden Age
passage, referred to this term, which he translated "Charité"; Pantagruel's translation is the Evangelical humanist one: "amours et
dilection mutuelle" (love and mutual affection).

These initial chapters set the scene for the rest of the *Tiers
Livre*, in which Panurge is both the dishonest and one-track-
minded orator, like Erasmus's Lady Folly in the early part of the
Encomium, and the brilliantly versatile actor we saw in Chapter
2. He is by no means the book's only orator; in this actionless story,
every episode opposes one orator to another. Each individual
authority consulted speaks his own language, sometimes severe-
ly technical (Herr Trippa, Rondibilis), sometimes a pastiche of
technical language (Trouillogan, Bridoye). Rabelais here demon-
strates his mastery of *ethos*, the conformity of speech to character. For a modern reader, it is hard to make a distinction between
the sometimes tediously erudite speech of Pantagruel and the
self-serving, tricksy argumentation of Panurge, but Rabelais's
intended reader would have had no problem. Panurge's ability
to twist the most ominous prediction into an omen favorable to
himself is what keeps the plot, such as it is, moving; that and Pantagruel's heroic patience and forbearance with him.

The *Quart Livre*, despite the rhetorically oriented letter of
Odet de Châtillon that prefaces it, is less preoccupied with Panurge-
as-orator, and more interested in other uses of language; in
particular, as Nilles (1993) and Jeanneret (1994) have stressed, in
the function of language as sign. The whole saga, as critics
have noted, is a hilarious eventless epic quest: "the composition
of the book is again and again dependent on the composition of
language" (Cave 205); "une sorte de fable linguistique sur le pou-
voir générateur des mots" ("a sort of linguistic fable about the
generative power of words," Kritzman 195). From the initial
port of call at an island called Nowhere to the final exhortation
"Beuvons!" ("Let's drink!"), how much epic action is there? Mer-

chant, shepherd and sheep are drowned, in an explicitly rhetorical context (8); a storm engulfs the fleet but kills no one and destroys no ships; a whale is killed (34); sausages are massacred— but immediately revived by their miraculous mustard (42); frozen words land on deck (55) and cannons are fired (66). The great majority of episodes are about language or generated by language: the pictures of subjects which could be depicted only in words (2); the cliché couplings of Ennasin (9); the Bringuenarilles story stemming from an idiomatic expression, "Nous n'y trouvasmes que frire" ("We couldn't find anything to fry/fry with, because the giant has eaten all the cooking-pots," 17); the Andouilles episode which seems to have more to do with naming (Riflandouille, Niphleseth) than with action, and so on. There is, indeed, some violence, but almost all of it is recollected in tranquillity (the Chiquanous, the Villon story).

Critics have given very different emphases to this preoccupation with language. Some I find untenable, like Berry's "breakdown of language in the *Quart Livre*," Nakam's "la peur domine le *Quart Livre*" (fear dominates the Fourth Book), or Randall's "despairing skepticism" (104) Others leave me intrigued but undecided: is this pseudo-epic really more of a commentary on the Eucharist than a genuine quest (Duval 1988, Smith 1987)? What is quite clear is that Panurge as character has not changed, inasmuch as his reaction to any crisis, storm, menacing sea-monster, inhabitants of Ganabin, is to express his feelings in a flood of words.

It is interesting that despite the book's preoccupation with language, Panurge comes across as less of a dishonest orator than in the *Tiers Livre*. In the Dindenault episode, indeed, the roles are reversed; Dindenault is the dishonest snake-oil salesman, and Panurge plays the part of a terse, sometimes monosyllabic bystander. As we saw in Chapter 2, Panurge the orator is at the same time Panurge the actor, and it would be pointless to attempt a distinction between the two. But the *Quart Livre* does retain, and even emphasize, one aspect of rhetoric already mentioned: the close ties between rhetorical and sexual potency. In the Prologue, Couillatris's flood of words is explicated, in a sense, by Priapus, who speaks "en toute courtoisie et joviale honesteté"— just like an Erasmian orator. And Priapus is recalled later in the book, as Cave notes (202), by the phallic/feminine Andouilles, although their specialty in the episode is rather action than words.

This chapter has made no attempt to cover every aspect of Rabelais the comic rhetorician. While it has often repeated or confirmed the opinions of other Rabelaisants, it has also tried to show that rhetoric is even more central to Rabelais, and especially to Panurge (the sophist, as Defaux identified him years ago), than has been realized. It has also proposed that to recognize the importance of rhetoric, for instance in Panurge's siege of the Parisian lady and his indefensible defense of borrowing, is at the same time to increase their potential for making us laugh.

CHAPTER 5

The Comic Doctor

They sent for some doctors
In sneezles
And wheezles
To tell them what ought
to be done.

A. A. MILNE

Doctor Rabelais

This book has not, until now, radically changed subjects from one chapter to the next, for literature, humanism, and rhetoric are all very closely interconnected. From rhetoric to medicine does seem like quite a jump, but let us remember that sixteenth-century intellectuals were "universal men" (and women, occasionally) to a degree difficult for us to grasp. Even if Rabelais had not been a qualified doctor, he might very well have been interested in, and quite knowledgeable about, medical subjects. Medicine formed part of the cultural baggage of most educated men, and it is not uncommon for literary authors to demonstrate quite detailed medical knowledge—Du Bellay, for instance, was apparently familiar with current anatomical theory relative to his deafness (Mcadoo), and Béroalde de Verville included among the speakers of his *Moyen de Parvenir* Fracastoro, Rondelet, Asclepiades, Avicenna, Fernel, Galen, Hippocrates, Linacre, Nicander, and Paracelsus. There can even be, as I have shown elsewhere, a surprising rhetorical dimension to some aspects of Renaissance cookery (Bowen 1995). But first we need to look at the discipline of medicine in general.

Molière, who must bear a share of responsibility for the relative neglect, even today, of Renaissance medicine, has left posterity with a hilarious but entirely misleading impression of medical science in his time. His doctors, whether phony like Sganarelle and Toinette, or genuine like Tomès and Diafoirus *père et fils*, know of no treatment beyond bleeding, purges and enemas, parrot imperfectly understood jargon from outdated authorities, and generally combine monumental stupidity with outrageous self-satisfaction. Who, after meeting any of these characters, could possibly take Renaissance medicine seriously? Modern works intended for the general reader seldom devote much space to sixteenth-century medicine. The outsize coffee-table book by Albert S. Lyons and R. Joseph Petrucelli, *Medicine: An Illustrated History* (New York: Abrams, 1987 [1978]), devotes only fifty-five pages to "The Renaissance," and most of those are illustration. Leoniceno is treated in one paragraph (369), Fernel and Fracastoro share a paragraph (376), and the half page on surgery mentions only Paré (381).

There is a general tendency to look down condescendingly on premodern medicine (as though today's medicine were all-knowing and infallible). In fact, as recent works both general (Siraisi, Conrad, Nutton) and specific (Antonioli, Fontaine) have shown, sixteenth-century medicine bears little relation to the gross caricature presented by Molière (who, whatever his personal grudges against the medical profession may have been, knew perfectly well that his portrait of Diafoirus was no closer to real life than those of Ortwin and Eck had been, a hundred years earlier, in the EOV). The early sixteenth century, in particular, was a relatively exciting time for medical humanism, which saw the first publication of the complete works of Galen in Greek (1525), and of Hippocrates in Latin (1525) and Greek (1526), and some lively quarrels among the supporters of Greek and Arabic medicine. Rabelais's own edition of the *Aphorisms* of Hippocrates made a contribution to this rediscovery of ancient medical authority. There was already at least one illustrated anatomy text in print, by Berengario da Carpi (French), and the "new humanist surgery" was beginning to flourish in France (Nutton 1985).

My intention in this chapter is not to add anything of substance to Antonioli's very valuable 1976 study on Rabelais, but to examine specifically how Rabelais's medical expertise is used to comic effect, and along the way to correct some misconceptions. Like Antonioli, I shall be relying a great deal on the information provided by Screech and others on the medical quarrels of the time, but I shall also be quoting medical authorities contemporary with Rabelais, who can provide useful background to Rabelais's own medical comments. Laughter, as we shall see, had closer connections with medicine in Rabelais's time than it does today. Readers are asked to approach this discussion with open minds; while there were no revolutionary discoveries in Renaissance medicine, and while theorists were by necessity still dialoguing with Hippocrates, Plato, and Galen, the whole subject is of much more interest than it has been given credit for.

Some of the basic principles of ancient and Renaissance medicine are still well known today. Medical practice was based on the theory of the four humors: blood, phlegm, black bile, and yellow bile. Picrochole's name indicates that his outrageous behavior stems from his overabundance of black bile; the subtitle of *Le Misan-thrope* is the oxymoronic *L'Atrabilaire amoureux* (The Irascible Man in Love), and Philinte can say to Alceste: "Mon phlegme est philosophe autant que votre bile" ("My phlegm is as philosoph-ical as your bile"). Hamlet's "melancholy" has been frequently analyzed, and we can still refer to a person as a "sanguine" char-acter. Medicine (or therapeutics) is traditionally divided into three parts (or "instruments of medicine"): surgery, pharmacology, and diet, but an even more fundamental distinction is that between restorative medicine, which counters illness by means of contrary things, and conservative medicine, which maintains good health by means of similar things (Céard 1982; this is based on the Hip-pocratic naturals, nonnaturals, and contranaturals).

Other basic principles are less well known, and an important one for understanding Rabelais is the whole question of medical "sects," for which I refer to the *Methode ou brieve introduction pour parvenir à la congnoissance de la vraye & solide Medecine* (Method or Brief Introduction to Arrive at the Knowledge of True and Solid Medicine) first published by Leonard Fuchs in 1531 (*Meden-di methodus*), and translated into French by Guillaume Paradin in 1552. In the fourth of his forty-eight chapters, Fuchs explains succinctly, following Classical medical theory, "combien il y ha de sectes de Medecins" ("how many medical sects there are"). There are three: first, the *Empiriques*, who say that "la seule expe-rience est suffisante" ("experience alone is sufficient"); second, the *Methodiques*, who claim that nothing (experience of the patient, etc.) is relevant except "laffection ou passion"; and, third, the *Rationaux* or *Dogmatiques*, who preach a combination of experi-ence and reason:

> Combien toutefois quilz ne veulent nier que lexperience ne soit nec-
> essaire aussi bien que le reste, mais ilz nient que le tout ne gist pas
> en elle: & par ce veulent affirmer, que lon ne pourroit paruenir a lex-

perience, sinon par le moyen de quelque raison: par ce que autrement elle seroit incertaine, & ny auroit nulle, ou bien peu dassurance

᧿

However, they don't wish to deny that experience is as necessary as the rest, but they deny that it is the whole story: and by this they wish to affirm, that we could not arrive at experience except by the means of some reason: because otherwise it would be uncertain, and we could put no, or very little, trust in it (22).

Hippocrates, "sans doute Prince de tous les Medecins," is their hero, and it is clear that Fuchs's sympathies, like Rabelais's, those of Charles Estienne in his *Dissection des parties du corps humain*, 1545, and those of many others, are with this third group. Screech (1976) thought that Rabelais believed Hippocrates to be infallible, thanks to a special revelation; I rather doubt this.

The Fuchs passage immediately throws some curious light on the child Gargantua's "experiences"[32] in search of the perfect *torchecul* (G 13; Bowen, "Rabelais et le propos torcheculatif"). Critics have assumed that he is being patted on the back, by Rabelais as well as by Grandgousier, for using experiment rather than authority in search of an answer to his problem, but the medical point of view is rather different. Among the various comic devices in this chapter we must count the obvious fact that if Gargantua had been able to use reason *as well as* experiment, he could have spared himself some painful experiments/experiences (with the embroidered cloth, the cat, and the basket), and could perhaps even have deduced that the most plausible solution was a nice soft bird.

But the sect question has further implications, in the traditional hostility between the "Greeks" and the "Arabs." The question is complex (Antonioli chap. 3), but for our purposes can be simply stated: "Greeks" usually designates the followers of Hippocrates, that is to say the *Rationaux* or *Dogmatiques* mentioned above, whereas "Arabs" or *Empiriques* refers to those followers of Avicenna and other, mainly Arabic writers who are interested only in practical remedies, and most often in the use of herbal remedies or *simples*. It is clear from the texts that a veritable Greek–Arab war was being waged during the years Rabelais was writing his first books. Fuchs was very anti-Arab, although he does not, like some authorities, lump them with the other *Empiriques* in group 1. But he attacks them specifically in chapter 5, à propos of "lintelligence des simples" (the understanding of medicinal herbs), though his disapproval is mild compared to Symphorien Champier's "Primordium omnium malorum ex Arabia fuit" ("The source of all evils came out of Arabia," *Symphonia Galeni ad Hippocratem*, Lyon, 1528, p. 10). A few pages later Champier fulminates against "Auicennistae, hoc est, ij qui malunt Arabice quàm Latine aut Graece medicari" ("Avicennists, that is to say, those who prefer to practice medicine according to the Arabs rather than the Romans and the Greeks"), and concludes "Quis non uideat plus esse ab Auicennistis quàm a morbo periculi?" ("Who cannot see that more dangers come from the Avicennists than from the disease?" [17]). Sebastian Colin attacks "empiriques" in his *Bref dialogue contenant les Causes, Iugemens, Couleurs & Hypostases des Vrines* (1558 ed., 45) and castigates "vieux resueurs Arabistes" (old Arab dreamers) in his *Declaration des abvz et tromperies qve font les Apothicaires* (Declaration of the Abuses and Deceptions Practiced by Apothecaries, Lyon, 1556). Canappe's translation of Chauliac's "Chapitre singulier" discusses sects, and attacks the "Empiriques, qui sans doctrine & Methode veulent curer" ("Empiricals, who want to cure without doctrine or method," 144), describing them as "promettans guerir de toutes maladies, & plusieurs autres" ("promising to cure all maladies, and several others," 38), like the charlatans of contemporary farce. Fuchs himself is more trenchant in his *Paradoxo-*

rum medicinae libri tres of 1534, and a delightful dialogue called *Barbaromastix* was devoted to demolishing the credibility of the Arabs; this dialogue was printed in 1534 in a collective volume aggressively entitled *Novae Academiae Florentinae opuscula. Aduersus Auicennam, & medicos neotericos, qui Galeni disciplini* [sic] *neglecta, barbaros colunt* (A Little Work of the New Florentine Academy. Against Avicenna, and the Newfangled Doctors, Who, with the Instruction of Galen Neglected, Cultivate Barbarous [disciplines]).

It is thus particularly intriguing to see, in the detailed humanist program for Pantagruel's education (P 8): "Puis songneusement revisite les livres des medicins Grecz, Arabes, et Latins" ("Then carefully review the books of the Greek, Arabian, and Latin doctors"). The Hippocratic Rabelais, trained at Montpellier where the emphasis in medical studies was on experience/experiment (Antonioli 38), does not, at least at this stage in his career, reject the authority of Avicenna, Mesue, and Serapion. Nevertheless, most medical allusions in Rabelais are to Greek, not Arab, sources, and Hippocrates, Galen, and Plato remain central.

In fact, as both Screech and Antonioli have stressed, Rabelais remains fairly conservative on medical subjects. He certainly accepts the theory of humors and the three traditional divisions, and his attitude to all three is more likely to be conservative than revolutionary—although he is credited with the invention of two new surgical instruments (Antonioli 99), was certainly in favor of dissection (the "frequentes anatomies" of P 8), and was aware of current arguments about the treatment of syphilis. I should mention here that not all writers on medicine in Rabelais are agreed; Evelyne Berriot-Salvadore (1995) proposes to modify both Screech's view of Rondibilis and Antonioli's stress on Rabelais's "optimisme médical."

Medical themes and references are frequent in all four books, but our author is most obviously Dr. Rabelais in two liminary pieces to the *Quart Livre*: the Epistle to Odet de Châtillon, and the 1552 Prologue. The Epistle begins by picking up the "reading-my-books-will-cheer-you-up" theme of the Prologue to *Pantagruel*. It then quotes Hippocrates, as we have already noted in Chapters 2 and 4: the ideal doctor is an actor/orator, and "la practique de Medicine . . . est par Hippocrates comparée à un combat, et farce jouée à trois personnages: le malade, le medecin, la maladie" ("the practice of medicine . . . is compared by Hippocrates to a combat and farce played by three personae: the patient, the doctor, and the illness"). Rabelais does not say, in this Epistle, that the ideal doctor is a laughing doctor; the word he uses a number of times is *joyeux*: "la face joyeuse," "esperitz . . . joyeux," and "resjouir." So that Rabelais's own "folasteries joyeuses," which are "le subject et theme unicque d'iceulx livres" ("the subject and only theme of these books"), can be assumed to have a therapeutic function.

In the 1552 Prologue the medical theme continues. The *santé* the speaker wishes for his readers can result only from *mediocrité* (the golden mean), the contentment with one's own modest station in life exemplified by Couillatris's refusal of the gold and silver axes. Those who prefer to pursue gain rather than health will end up with neither, but the wise reader will follow the speaker's final advice: "Or en bonne santé toussez un bon coup, beuvez en trois, secouez dehait vos aureilles, et vous oyrez dire merveilles du noble et bon Pantagruel" ("Now, in good health cough one good cough, drink three drinks, give your ears a cheery shake, and you shall hear wonders about the good and noble Pantagruel").

It seems odd, in view of all this, that medicine in Rabelais, like Renaissance medicine in general, has always been short-changed, despite the numerous references to it throughout his work. Even the solid and interesting overview by Antonioli has never received the acclaim it deserves; "Rabelais médecin" seems

simply not as interesting to modern readers as "Rabelais humaniste" and "Rabelais évangélique." This chapter will at least attempt
to redress the balance.

There are three different types of medical passages in Rabelais,
not all of which are comic. First, there is the very obvious medical explanation, for instance of baby Gargantua's birth when the
usual downward passage from the womb is blocked (G 6):

> Par cest inconvenient feurent au dessus relaschez les cotyledons de
> la matrice, par lesquelz sursaulta l'enfant, et entra en la vene creuse,
> et gravant par le diaphragme jusques au dessus des espaules (où
> ladicte vene se part en deux) print son chemin à gauche, et sortit par
> l'aureille senestre.

❧

> By this mishap were loosened the cotyledons of the matrix, through
> which the infant sprang up into the vena cava; and, climbing up
> by the diaphragm up above the shoulders, where the said vein
> divides in two, took the route to the left, and came out through the
> left ear.

The (presumably correct) anatomical precision is comic because
of the physical impossibility of such a birth, and because the technical terminology contrasts amusingly with the context of tripe,
peasant carousing, and the "horde vieille"'s "medical" procedures.

The *Tiers Livre*, the most medically preoccupied of the four
books (medicine has close ties with both marriage and folly), contains two lengthy passages of medical explanation which have
been thoroughly analyzed by Screech, in *The Rabelaisian Marriage* and in the notes to his edition. Panurge's praise of debts is
not only a magnificent paradoxical encomium (see chapter 4); it
includes a detailed account of how the different parts of the body
work together to "forge" blood, the principle of life, which in its

turn forges semen. This description of the progressive refinement of the blood sounds foolish to modern readers, but is in fact perfectly orthodox medical theory of its time; Panurge is comic because he is misusing this scientific material for his "argument," and also because the unlearned trickster of *Pantagruel* has suddenly become an expert anatomist. And his generally pejorative image in the *Tiers Livre* does not prevent him, in this instance, from being a mouthpiece for Rabelais's anti-Galenism.

The same support for the medical principles of Hippocrates and Plato against those of Galen is evident in the *Tiers Livre*'s other long medical passage: Dr. Rondibilis's definition of what used to be called uterine hysteria in chapter 32. Modern readers have to laugh on learning that the uterus qualifies as an animal because it has independent movement and a sense of smell, but there is nothing laughable here to educated Renaissance readers; this had been standard medical "knowledge" since antiquity, and Vesalius in 1543 still likens the uterus to "a sort of animal" (Screech 1958, 92).

The second type of medical reference in Rabelais is much harder to identify. We have only recently learned that the medlars of P 1 were considered efficacious against bleeding, especially menstrual and hemorrhoidal bleeding, and also sometimes identified with female genitalia (Nilles 1989), and that the series of surrealist comparisons making up the "anatomie" of Quaresmeprenant (QL 30–32) is a parody of contemporary vernacular physiological terminology (Fontaine). I was astonished, a few years ago, to discover that all the plants essayed by the child Gargantua as toilet-paper substitutes are present in herbals from antiquity through the Renaissance with a variety of medicinal properties, most frequently connected with diarrhea or other intestinal problems; part of the comedy here must be in Gargantua's use, raw, on one end of his body, of leaves which are normally cooked and absorbed at the other end. In all these cases, a little specialized medical knowledge greatly enhances Rabelais's comedy; there are certainly more such references awaiting identification.

Most readers probably do not even notice what I consider as a third type of medical reference: the casual remark which is evidence that medicine is frequently in our narrator's mind. For instance, we learn in passing that roasting cures sciatica (P 14) and that chestnuts cause farting (G 40); we are told that a conqueror must treat his newly acquired subjects as a doctor would treat convalescent patients (TL 1). Medical references occur in the most apparently unpromising contexts; are most of us reminded of Galen by the sight of a dog gnawing on a marrow-bone (G Prologue)? The only farce plot recounted fully (TL 34) is a medical one involving a doctor, a surgeon and an "encyliglotte . . . soubs la langue" (restricting chord . . . under the tongue). Screech concludes that for Rabelais medical science is in harmony with "le bon sens de la farce française" ("the sound common sense of French farce," TL ed. 240). This chapter marks the end of the Dr. Rondibilis episode, so a medical farce is certainly appropriate, but it is Epistemon, not Rondibilis, who supplies the medical details. And it is the always irreverent Panurge who throws out the standard scatological joke against medical students: "Stercus et urina Medici sunt prandia prima" ("Urine and dung for doctors make fine meals"), immediately countered by Rondibilis with the standard retort: "Nobis sunt signa, uobis sunt prandia digna" ("Mere signs to us, to you they're worthy dishes"). Jokes about doctors and excrement go back to antiquity; Erasmus (not a fan of gross comedy) mentions in passing that in old comedy doctors were jokingly called *skatophagoi* (excrement-eaters, *Encomium medicinae*, 1499, 184).

Given the passion with which Rabelais as narrator expresses his views on true religion and the conduct of the Ideal Prince, we might have expected him to engage in some of the burning medical controversies of the day, like the battle over the nature of syphilis. Is it an entirely new disease, as Symphorien Champier claimed (*Castigationes*)? Or is it just a modified form of a disease long known, like lichen (Leoniceno) or impetigo (Fuchs)? Rabelais must have seen enough syphilis patients during his hospital stint in Lyon to have his own opinion on the matter. But his books' engagement in medical polemic seems to be limited to the reproductive questions we have just seen treated in the *Tiers Livre*, and to a few references to therapeutic laughter, of which more will be said shortly. The other, very frequent, mentions of medicine are nearly always comic applications of his medical expertise, most outrageously with an exaggerated display of his surgical and anatomical knowledge. The itemization of Quaresmeprenant contains almost as many technical anatomical terms as Charles Estienne's *Dissection des parties du corps humain* (1546); there are also quite a number of such terms in the *Tiers Livre*'s double set of epithets for *couillon* (26 and 28); and numerous violent incidents use precise anatomical detail with great gusto: the deaths of Panurge's Turk (P 14), Loupgarou (P 29), the invading soldiers massacred by frere Jean in the cloister (G 27), Tripet (G 35), Tyravant (G 43), the archers guarding frere Jean (G 44), and Tappecoue (QL 13), and the wounding of Marquet (G 25) and the Chiquanous (QL 15). Only once, for the resurrection of Epistemon by Panurge (P 30), is Rabelais's anatomical precision used constructively rather than destructively (we note with amusement, in passing, that there are no doctors in Epistemon's Hell).

Surgery, and the anatomy necessary to it, are not in any case nearly as frequent as medicine's traditional second division: pharmacology (and the general medical theories it requires). References to disease and its cure are pervasive in Rabelais, starting from the Prologue to *Pantagruel*, which presents the *Grandes et inestimables Chronicques* as a sovereign remedy for disappointment, toothache, and the miseries of treatment for syphilis. Throughout the four books, we learn in passing of drugs and remedies, some of them surprising: moss for plugging a wound (P 15), Panurge's diuretic for Pantagruel (P 28), the medical properties of clothing (G 8 and 20), a *cuisse de Levrault* (young hare's drumstick) for the gout (G 39), Pantagruelion for all sorts of ills (TL 51), paper on the stomach for seasickness (QL 1), the droppings of Dindenault's sheep for seventy-eight different maladies (QL 7).

Venereal disease is the most commonly mentioned illness, naturally enough in an age where its threatening presence was roughly that of AIDS in our own (but it is not referred to as often as Berlioz claims it is). Oddly to our ears, syphilis was sometimes known as the "gay disease" ("gay" in the older sense of that term), and Panurge at one point refers to the fool Triboullet as "fol riant et Venerien" ("laughing and venereal fool," TL 38). Numerous other diseases are mentioned, including of course folly, which is central to the *Tiers Livre*, where Panurge not only consults fools, he *is* a fool—though Rabelais does not advocate any of the gruesome medical procedures common, at least in the visual arts, at the time, like surgical removal of the "stone of folly" from the forehead.

As with syphilis, so with other diseases, descriptions of the malady and its suggested remedies are commoner than abstract theorizing about its nature. We have noted a few exceptions to this rule: the formation of semen in the body, and the nature of "uterine" hysteria, and there is one more such general subject on which Dr. Rabelais has a few (surprisingly few) things to say: the physiological origin and nature of laughter.

Therapeutic Laughter

As already mentioned (chapter 1), medical authorities since Aristotle had discussed the *risus* which is a *proprium hominis*. The sixteenth century, for some reason, produced an unusually large number of medical theorists interested in the question, although there are as always some who are not interested. The most surprising of these is perhaps Cardano, who discusses so many different subjects (including tears, in *De propria vita*, 1654 ed. 208). In his "De praeceptis ad Filios libellus" (Little Book of Precepts to His Children) he warns against "ridere cachinno" ("boisterous laughter") because "risus enim abundat in ore stultorum" ("laughter abounds in the mouths of fools"), but in the *De sapientia*, he admits the necessity of "ludus vel relaxatio animi" ("play or relaxation for the mind," 1624 ed. 62). Satirical and comic, as well as historical writers are "utiles ad humanam sapientiam" ("useful for human wisdom"); he even has the good taste, rare at the time, to prefer Plautus to Terence (219), but is still careful to disapprove of excessive or unkind laughter—laughing at present company is *inurbanum* (unrefined, rustic) as well as *periculosum* (dangerous).

Objective discussion of this topic is tricky, because no critic can (or at least none has to date) read all the sixteenth-century authorities on laughter. Because Screech and Calder, De Rocher and Ménager all come to different conclusions prompted by their particular knowledge of relevant texts, let me state before beginning my own discussion that it is based on the authors with whom I am familiar: Ambroise Paré, Laurent Joubert, and Nicolas Nancel in France, Fracastoro (plus the philosopher Celso Mancini) in Italy, and Rudolph Goclenius the Elder in Germany. De Rocher quotes some of these authors, but his almost exclusive emphasis on Joubert is misleading; each authority has his own perspective on the question. De Rocher's argument is also weakened by his ignorance of Cicero; the most astonishing thing about all the medical discussions is that they take place in a rhetorical context, as though Ciceronian rhetoric still provided the only possible general framework for a discussion of laughter. Thus Joubert's distinction between "fais ridicules" (comic actions, I.2) and "propos ridicules" (comic speech, I.3) corresponds to Cicero's separation of the comic into *in re* (in deed) and *in dicto* (in word), and Joubert's main examples of verbal wit are rhetorical devices, "comme d'amphibologie, enigme, comparaison, metaphore, ficcion, hyperbole, feintise, allegorie, emphase, beau-semblant, dissimulation" (I.3). Mancini chides Cicero for overlooking "admiration" (*admiratio*) and novelty as causes of laughter, but Nancel quotes him extensively.

Two specific problems are stressed by all or most of these authors. First, to which "passion of the soul" does laughter belong? To joy, according to Joubert and Paré; to a combination of joy and "admiration" (Fracastoro); definitely not to joy, according to Mancini; to a mixture of different passions, according to Nancel. The relationship between laughter and joy is a curious one; Rabelais mentions *joie* much more often than *rire* and its cognates (Bowen 1988), and some authors who do not mention laughter at all are interested in joy. Cardano, in the *De subtilitate*, devotes a passage in his book on the soul (XIV) to "la ioye vehemente," and concludes that "la ioye est la medecine & remede d'ire, & encor plus de la crainte" ("joy is the medicine and remedy for anger, and even more so for fear," 350–50v).

Second, although there is general agreement that those of "sanguine" humor are more apt to laugh (according to the *Regimen sanitatis*, sanguine characters laugh easily "a cause que le sang de soymesme prouoque a rire" ["because blood by its nature encourages laughter"], lvijv), there is much dispute about which bodily organ is the physiological origin ("siege") of laughter. Candidates are the heart, the brain, the spleen, or the diaphragm (because gladiators, we are told, died laughing if their diaphragm was pierced with a spear). Joubert and Mancini decide for the heart, Nancel for the brain, whereas Goclenius hesitates between the heart and the diaphragm. Dr. Rabelais was obviously not interested enough in these arguments to devote much space to them, but we can tell where he stood on the two basic issues.

Because, as noted in Chapter 1, *joie* and *joyeux* are more frequent in his text than laughter words, and because a large majority of them are not accompanied by laughter, it seems reasonable to assume that he did not think of laughter as inseparable from joy. With regard to the origin of laughter, Rabelais presents us with two possibilities. Two passing references in the *Quart Livre* take the spleen as "siege": in chapter 1 we are told that nobody could be so melancholy "qui n'entrast en joye nouvelle, et de bonne ratte ne soubrist" ("who would not have rejoiced afresh, and smiled in good humor [smiled with a hearty spleen]") on seeing the fleet ready to sail; and in chapter 17 that Philomenes, watching his donkey eating figs, "entra en si excessive guayeté d'esprit, et s'esclata de rire tant enormement, continuement, que l'exercice de la Ratelle luy tollut toute respiration, et subitement mourut" ("was seized with such excessive merriment of spirit, and burst into such uncontrollable laughter, that such overexertion of the spleen stopped his breathing entirely, and suddenly he died").

So we have two examples of "splenetic" laughter, one therapeutic and one fatal, but neither described at any length. The only detailed account of what happens inside our bodies when we laugh is in G 20, which is worth examining in some detail. First we learn that "Le Sophiste n'eut si toust achevé que Ponocrates et Eudemon s'esclafferent de rire tant profondement, que en cuiderent rendre l'ame à dieu" ("The sophist had no sooner finished than Ponocrates and Eudémon broke out laughing so heartily that they nearly gave up their souls to God"), like two Classical characters, including Philemon, who is the same person as the QL Philomenes. Then,

> Ensemble eulx, commença rire maistre Janotus, à qui mieulx, mieulx, tant que les larmes leurs venoient es yeulx: par la vehemente concution de la substance du cerveau: à laquelle furent exprimées ces humiditez lachrymales, et transcoullées jouxte les nerfz optiques.

En quoy par eulx estoyt Democrite Heraclitizant, et Heraclyte Democritizant representé.

♃

Together with them Master Janotus began to laugh, all three competing, so that tears came to their eyes through the violent concussion of the substance of the brain, at which were squeezed out these lachrymal humidities and made to flow through next to the optic nerves. Wherein by them was Democritus shown to be Heraclitizing and Heraclitus Democritizing.

This passage, which might easily strike a modern reader as comic, is probably entirely serious; its erudite vocabulary is simply explaining that laughter arises in the brain ("la substance du cerveau"), and that laughter and tears are very closely allied. Democritus, who laughed at the world's follies, and Heraclitus, who wept over them, are presented as neighbors rather than (as they usually are) polar opposites; and several of our medical authorities juxtapose their chapters, or separate treatises, on laughter and tears.

But to what extent is laughter in Rabelais practically therapeutic? The laughter of Janotus, Ponocrates, and Eudemon (not Gargantua, we notice) does not cure Janotus's stupidity or greed, or get him his bells back (because Gargantua has already agreed to return them). There is no episode in Rabelais analogous to the kind of anecdote told in both joke collections and medical treatises, in which a sick person is actually cured by laughing (at the antics of a monkey in the sickroom, for instance, or at the stupidity of an ignorant doctor).

Moreover, as we have already seen, not all laughter in Rabelais is healthy and good. Philemon's merriment over his donkey was the immediate cause of his death; Panurge's laughter is more often mean and vengeful (like that of the medieval characters we met in Chapter 1) than healthy and joyous, and there is at least one case in Rabelais of the *immodicum risum* against which doctors warn us: "Icy commença Homenaz rocter, peter, rire, baver, et suer" ("Here Grosbeak began to burp, fart, laugh, drool, and sweat," QL 53). This is to reduce laughter to its role of involuntary physical effluvium; Homenaz is emphatically not an admirable character.

We need to read only a few of the laughter theoreticians I have quoted to wonder why Rabelais doesn't have more to say on this controversial subject. Joubert is more fascinated than most by the physiology of laughter; of the twenty-seven chapters in the first book of his *Traité du ris* (1579), only the first four deal with a general definition of laughter, based as we have seen on Cicero. The other chapters analyze in minute detail such matters as the movement of heart (15) and diaphragm (16), the formation of laughter lines on the face (19), and why we can sweat, urinate, and defecate while laughing (26). Nicolas Nancel (*De risu libellus*, 1587) also discusses physiology, but raises numerous other aspects of the question, including the etymology of *risus*, why laughter is proper to man, why some people do not laugh, the nature of the soul and the passions, Cicero's categories of the comic, and why we don't laugh while making love. Laughter for him is an intellectual reaction: "Quis enim risit vnquam, nisi qui priùs perceptum haberet, cur esset ridendum?" ("For who has ever laughed, unless he has first perceived why something was laughable?" [86]). Both these authors wrote well after Rabelais, but it is clear that the whole century engaged in discussion and argument on the topic; why is Rabelais not interested?

Although Rabelais's fictional characters do not cure each other by laughing, and although their creator has little to contribute to medical theorizing about the causes and mechanism of laughter, there can be no doubt that Doctor Rabelais's book is intended as a *pharmakon* for us, the "lecteurs bénévoles." Like a good orator, Rabelais keeps a straight face while recounting his health-giving *facetiae*—and also while presenting one further aspect of comic medicine that modern readers find unexpected.

Comic Diet

The adjective "Rabelaisian" is essentially based on two myths. Earlier chapters of this book have attempted to counter the myth of giants who laugh constantly; but giants-who-eat-constantly is also a myth, equally firmly entrenched. This is obvious from the sheer number of French restaurants called "Gargantua" or "Pantagruel," as well as from the cliché phrases "a Gargantuan appetite" or "un repas pantagruélique," and frequent critical judgments to the effect that the words "Nous banquetans" ("as we were banqueting," QL 55) "pourraient résumer l'oeuvre entière" ("could summarize the entire work," Hansen 82). The text, as so often, does not support the myth.

There is, certainly, some impressive eating in the four books, and, more to the point for the myth, there are some impressive enumerations of edibles. Pantagruel's birth is preceded by the appearance of a mule carrying salt, nine dromedaries with ham and smoked beef tongue, seven camels with eels, and twenty-five carts of leeks, garlic, onions, and scallions, all issuing from his mother's womb (P 2); after the defeat of the 660 Dipsode knights in P 25, the companions feast on

> quatre grandes Otardes.
> Sept Bitars.
> Vingt et six perdrys grises.
> Trente et deux rouges.
> Seize Faisans.
> Neuf Beccasses.
> Dix et neuf Herons.

Trente et deux Pigeons ramiers . . .
dix ou douze que Levraulx que Lapins . . .
Dixhuyt Rasles parez ensemble.
Quinze sanglerons.
Deux Blereaux.
Troys grands Renards

♋

Four great bustards,
seven bitterns,
twenty-six gray partridges,
thirty-two red ones,
sixteen pheasants,
nine woodcocks,
ninenteen herons,
thirty-two ringdoves . . .
ten or twelve young hares and rabbits . . .
eighteen coots, paired together,
fifteen young wild boars,
two badgers,
three big foxes,

plus "un beau grand chevreul" ("a fine big roebuck"), all caught "en un moment" by Carpalim; and the arrival of Gargantua and his reinforcements for the war against Picrochole (G 37) is celebrated by Grandgrousier with a banquet consisting of:

seze beufz, troys genisses, trente et deux veaux, soixante et troys chevreaux moissonniers, quatre vingt quinze moutons, troys cens gourretz de laict à beau moust, unze vingt perdrys, sept cens becasses, quatre cens chappons de Loudunoys et Cornouaille, six mille poulletz et autant de pigeons, six cens gualinottes, quatorze cens levraux, troys cens et troys hostardes, et mille sept cens hutaudeaux

❦

sixteen oxen, three heifers, thirty-two calves, sixty-three fat kids, ninety-five sheep, three hundred suckling pigs stewed in must, eleven score partridges, seven hundred woodcocks, four hundred capons from Loudun and Cornouaille, six thousand chickens and as many pigeons, six hundred Guinea hens, fourteen hundred young hares, three hundred and three bustards, and seven hundred cockerels,

plus venison, twenty-one different varieties of birds (including flamingos, which must be fairly rare in Touraine), "force Coscossons, et renfort de potages" (lots of couscous,[33] and a store of broths). But these chapters of "grande bouffe," however memorable they may be, are very few. Much more common are mentions of feasting and drinking ("Et Dieu sçayt comment il y eut beu et guallé" ["And Lord only knows what drinking and feasting went on"], QL 25), food similes ("eximé comme un haran soret" ["as dry and emaciated as a red herring"], P 14; "S'il toussoit, c'estoient boytes de Coudignac" ["If he coughed, it was jars of quince marmalade"], QL 32), and passing references to ham, sausages, tripe, or *fouaces*.

There is sufficient food in Rabelais for us to assume his debt to Folengo, whose *Baldus* is inspired by the Muses of cooking and feasting (see chapter 2). But Rabelais the Erasmian is certainly familiar with a diametrically opposed culinary tradition, in the *Colloquies* and elsewhere, where Evangelical intellectuals eat only eggs, lettuce, and a little roast meat, and the true "Sober Feast" is the philological discussion of the Word of God.

One more literary food context should be mentioned here, and that is the epic. The *Iliad* seldom refers to food, and usually to ritual meals, where parts of a sacrificial animal are offered to the gods and the rest consumed by the worshippers (who of course drink wine to accompany it). The actual eating is preceded by the formulaic account of the ritual and followed by a formula like:

"and when they had satisfied their desire for eating and drinking . . ." The only food ever mentioned is meat, occasionally with salt, and bread. The *Odyssey*, in striking contrast, has a great many meals. When its protagonists are not fighting or plotting, they are frequently sitting round the table. Some are ritual meals, many are not, but again they consist almost exclusively of meat and bread (the poor eat only bread, we learn in Book XVII). Not only do the heroes of "Homer" apparently scorn vitamin C; they eat fish only as a last resort, when they are close to starvation on the Island of the Sun. The only fish-eater in the *Odyssey* is the monster Scylla. This rejection of fish, odd indeed in people who live so close to the sea, provoked some comment much later in the *Deipnosophists* of Athenaeus, who concluded that the eating of vegetables, fish, and birds would be considered a mark of greed (I.9, 13, 18, 25; and besides, heroes do not cook).

Virgil's *Aeneid* is more like the *Iliad* than the *Odyssey*, at least in this respect; the few meals described are again meat, wine and bread, although apples are mentioned once as an accompaniment (Book VII). It seems clear that the warriors' banquet of roasted game and "force vinaigre" in chapter 26 of *Pantagruel* is a nostalgic reminiscence of the feasting of Homeric and Virgilian heroes. I hesitate to conclude, along the same lines, that the strong emphasis on meat in Rabelais is a literary recollection; he may simply, like Erasmus, have disliked fish.

In *Pantagruel*, an important distinction between upper-class and lower-class food is already apparent, and the emphasis placed squarely on the latter. References to "jambons, et pastez" (hams and pasties, 5), fish (11), *Myrobolans* (East Indian Emblic plums, 14), and game (26) are much less frequent than those to smoked beef tongue (2 and 3), onions (3, 12, and 30), tripe (7, 12), *boudin* (blood pudding, 7), *poys au lart* (peas with bacon, 7), and *potée de chous* (potful of cabbage, 11). Both the cartloads of food emerging from Badebec before the birth of Pantagruel (2) and especially the wedding feast for Anarche (31: "belles testes de mouton, bonnes hastilles à la moustarde, et beaulx tribars aux ailz" ["fine sheep's heads, good slices of roast pork with mustard, and other good roast meat with garlic"]) stress the cheap, copious food characteristic of the peasant and working classes. It is instructive to compare Anarche's meal with a contemporary feast of a kind Rabelais must often have attended in Italy; given in Ferrara on May 20, 1529, it was a fish banquet for fifty-four noble and ecclesiastical guests (Messisbugo). The table was sumptuously appointed, strewn with flowers and decorated with fifteen two-foot-high mythological figures made of spun sugar, gilded and painted. The menu consisted of seventeen separate courses. Here is course number two, each dish served in fifteen separate platters while musicians played in the background: trout in pastry; stuffed hard-boiled eggs with sauce; fish entrails fried with orange juice, cinnamon, and sugar; sturgeon with garlic (decorated with the Este arms in red sauce); sixty large fried river fish; white almond soup; pizza; and little fried river fish. The seafood served included tuna, mullet, lamprey, stuffed crab, shrimp, squid, pike, and caviar, as well as a thousand oysters.

This description is one of only a few detailed accounts of upper-class food in the sixteenth century. But we know that aristocratic cooking and eating habits had not changed a great deal for centuries, and that the Renaissance still reveled in the exotic and surprising food dear to the Middle Ages. The most outrageous items are well known: the roast boar stuffed with a roast quail, the half-hare sewn to the half-capon and roasted to produce a composite monster, the roast peacock with its skin and feathers replaced so that it looked alive on the table, the "four-and-twenty blackbirds baked in a pie" (actually placed inside an already-cooked pie and released at the table; Blond, Cosmer, Wheaton, Scully). Rabelais's "grande Truye" ("great sow," QL 40) in which frere Jean secretes 157 cooks is a glancing reference to the Erasmian adage "Porcus Trojanus" (IV.x.70), which describes a pig (or ox or camel) stuffed with an assortment of smaller animals; Bruyerin Champier still lists this dish in 1560 (688). Such marvels were apparently expected, when the aristocracy dined in state; during the Roman festivities of September 1513 connected with the conferral of Roman citizenship on Giuliano and Lorenzo de' Medici, a feast in the Campidoglio theater featured peacocks and other birds and animals with their skins replaced "as if they were alive," set-pieces including an eagle holding a rabbit in its talons and the wolf with Romulus and Remus, real tame rabbits hopping round the room, and live birds that flew out of the napkins when they were unfolded. As the editor of the contemporary account sums it up, "all'abondanza dei cibi si unì la sorpresa e la meraviglia della loro presentazione" ("to the abundance of foodstuffs was added the surprise and wonder of their presentation," Cruciani, lxviii–lxix). The surprise was certainly sometimes accompanied by laughter; Platina explains, while describing how to make the cooked peacock look still alive, that "Aulcuns y a qui pour faire rire et esmerueiller les gens" ("There are some who, in order to cause laughter and astonish those present") put something flammable in its mouth and set light to it (1528, lxiiiv).

So the abundance of homely or peasant food, in Rabelais, is already amusing in the context of a prince and his companions, whom we would expect to eat more refined food, presented more elegantly. In the titles of books in the St-Victor library there are several suggestions that intellectuals, and scholastics in particular, are peasants at heart: wine, cheese, mustard, a *marmite* (cooking-pot), *marmitons* and *marmiteux* are all mentioned; frere Lubin likes *lardons* (chunks of bacon) and Pasquin goat with *chardonette* (thistles); Mayr is associated with blood pudding and Béda, as we saw in chapter 3, with tripe; and *pois au lard* (peas with bacon) are accompanied by a gloss. Baisecul and Humevesne, in their delightfully inscrutable speeches (11–12), name assorted foods, including eggs, *potée de choux*, salt beef, sheep's heads, *fraize de veau* (calves' chawdron*)*, onions, and garlic. We are not given the recipe for the green sauce Anarche is condemned to sell (as mentioned in chapter 4, there are numerous different recipes for it*)*, but we are given a thoroughly nauseating recipe for a *tartre Borbonnoise* (16), guaranteed to make anyone smelling it throw up on the spot; a *tarte bourbonnaise* was a well-known pastry.

But we must not forget the close ties between Renaissance cookery and medicine, which may seem less surprising in the 1990s than they would have a generation ago. The most often reprinted "cookbook" of the period is Platina's, originally titled *Platynae de honesta voluptate et valitudine* (On Honorable Pleasure and Health, by Platina), and sixteenth-century editions are sometimes titled *De tuenda valetudine*, "On Conserving Health." Its recipes are frequently accompanied by medical information; of bear meat, for instance, we learn that "its flesh is slow to be digested and does not agree with the spleen or the liver. It generates many bad humors, takes away the appetite, and makes those who eat it squeamish" (Platina 1967).[34] A recent Italian historian of cooking, Massimo Alberini, congratulates Platina on this "discovery" and hails him as the grandfather of modern dieticians. This is putting it the wrong way round; Platina is not the initiator of a modern trend, but the inheritor of a long medical tradition.

Since antiquity, dietary manuals had been based on four criteria for the quality of food: temperature, consistency, ease of digestion, and excremental nature. The medieval *Tacuinum sanitatis*, sometimes reprinted today because of its beautiful illustrations, enumerates for every item of meat, plant, or other food its nature, usefulness, dangers, and the recommended neutralization of these dangers. Thus watermelons and cucumbers are "cold and humid in the second degree. . . . They cool hot fevers and purify the urine . . . they cause pain in the loins and in the stomach," but these dangers can be neutralized with honey and oil (Paris, f. 38v, in Arano). So we need not congratulate Platina on any novelty in his instructions in the section on "What should be done to further the enjoyment of life," to the effect that "all foods are not suitable for all persons. As the elements vary, so men are different in their humors and appetites and tastes as well." Each of the four humors is dominant at a season of the year; thus "warm and moist blood accompanies the spring time," and so forth. We should therefore regulate our eating and drinking, and even our "contact with women," accordingly. The man "who carefully observes all these things with Nature, not I, to teach him what is beneficial and what is harmful, may easily for all his years live a pleasant life, safe and sound, without needing the care of doctors."

All this explains why, though *Gargantua* continues to enumerate large quantities of food, a new, medical element appears. Although the joyous consumption of vast quantities of tripe (Gargamelle eats "seze muiz, deux bussars et six tupins" [sixteen hogsheads, two bushels, and six pecks], which Demerson estimates at about three thousand liters) is presented as a healthy peasant pastime (4–6), Janotus de Bragmardo's preoccupation with sausages (19–20) adds to the satire on lazy, ignorant, greedy theologians. The child Gargantua's outdated and stultifying educational régime includes "bad" food: "belles tripes frites, belles charbonnades, beaulx jambons, belles cabirotades, et force soupes de prime" ("fine fried tripes, beautiful carbonadoes, fair hams, fine game stews, and many early morning dips as snacks," 21).

In 1913 Emile Roy pointed out the discrepancies between Gargantua's upbringing and what we know about the care given to aristocratic small children. The little treatise he reprinted emphasizes the importance of choosing the right food (fish is not advisable "car il seroit trop fleumaticque" ["for it would be too phlegmatic"]) and in the right quantities: "Item ne soit point induit a plenté mengier et soit accoustumé de pau boire et a petis trais" ("Item, let him not be encouraged to eat copiously, and let him be accustomed to drink little and in small mouthfuls").

Rabelais, moreover, knew that Erasmus and Vives strongly recommended that mothers suckle their own babies, so that Pantagruel's consumption at each meal of "le laict de quatre mille six cens vaches" ("the milk of four thousand six hundred cows," P 4), and Gargantua's of the milk of 17,913 (G 7) are comic nose-thumbing at humanist theory, as well as reminiscences of the *Grandes Chroniques*.

Gargantua's eating habits are corrected by Epistemon along with his learning habits. Food is seldom mentioned, and when mentioned is of the simplest: bread, wine, water, salt, meat, fish, fruit, herbs, and roots (23). At the monthly picnic in the country, the emphasis is on playing and drinking, not eating, and on wet days (24) "mangeoient plus sobrement que es aultres jours, et viandes plus desiccatives et extenuantes: affin que l'intemperie humide de l'air, communicqué au corps par necessaire confinité, feust par ce moyen corrigée" ("they ate more soberly than on other days and foods more desiccative and attenuating, so that the intemperate humidity of the air, communicated to the body by necessary proximity, might by this means be corrected"). Rabelais might be quoting Platina; he is certainly speaking as a doctor here.

Once the animal-like child has become a rational humanist, he no longer stuffs himself with indigestible food, just as he no longer delights in excreta and excretory jokes; after G 13, scatology will be associated only with despised or disapproved figures. There is, certainly, plenty more food in this second book, from the mouth-watering *fouaces* to the enormous banquet already mentioned, but in the triumphal banquet after the Picrocholine War (51) no food is mentioned; the emphasis is on the magnificent presents given by Grandgousier to the conquering heroes. And the Thelemites, apparently, do not eat at all.

The *Tiers Livre*, the most overtly humanist of the four books, is also the least food-oriented. The central symposium (29–36), called a *dipner*, so spelled no doubt to recall the Hellenistic *deipnon*, or discussion session after the main meal was over, involves much more talk than food, although there are mentions of the *seconde table*, *massepain* (marzipan), *pasté de Coins* (quince pastry) and its medical properties, *hippocras*, and *rislé (rillettes,* a kind of pork pâté[35]). Bridoye, not an admirable character (see chapter 6), presents in an anecdote Perrin Dendin as a regular attendee at a "banquet, festin, de nopces, de commeraige, de relevailles" (banquet, a wedding feast, a christening, a churching), or at the tavern (41), and Gargantua receives the suggested voyage to the Dive Bouteille with a promise to prepare a feast for Pantagruel's wedding (48).

The *Quart Livre* returns both to an epic *ambiance* and to a preoccupation with food; only fifteen of its sixty-seven chapters contain no reference to food. The fleet departs on its epic quest only after a meal (*vivres et vinaige*) on the deck of the flagship Thalamège. At the first port of call, Medamothi, Pantagruel orders a *collation* (4); Panurge throws a supply of ham, sausage, and caviar into the monks' ship (18), and the Macraeons offer a *repas* after the storm episode (25: "Et Dieu sçayt comment il y eut beu et guallé" ["And Lord only knows what drinking and feasting went on"]). The banquet offered by Homenaz and the Papimanes (51–54) is the most detailed, but even it has few specific items of food, except the "poires de bon Christian" whose major meaning is not culinary (Screech 1988). The companions are "banquetans" when they first hear the frozen words (55), and the book ends with a meal on board ship (64), involving four enormous *pastez de jambons* (ham pies) which remind the narrator of the bastions of Turin, *desserts* and *fruict*, but more essentially involving the bread and wine that, according to Duval (1988) and Smith (1987), make of this meal a eucharist.

This is already a significant number of meals, but there are many more, and more important, allusions to food in the *Fourth*

Book. Among the very numerous *contes* told by all and sundry, a number involve food, from the contemporary seigneur de Guyercharois and Bernard Lardon to the Classical poet Antagoras and the imaginary Chiquanous and Lucifer (who is tired of eating lawyers because so many of them end up in hell, 46). All these could be counted as food references, but they pale beside the two chapters enumerating all the food offered to Gaster by his Gastrolâtres (59–60) on feast and fast days. This is the only passage in Rabelais where elaborately prepared food is described in detail; the other enumerations merely list edible items. Gaster is offered, among many other things, "longes de veau rousty froides sinapisées de pouldre Zinziberine" ("shanks of roast veal, cold, spiced with powdered ginger"), "confictures seiches et liquides soixante et dix-huyt especes" ("dry and liquid preserves, seventy-eight species"), "Sallades cent diversitez" ("a hundred varieties of salads," of which seven are enumerated), and eggs "fritz, perduz, suffocquez, estuvez, trainnez par les cendres, jectez par la cheminée, barbouillez, gouildronnez, *et cet.*" ("fried, lost, stifled, steamed, dragged through the ashes, thrown down the chimney, jumbled [scrambled?], calked, etc."). Real men, in Rabelais's fictional world, don't eat quiche; nor do they care for the exotic salads and fancy, spicy sauces so often used for elaborate banquets, like the one in Ferrara quoted above. Gaster also eats peacocks, and is the only character in Rabelais to do so; since Roman times peacocks had represented the ultimate in gastronomic refinement, or decadence, depending on one's point of view (Budé). Gaster's refrain of "Tout pour la trippe!" ("and all for the gut!") comically recalls the simple peasant tripe feast which represents the antipodes of his culinary excess.

As well as quantities of "real" food, in the *Quart Livre*, we encounter much more metaphorical food than in the earlier books. The Bringuenarilles episode (17) is based on the metaphorical "nous ne trouvasmes que frire," meaning "we couldn't find anything at all" (because the giant had eaten all the pots and pans),

and many of the outlandish comparisons that purport to describe
Quaresmeprenant are culinary. Perhaps the best banquet joke in
the book is the island of Ruach whose inhabitants "ne vivent que
de vent." *Ruach* is the Hebrew word for breath or spirit, known
to every student of Biblical Hebrew from the beginning of Gene-
sis where the spirit of God moved on the face of the waters. Quite
apart from the polemical implications of the episode (Weinberg
1995), to portray the Ruachites as gourmets in search of the tasti-
est wind was a delightful idea.

The longest, and some think most successful, *Quart Livre* episode
is the battle with the Andouilles (35–42). Here we certainly have
the largest number of food jokes crammed into a few chapters.
The *andouilles* as sausages (not chitterlings, as in too many translations) are accompanied by *boudins* (blood puddings), *cervelats*
(saveloys[36]) and *guodiveaux* (veal patties), and are at the same time
warriors, phallic symbols, metaphors ("rompre les andouilles au
genou" means literally "to break sausages over one's knee," that
is, to undertake something futile or pointless), and reminiscent of
eels. Their healing mustard, their tutelary flying pig, and frere
Jean's Grande Truye in which many of the cooks, naturally enough,
have food-related names like Raclenaveau and Potageouart, are
all elements of the surrealist carnival-feasting ambiance.

If the traditional view of Rabelais's heroes as constantly stuff-
ing themselves is in serious need of revision, it is true that the four
books are often preoccupied with food, and that this food is comic
more often than not. The bad and good diets of the young Gargantua are contrasted in order to draw a humanist lesson, but
typically Rabelais draws as comic a picture as possible of the "bad"
food that must be superseded. The symposium of the *Tiers Livre*,
though certainly containing references to a venerable symposium
tradition (Jeanneret 1987, Hansen), is less interested in food than
in the "advice" given to the incorrigible Panurge. And the excessive and over-elaborate food offered to Gaster seems fundamen-

tally ambiguous. Are we to admire Gaster because of all of his beneficial inventions for humanity (hunger is the mother of invention), or disapprove of his conspicuous consumption? I am attempting here only to claim that discussions of food in Rabelais need to be based on knowledge of what the period actually ate, and in what terms it was accustomed to discuss food, cooking, eating, and diet.

Rabelais is a comic doctor, as I hope to have suggested, in a variety of ways—and certainly in more than are covered by this chapter. Unlike Molière, who apparently found the entire medical profession grotesque, and thus a suitable butt for satirical laughter, Rabelais takes his medicine seriously, and occasionally expresses or implies serious opinions on it (Picrochole's name; the juxtaposition of Greek and Arabic medicine in P 8; the cheerful doctor of the *Epître* to Châtillon; recommendations about sober diet).

Some familiarity with Renaissance medical preoccupations can help us to a better understanding of which passages are more comic than we had thought (like Gargantua's *torchecul*), and which, though appearing comic to a modern reader, are not (like Janotus and the companions laughing, Panurge's account of the formation of semen, or Rondibilis on uterine hysteria). It can also help us to a clearer picture of Rabelais as a person; although he enjoys occasionally displaying specialized knowledge and making standard medical jokes, he is not deeply engaged in current medical controversy on cures for syphilis or the physiology of laughter. But he certainly believed profoundly, like Erasmus and other humanists before him, in the necessity of laughter for mental health, and his book will continue to be good therapy, we can hope, for many more generations to come.[37]

CHAPTER 6

The Comic Lawyer

And that Nisi Prius *nuisance, who just now is
rather rife,
The Judicial humorist—I've got him on the
list!*

W. S. GILBERT

Law and Medicine

If Renaissance medicine is a seldom-discussed topic, Renaissance law is simply a closed book to all but a handful of legal historians specializing in the period. Today's Americans are apparently fascinated by courtroom procedure both real and fictional, if one may judge by the number of television programs devoting time to it, but very few people have any interest in the history of law. Modern U.S. law is in any case a descendant of British, rather than Continental law, while modern French law dates back mainly to Napoleon. And even to specialists, "the modern study of Roman law starts with the edition of the Corpus Juris

Civilis by Denys Godefroy" (Derrett 124), well after Rabelais. A law student today in England, the United States, or France would hardly understand Rabelais's legal preoccupations any better than the rest of us.

It is tempting to assume, with most critics, that law in Rabelais's four books is not sufficiently important to justify the time and effort required to elucidate it. Time and effort are indeed required. Most relevant texts are in Latin, many can hardly be found in university libraries, and as we shall see, the few experts who have tackled the subject are not good at explaining how they found their material and reached their conclusions.

This unwillingness to explore the topic of Rabelais and law is unfortunate. Numerous writers on Renaissance humanism have stressed that law was one of its important shaping forces. In 1500 about eighty European universities taught law (Kelley 1990, 131); Thomas More was trained as a lawyer, and French Renaissance writers who had studied law include Calvin, Dolet, Rabelais's friend Jean Bouchet, Noël du Fail, Louis Le Caron, Estienne Pasquier, Montaigne, Corneille, and Molière. Catherine des Roches's Placide, in "Le Dialogue de Placide et Severe," even claims that women should not be entirely ignorant of law (Guillerm, II.234). To the humanists, law was part of literature, often taught as part of the *studium liberale*, not a separate, esoteric discipline practiced by a few experts. It has been claimed that lawyers started the Renaissance (Roberto Weiss, *The Dawn of Humanism in Italy*, 1947, 5); and no one doubts that such legal experts as Valla, Poliziano, Budé, and Alciati crucially influenced its development. Modern European historiography, as George Huppert demonstrated years ago, began in the sixteenth century with historians trained in the law. La Garanderie calls Guillaume Budé's *Annotationes in Pandectas* the fundamental work of the French Renaissance (79), and, as we saw in chapter 3, many French humanists thought of Budé as the equal of Erasmus.

Law is often overlooked as an important theme or structural element in Renaissance literature. To give just a few examples: Shakespeare's sonnets contain a surprising amount of legal imagery, and according to Daniel J. Kornstein (*Kill All The Lawyers*, Princeton University Press, 1994), two-thirds of his plays include a trial scene; a number of French farces and *sotties*, including *Maistre Pierre Pathelin*, put legal procedure on stage; and a critic has estimated that one-quarter of the anecdotes in Pauli's *Schimpf und Ernst* are concerned with law. As late as 1668 Racine, in *Les Plaideurs*, can have fun with an imaginary "loi *Si quis canis*, Digeste, *De vi*, paragrapho . . . *Caponibus*" (III.3). This should not surprise us, inasmuch as Renaissance literature is much closer to its rhetorical origins than later literature (see Chapter 4), and Cicero's orator was usually considered as first and foremost a lawyer.

Nor is law, as an intellectual domain, as far removed from medicine as a modern reader might assume. As two of the three superior disciplines (theology being the third) to which the educational program of the seven liberal arts served as preparatory ladder, law and medicine were often considered either as complementary, or as serious rivals—and are dismissed in the same breath by Marlowe's Dr. Faustus: "Both Law and Physick are for petty wits." Garin lists nine fifteenth-century Italian works, including contributions by Alberti, Bruni and Poggio, on the relative merits or "dignity" of law and medicine, and there may well be more. According to E. Berriot-Salvadore, the debate concluded in 1492 with Antonio de Ferraris's *De dignitate disciplinarum*, which stated that medicine is superior to law, but it was certainly not forgotten in the following century; in no. 50 of Pauli's *Schimpf und Ernst* a fool decides that the law faculty should precede the medical faculty, because judges precede executioners.

All the Italian works were presumably inspired by the celebrated tract by Salutati, *De nobilitate legum et medicinae* (1400), whose thirty-nine chapters are almost exclusively devoted to the superiority of law over medicine. Salutati's reasoning ranges over every possible aspect of the two disciplines—their origin, founders, development, aims, moral and scientific content, and "certainty" (*certitudo*). Among many specific arguments, he claims that the active life is necessarily superior to the contemplative (Rabelais would certainly agree), and that the will is nobler than the intellect. Rabelais need not have read this work, or any of the others, to be aware of the comparison of law to medicine as a *topos*; Screech (1976) is convinced that his "commitment to humanist law was . . . a deeper and more passionate one than his commitment to his art" (157).

Law and medicine are often mentioned together in *Gargantua and Pantagruel*, and it is no surprise that one of Rabelais's favorite sources is *Maistre Pierre Pathelin*, a play about both medicine and law. Pantagruel's tour of French universities, in P 5, is basically a search for legal training (Screech 1979, 73), but he drops in on Montpellier, one of the great medical centers of Europe, "et se cuida mettre à estudier en Medicine, mais il considera que l'estat estoit fascheux par trop et melancholicque et que les medicins sentoyent les clisteres comme vieulx diables" ("and he thought of starting to study medicine; but he considered that doctors smelled like old devils of enemas"). In the paternal letter-cum-humanist-manifesto of P 8, law and medicine are separated only by "la congnoissance des faictz de nature" ("the knowledge of nature's works"). The discussion of eleven-month pregnancies, in G 3, quotes Roman and canon law as well as medical authorities (Hippocrates and Aristotle). Three episodes in the *Quart Livre*: the Chiquanous, the Papimanes, and Gaster, combine legal and medical joking.

But the most interesting book, from this perspective, is the *Tiers Livre*. As we saw in the previous chapter, it is fundamentally a book about medicine, since both marriage and folly are medical subjects. At the same time, it is fundamentally a book about law, and aimed at readers with some knowledge of law (Screech 1979, 217). And surprisingly often, medicine and law are both in question. In his praise of debts (TL 2), Panurge cites Hippocrates to bolster his argument about distributive justice; he quotes Galen in his explanation of Mosaic law in chapter 6, and both Galen and Justinian in his apology for the codpiece in chapter 8. The symposium planned by Pantagruel (29) is to include both a lawyer and a doctor; Panurge uses both medical terminology and a legal tag in his "debate" with Trouillogan (36); several items in Bridoye's torrent of legal references (of which more later) deal with medicine; and Pantagruel invokes both law and medicine to explain the behavior of Triboullet (45).

Roman and Canon Law

We have here the most acute case of a problem mentioned already: the frequent necessity, when reading Rabelais, for detailed and lengthy explanation of specialized material before laughter becomes possible. This problem, as stated earlier (in chapter 3), is at its worst when humanist topics are at issue, and law is the humanist topic par excellence.

A few specialists have, indeed, attempted to explicate law in Rabelais, the three most helpful within a year or two of each other. In 1962 Enzo Nardi's dense and very useful work on Roman law in Rabelais appeared, in Italian; in 1963 an immensely learned article by J. Duncan Derrett on the Bridoye episode; and in 1964 Screech's article on Bridoye (the last two will be discussed in detail later in this chapter). Not one of these authors gives directions for finding relevant legal texts, starting from Rabelais's off-putting abbreviations like *Spec. tit. de instr. edi. et tit. de rescrip. praesent.*[38] Nor is much enlightenment available in the little primer by Michel Reulos (*Comment transcrire et interpréter les références juridiques*, Geneva: Droz, 1985) which purports to be a guide to Renaissance legal references. The most helpful work I have found is a small volume often reprinted in the sixteenth century, called *Modus legendi abbreviaturas in utroque iure* (Method of Reading Abbreviations in Civil and Canon Law), usually printed in blackletter with numerous abbreviations. Thus I hope that the following brief manual, with the list of legal abbreviations in the Appendix, will be found useful by interested neophytes; readers already familiar with all this will simply skip it. In 1953 H. Janeau said: "Je crois qu'une étude reste à faire sur 'le droit dans Rabelais'" ("I think a study remains to be done on 'law in Rabelais,'" Nardi 9); it still does. I should also explain the variety of editions of civil and canon law quoted here; few libraries own sixteenth-century editions of these works, and I was obliged to use whichever editions were to hand in the library where I happened to be.

Law, in Renaissance France, has three standard meanings: Roman law, canon law (the law of the Catholic church), and customary law. Rabelais's interest in the subject is shown by his passing references to other, very different kinds of law: "l'institution des druydes" in ancient Gaul (TL 3); Plato's *Laws* (TL 5); Mosaic law (TL 6 and 16, QL 16); the laws of the Aeropagites (TL 37 and QL 27); the Twelve Tables (TL 44 and QL 16); "droict naturel" (natural law), G 10, 29), *ius gentium* or the "droict des peuples" (universal law,[39] G 10, TL 44, 48), and whatever he means by "la loy totale" (total law, TL 44). He is apparently not concerned with customary law, but his knowledge of Roman and canon law is obvious, and often important. A modern reader is likely to find this very odd, especially in the case of Roman law; law and literature seem to us so far apart that they cannot possibly have any connection, and in any case how can the great law books compiled by order of the Emperor Justinian in the sixth century possibly be relevant to sixteenth-century France?

In fact, both Roman and canon law still reigned as supreme authorities in their respective domains, and Rabelais's intended reader would have had no trouble identifying Bridoye's references to either, whether or not he wanted to pursue Bridoye's train of thought by looking them up. The interested reader of this book, with the aid of the index of legal abbreviations in Rabelais (appendix 2), should be able to do the same.

The majority of Rabelais's legal sources are in Roman law, namely, what is now known as the Corpus Iuris Civilis, compiled on the initiative of the Emperor Justinian in the sixth century C.E. This corpus consists of four separate works. The *Institutions*, quoted only twice by Bridoye, is an elementary law manual in four books. Bridoye's *Instit. de re di. § is ad quem.* (S 28, D 56[40]) means *Institutiones* book II (the book's title is *De rerum diuisione*), paragraph beginning "Is verò ad quem" (1549, col. 118).

The *Codex* consists of twelve books of *tituli* and *leges*, and is referred to by Bridoye as C. So *l. maximum uitium. C. de lib. praeter* (S 3, D 7), refers to the section beginning *Maximum vitium* in title 38 (*De liberis praeteritis*) in book VI. One can find it by looking up *maximum vitium* in the *Index legum*, or *Liberis praeteritis* in the *Tabula titulorum*, of the 1532 edition.

Bridoye cites most frequently the Digest or Pandects, fifty books containing the decisions of jurists. Many sixteenth-century editions are in three volumes, respectively titled Digestum Vetus (twenty-four books), Infortiatum (fourteen) and Novum (twelve). Each book is divided into titles, subdivided into paragraphs and fragments. Most pages consist of a small central text, surrounded by a much larger amount of commentary, in several different type-faces (this is Rabelais's "belle robbe d'or triumphante et precieuse à merveilles, qui feust brodée de merde" ["beautiful golden gown that was bordered with shit"] in P 5). The abbreviation for the Digest is ff, for reasons not known. So Bridoye's *ff. de re milit. l. qui cum uno.* (S 2, D 2) sends us to paragraph 4, beginning "Qui cum vno testiculo" in title 16, *De re militari*, of Book 49 (col. 1682 of the Novum volume in the 1566 edition). *Qui cum uno testiculo* is in the *Index legum*, *Re milit.* in the *Index titulorum*.

The fourth and last work of Roman law is variously designated as *Novellae* (that is, *leges novellae*, not to be confused with the Digestum Novum), *Authentica*, or *Volumen*. It has nine *Collationes* with numbered *tituli*. Bridoye's *Autent. de restit. et ea quae pa.* (S 26, D 51) sends us to title VI, *De restitutionibus, & ea quae parit in XI. mense post mortem viri*, in the fourth *Collatio* (1550, col. 176).

Canon law is more complicated, and usually consists in Rabelais's time of six separate works. The earliest and (by the humanists) most respected of these was the Decretum of Gratianus (1139–48), modeled on the Digest and in the sixteenth century often similar to it in form, that is, folio pages with text in the center and glosses in smaller type in the margin. Part I, on the nature and sources of canon law, ecclesiastical offices and conduct, consists of 101 distinctions with canons. Bridoye's *d. .LXXXVI. c. tanta* (S l, D l) refers to distinction 86, canon 24, beginning "Tanta nequitia" in Part I. Part II contains thirty-six causes with questions and canons, on Christian behavior, penal law, church property, religious orders, marriage, and penance. This last is apparently considered the most important, in that the title of question 3 of cause 33 is *Tractatus de penitentia*, sometimes designated *p.* or *De pen.*

Bridoye's *ut ait gl. VI. q. I. c. Si quis* (S 31, D 65) refers us to the gloss on question l in cause 6, where canon 22 begins "Si quis cum militibus vel priuatis" (1538, 212r). Part III, known as the *De consecratione*, on sacraments and doctrine, has five distinctions. Bridoye's *de cons. d. V. c. I. fi.* (S 31, D 66) ought to refer to distinction 5 in part III, canon 1, but seems not to do so (see Derrett, p. 152).

Rabelais and his fellow humanists had on the whole no quarrel with the *Decretum*, but they objected strongly to the other five compilations included in canon law, and which are savagely satirized by Rabelais in the Papimanes episode of the *Quart Livre* (48–54). The so-called *Decretals* of Gregory IX (Homenaz's "dives Decretales"), compiled by Raymond de Penafort in 1234, are divided into five books: *judex, judicium, clerus, conubium, crimen*. Each book's *tituli* have *capituli, paragraphi*, and *versiculi*. Bridoye's *no. gl. in c. fin. de sortil.* (S 4–6, D 11) means the last *capitulus* of the title *De sortilegiis* in book V.

The next book of canon law (taking them in chronological order) is the *Liber Sextus* (Homenaz's "seraphicque Sixiesme") of 1294, which has five books corresponding in content to the five books of the *Decretals*. Bridoye's *in c. cum sunt eod. tit. lib. VI.* (S 10, D 18b) means the *capitulus* beginning "Cum sunt" under that title, which is in book V. Most of the *Liber Sextus* is divided into *capituli*, but the end of book V has a separate title, *De regulis iuris*, and is divided into *regulae* instead of *capituli*; so that Bridoye's reference in fact runs: *de reg. jur. et in c. cum sunt*.

The last canon-law work quoted by Bridoye is the *Clementinae* (Homenaz's "cherubicques Clementines") of 1317, prepared by Pope Boniface VIII and "published" by John XXII. It again has five books and the same plan. Bridoye quotes *Cle. I. de baptis.* (S 22, D 45). He never quotes from the last two canon-law works, the *Extravagantes* of John XXII and the *Extravagantes communes* (although Homenaz apostrophizes the "Extravaguantes angelicques"), so that the usual abbreviation *extra* cannot (in Rabelais) refer to them; it refers in fact to the Decretals.[41]

These examples are far from exhausting the abbreviations used by Bridoye, of which a complete list will be found in the appendix. Rabelais is assuming a reader who is familiar, not only with the standard abbreviations for the basic works of civil and canon law, but with the major glosses and commentaries on both; who knows that *Alex.* is Alexander Tartagno de Imola, a famous fifteenth-century legal authority, and that *Spec.* (short for *speculator*) means Guglielmus Durandus. Rabelais undoubtedly sides with the jurists of what is known as the *mos gallicus* school, of whom Alciati is considered the leader, who wanted to remove all glosses from both civil and canon law, whereas the more old-fashioned *mos italicus* jurists were as likely to accord authority to the gloss as to the text. This is one reason why Bridoye quotes so many glosses.

Rabelais and Law

Let us, with a sigh of relief, return to the question of law and Rabelaisian comedy. But first we must note that the specific references to civil and canon law are not Rabelais's only (according to Screech, not even his most important) legal references. We need to take into account at least three other kinds of "legal" text. And first, Bridoye's references are nearly always accompanied by a *brocard* or legal tag: *Gaudent brevitate moderni* (The moderns delight in brevity), or *Qui prior est tempore, potior est jure* (That which is prior in time, is more powerful in law). These tags, from either civil or canon law, were readily accessible in alphabetized lists. Screech relies heavily on three such lists for his explanation of the Bridoye episode: the *Brocardia Juris* (hence Bridoye's law professor Brocadium Juris, and the second title of the Library of Saint-Victor: *Bregueta iuris*); the *Flores legum*; and Albericus de Rosate's *Lexicon utriusque juris*. I shall have more to say about these *brocards* shortly.

Second, we must remember that sixteenth-century humanists had very different reading habits from ours. What to us look like heavy, indigestible volumes of technical material were probably often considered agreeable light reading. Such volumes include not only Budé's *De asse* (see chapter 3), but his *Annotationes in Pandectas*, which we have seen La Garanderie call the fundamental work of the French Renaissance. Rabelais's friend Tiraqueau produced a number of legal commentaries, the best-known of which are the *De legis connubialibus* and the *De nobilitate*, which are unlikely to strike a modern reader as in any way attractive.

Both *brocard* dictionaries and learned legal commentaries were fundamentally serious, but Rabelais was also familiar with a pervasive use of law and legal themes in comic literature; a use which tends to get overlooked altogether by modern critics. I have mentioned a few examples, several of which preceded Rabelais. Of these, *Pathelin* is most obviously playing with a law-court setting, but it uses few specific legal terms and may not have been intended for a law-conscious audience. Plattard mentions briefly several other examples, including the (partly comic) morality play *La Condamnation de Banquet*, in which both the Docteur Prolocuteur and Experience make specific references to both civil and canon law, and also mentions the *Arrêts d'Amour*, a more intriguing case. Probably dating from the 1460s (Rychner xxiv), this mildly amusing prose work is an extended pastiche of the style of the courts. Each of its fifty-one *arrêts* concerns a lawsuit with love as its theme: a lover charges that his lady kissed him so roughly that she made his nose bleed (II); a lover charges that while he was serenading his lady, she dropped a bowl of blood all over him, so that he was subsequently arrested by the watch on suspicion of having committed a murder (XXI); "plusieurs galants amoureux" ("several lovesick gallants") want an injunction against local "gauffriers et patissiers" ("waffle-makers and pastry-cooks") who set up shop around churches, because the smoke from their ovens hurts the lovers' eyes so that they cannot properly enjoy the sight of their ladies (an early example of a class-action suit? XLVII).

This parody is already evidence of a reading public at ease with the standard vocabulary of plaintiff and defendant, lawyer and judge. Still more convincing is the Latin commentary on it produced in 1533: *Arresta Amorum, cum erudita Benedicti Curtii Symphoriani explanatione* (Lyon: Gryphe). As Plattard points out (115), most of Bridoye's *brocards* are in this work, which quotes copiously and accurately from both laws. So Bridoye's habit of "legal" quotation could not have been entirely unfamiliar to his readers, even if no previous work exploits them in such dizzying quantity.

In this connection we should also note the work of Coquillart, which I believe is worth more attention than Plattard gives it. Of the fourteen works in the Freeman edition, Plattard quotes only the *Droits nouveaulx*, a long poem which amusingly mixes earthy and obscene vocabulary with legal terminology; the titles of the seven *droits* are in Latin. Often very similar in tone to Rabelais, this lengthy (2,329 lines) joke is fully intelligible only to readers with some knowledge of the law. Law is also essential to the *Plaidoyé d'entre la Simple et la Rusée* (Lawsuit between the Simple Girl and the Crafty Girl), a dramatized lawsuit that has sometimes been listed among the farces of the period. There are only a couple of specific legal references, to the Codex and the Digest (ll. 422–23), but much of the vocabulary of the Judge and both lawyers is riddled with legal terms, which again make a comic contrast to colloquial and obscene words and turns of phrase. There are also legal references in the *Drois nouveaulx establis sur les femmes*, so that Coquillart is obviously aiming at a legally literate reading public.

Brocard collections, legal treatises by contemporary writers, and a number of literary works, all make very clear that the legal expertise of Rabelais's intended readers was much broader than we can easily imagine.

Rabelais's preoccupation with law becomes clear early in his first book, *Pantagruel*, whose title page deliberately recalled a common format for law books (Screech 1979, 24). Chapter 5 contains not only the slighting reference to law at Montpellier, but a compliment to the law faculty at Bourges (where Alciati was teaching in 1532), and the celebrated description of the Digest quoted above. The next sentence makes the import of this clear to the meanest intelligence:

> au monde n'y a livres tant beaulx, tant aornés, tant elegans, comme
> sont les textes des *Pandectes*, mais la brodure d'iceulx, c'est assavoir
> la glose de Accurse, est tant salle, tant infame, et punaise, que ce n'est
> que ordure et villenie

𝕽

> There are no books in the world so beautiful, so ornate, so elegant,
> as are the texts of the *Pandects*; but their border, to wit, the gloss by
> Accursius, is so foul, unspeakable, and smelly, that it's nothing but
> sewage and sludge.

The deliberately gross analogy is undoubtedly comic, but the point being made is the ultra-serious humanist one: keep the text, scrap the gloss. In chapter 8, Gargantua will instruct his son: "Du droit civil" ("Of civil law," implicitly rejecting canon law), "je veulx que tu saiche par cueur les beaulx textes" ("I want you to know the fine texts by heart," implicitly rejecting all glosses).

This does not mean, by the way, that humanists did not feel free to comment on Justinian. Budé's *Annotations on the Pandects* begins with an attack on Accursius ("Ivs est ars boni & aequi. Accursius hunc locum enarrans aliud bonum esse censet, aliud aequum: nec satis hoc explicat" ["Law is the art of the good and the equitable. Accursius, expounding this passage, thinks that the good is one thing and the equitable another thing, but he doesn't explain this adequately"]), but goes on to provide twenty-five pages of his own discussion of the first law, *De iustitia et iure*—much longer than Accursius's gloss. The difference of course is in the content of the discussion. Note too that the 1535 edition of the *Annotations* has no index of laws or titles, and that Budé can casually refer to a law "Si quis," knowing that his reader will immediately situate the allusion, despite the fact that the index to the Digestum Vetus lists ninety-four *leges* beginning "Si quis."

The hilarious list of imaginary books in the Saint-Victor library (see Chapter 3) is directed mainly at scholastic theology and the Reuchlin affair, not at law, but it has a few legal titles at which Latinists would have to smile. As we have seen, the second item on the list is *Bregueta iuris*, an obvious parallel to the opening theological title *Bigua salutis*, "The cart of salvation." *Bregueta* is not a genuine Latin word (and no Classical Latin word begins with *brag-* or *breg-*), but it is obviously the French *braguette*, codpiece. Why the codpiece of the law? No doubt because of the popular tag phrase "Les femmes aiment bien le droit," in which the noun *droit* means "law," but the adjective *droit* "right," "upright," or "erect." *Bregueta iuris*, as mentioned above, also recalls the *Brocardia juris* on which the Bridoye episode will be based.

The other legal titles in this library are: *Pantofla decretorum* (the slipper of the decrees); *Decretum uniuersitatis Parisiensis super gorgiasitate muliercularum ad placitum* (Decree of the University of Paris concerning the gorgiasity of harlots); *"Le cabat des notaires"* (The Notaries' Sweet Spot); *"Les fariboles de droict"* (The Balderdash of Law); *"La complainte des advocatz sus la reformation des dragées"* (The Advocates' Lament over the Reform of Goodies); *"Le chatfourré des procureurs"* (The Pettifoggery of the Attorneys); *"Le maschefain des advocatz"* (The Insatiable Appetite of the Advocates); *"Les happelourdes des officiaulx"* (The Booby Traps of the Ecclesiastical Judges); and "Iustinianus *De cagotis tollendis*" (Justinian, On the exaltation of hypocrites). Two longer titles stand out: "Magistri n. Fripesaulcetis *de grabellationibus horrarum canon-icarum*, lib. quadraginta" (Our Master Saucelicker, On scrutini-fications of the canonical hours, forty books), and "Preclarissimi iuris utriusque doctoris Maistre Pilloti Racquedenari *de bobeli-nandis glosse Accursiane baguenaudis repetitio enucidiluculidissima"* (The most Illustrious doctor of both branches of the law, Mas-ter Pilferus Scrapepenny, On coping with the idiocies of the gloss-es of Accursius, a most lucidly unraveled treatise—Accursius again.)

It is clear from these titles that Rabelais's interest in law is of two kinds. He knows the standard law texts and their glossators well enough to make fun of them, but he also mocks law-court procedure, its personalities (*notaires, avocats, procureurs, officiaulx*) and its customs (*dragées*). In chapters 10–13 court procedure will dominate, although there are also some learned references to the *Corpus*. We note first, in chapter 10, that there are lawyers among the audience for Pantagruel's public "thesis defense": not just *advocatz*, but *canonistes* (no Roman law specialists because there was no civil-law faculty at the University of Paris at this time). We then learn about the lawsuit between Baisecul and Humevesne, which has baffled national and international legal experts for forty-six weeks. The suggestion, by Du Douhet (a real person), to submit the case to Pantagruel, asking him to "leur en faire le raport tel que de bon luy sembleroit en vraye science legale" ("make his report to them on it as he should see fit to in real legal form"), implies that a broad humanist education, rather than spe-cific legal training, is the best preparation for sound judging.

On hearing that the two plaintiffs are still alive, Pantagruel launches into a tirade that permits Rabelais to show off his legal expertise. The giant insults Cepola, author of a notorious work called *Cautelae*; the glossators Accursius (yet again), Baldus, and Bartholus; and seven other legal commentators, well known at the time but forgotten today. Not content with this comprehensive condemnation, he then explains in some detail its threefold humanist justification: these commentators knew no Greek (whereas Roman law originated in Greece), wrote terrible Latin (whereas the Digest was written "en Latin le plus elegant et aorné qui soit" ["in Latin, the most elegant and ornate there is"]), and knew no philosophy (and we remember that in chapter 8 Pantagruel was urged not just to know the "beaulx textes" of civil law by heart, but to discuss and compare them "avecques philosophie").

Chapters 11 and 12 appear to have little to do with law or indeed with anything else. First Baisecul and then Humevesne delivers a long speech consisting entirely of non sequiturs (what in poetry is called *coq-à-l'âne*). Only a few words and phrases recall that we are ostensibly in a court of law: "Messieurs de la court," "les canonistes," "le sergeant," "le greffier," "Messieurs des Comptes" (chap. 11); "le notaire," "Messieurs les clercs," "une rubrique de droit," "la loy Salicque" (chap. 12). But Pantagruel's summing-up in chapter 13 gives Rabelais another chance to show off, by quoting from the list of difficult laws found in many sixteenth-century editions of the Digestum Vetus.

The humor of this episode is not as overtly legal as one might expect, but certainly the strings of nonsense produced by the two litigants are in part a satire on the often incomprehensible jargon of lawyers—now as well as then. There are several other lawsuits in the four books: Panurge's against women wearing high collars, against the workmen who emptied the latrines, and against slobbering mules (P 17); Janotus de Bragmardo's against his fellow theologians (sophists) (G 20); the *faquin* (porter) accused of consuming the smell of meat from the butcher's shop (TL 37); the woman of Smyrna accused of murdering her children (TL 44). All but the last of these are trivial and lighthearted.

It is intriguing that Panurge's largely gratuitous practical jokes, in P 16 and 17, should include at least three lawsuits. His ancestors Margutte (who also robbed churches, in MM 18) and Cingar (who also had pockets full of nefarious tools in *Baldus* II.49v; cf. chapter 2) were liars, cheats, and tricksters—but not lawyers. Panurge quotes "les legistes" in chapter 16 and uses a lawyer's verbal tic in chapter 17 in his defense of his literal interpretation of *Centuplum accipies* (Thou shalt receive a hundred-fold): "et *ibi* Bartolus." This is a complicated joke. Bartolus of Sassoferrato (1313–57) was the most famous of the commentators on Roman law known as the Post-Glossators. Jurists frequently quoted him, using this tag phrase, after a reference to a Roman law text—but Panurge pretends that he can also be quoted in support of commentators on the Hebrew Bible, which even if true would be irrelevant inasmuch as *Centuplum accipies* occurs in the New Testament, not in the Old (Matthew 19:29). Panurge will change a great deal between *Pantagruel* and the *Tiers Livre*, but will remain a lawyer; in TL 16 he claims that the advice of women is as reliable as "rubricques de droict" (rubrics of the law books); in TL 34 he includes himself among "nous aultres Legistes" (us jurists), and cites an authentic rubric from the Digest.

Immediately following the exploits of Panurge the Trickster, we have the episode of Thaumaste which, as is well known, is based on an anecdote recounted in a gloss—by the despised Accursius! Readers who do not have Screech's book open in front of them (to p. 89) might appreciate an account of this anecdote (Latin text in Nardi, 98–99). The Greeks sent a wise man to Rome to find out whether the Romans were worthy of receiving Greek laws. The Romans designated a fool to debate with him, on the grounds that if he lost, the Greeks would look foolish. The wise man began by raising one finger to signify one God; the fool, thinking this was a threat to poke out his eye, raised two fingers and his thumb in a defensive gesture, which the wise man took for a symbol of the Trinity. The wise man then extended his open hand, to signify that all things are open to God; the fool, again assuming that this was a threatening gesture, bunched his fist, which the wise man interpreted as meaning that God holds all things in the palm of his hand—and he concluded that the Romans were indeed worthy of receiving laws from the Greeks.[42] Budé had already pointed out that Accursius was foolish to take this anachronistic anecdote seriously (Nardi 100), and Rabelais's use of it here reinforces the legal atmosphere because it concerns the transfer of Greek law to Rome. Readers unfamiliar with the story have been tempted to take Thaumaste seriously, as a genuine seeker after esoteric knowledge, but the point of the story is that the fool's defensive or offensive gestures are taken by the naïve philosopher to refer to the mysteries of Christianity. So Thaumaste is supposed to be ridiculous, as well as morally in error: he recalls Christ's condemnation of "seekers after signs" (Screech 93), and I would add that his desire to elucidate "problemes insolubles" is also blameworthy. One of the Renaissance's favorite Latin tags was "Quod supra nos, nihil ad nos" ("What's up there is none of our business"), and Marlowe's Faustus will surely be damned in part because of his yearning to "resolve me of all ambiguities" (*Doctor Faustus* I.1); the human condition is by definition ambiguous, and we must learn to live with that fact.

Panurge behaves like a lawyer throughout the Thaumaste episode, and his audience includes "conseillers, legistes et decretistes" (counselors, jurists, and decretists [canon law specialists]). Apart from the mention of Justinian in Epistemon's account of the underworld (chap. 30), this is the last legal reference in *Pantagruel*, but we can see that there is already plenty of law in Rabelais's first book, as there will be in his second: legal pronouncements on eleven-month pregnancies (3); the lawyer's remarks among the *propos des bien-yvres* (5); mentions of "droict universel," "droict naturel," and Bartolus à propos of Gargantua's colors (10); Janotus's "plus n'en dict le deposant" ("And further deponent saith not," 19) and his lawsuit against his fellow sophists (20);

Gargantua listening to "les playdoiez des gentilz advocatz" ("the pleading of the nice lawyers") on rainy days (24); a couple of contemptuous remarks about the Decretals by frere Jean (42); and the exclusion of all lawyers from the Abbey of Thelema (54). Most of these references are either comic or trivial, or both. Probably more important is that Ulrich Gallet is a lawyer, Grandgousier's *maître des requêtes* (Master of Requests), "homme saige et discret" ("a wise and discreet man," 30), probably modeled on a real Jean Gallet who was a Chinon *avocat*. His speech to Picrochole (31) is a model Ciceronian lawyer's oration, and not, I think, intended to be comic.

The *Tiers Livre*, as already noted, is fundamentally concerned with law (Nardi has a chapter on "la miniera romanistica del *Terzo Libro*" ("the mine of roman law in the *Tiers Livre*"). Not only is marriage necessarily a legal subject, but folly is also an important legal issue (how is it defined? can fools testify?); so is *perplexitas* (Screech); and so, as Screech has shown, is language. One of the most delightful *contes* in all of Rabelais, the story of the fool's judgment about the porter and the smell of the roast meat (37), comes from canon law, as of course does Gargantua's virulent tirade against the marriage of children without parental consent (48). To the educated reader of 1546, the Bridoye episode, which we shall get to eventually, was no doubt as hilarious as the Saint-Victor Library to the 1532 reader. And throughout the book, Panurge the dishonest rhetorician (see chapter 4) remains very close to Panurge the dishonest lawyer. His imagined Golden Age of mutual indebtedness may have "nul procés" ("no lawsuit," 4), but it is not by chance that when he pleads with Pantagruel to leave him just a few debts, he invokes the example of Milles d'Illiers, who implored King Louis XI to leave him at least one lawsuit "pour se exercer" ("to practice on," 5).

The *Quart Livre* contains less law in proportion to its length, but still a sizeable amount. Apart from passing references (of which the funniest must be the little devil's statement that the

Devil is so tired of eating lawyers that they give him indigestion), there are at least two entire episodes devoted to law (three, if Saulnier [1954] is right that chapter 66 is about the Châtelet and the Conciergerie in Paris). In chapters 12–16 we meet the Chiquanous and their enemy, the seigneur de Basché, in a delightfully theatrical episode (the Seigneur calls it a "Tragicque comedie" and a "tragicque farce;" see Chapter 2) whose main import is satire of what Rabelais sees as a legal abuse (Marichal 1949). The satire does not require predominantly legal language, and the vocabulary here is fuller of medical terminology ("denudation de la luette, et perte insigne des dens molares, masticatoires, et canines" ["baring the uvula and knocking out a lot of teeth: molars, masticators, and canines"]), and of *fantaisie verbale* ("mordere-grippipiotabirofreluchamburelurecoquelurintimpanemens") than of legal technicalities. The only key legal terms are *procuration*, *record*, *citer*, and *exploit* (in both its legal and its heroic meanings).

Much more technical, and indeed incomprehensible to readers ignorant of canon law, is the Papimanes episode (48–54), a comprehensive satire by an apologist for the French king, and for a Gallican Church which strongly objects to being dictated to by Rome. Only here, as noted before, does Rabelais refer to all six books of canon law, and unlike the Chicanous chapters, these are aimed at readers familiar with the standard jibes against overzealous Catholics: that they have dropped the *quasi* out of the definition of a Pope as "quasi Deus in terris" ("almost God on Earth"); that they have replaced the respected Decretum with the later, and—to the humanists—unworthy Decretals, Clementines, and so forth; and that they have allowed the letter of the law to supersede God's commandments ("charité envers vostre prochain, pourveu qu'il ne soit Hereticque" ["charity toward your neighbor, provided he is not a heretic"] says Homenaz, 51). The grotesque, obsessive Homenaz is one of Rabelais's funniest minor characters, but the comedy intensifies, rather than attenuating, the satire.

It is clear, I hope, from this overview that law is seldom far from Rabelais's mind in any of the four books (and how interesting that there is very little law in the CL). But his law-inspired masterpiece is, obviously, the Bridoye episode, to which we must finally turn.

Bridoye

I hope this lengthy prologue has helped to explain how the 1546 reader would be able to make sense of Bridoye's ramblings in chapters 39–42 of the *Tiers Livre*. Confronted with Bridoye's first reference: *not. per Archid. d. .Lxxxvi. c. tanta.*, that reader would know that Archid. is the Archdeacon, Baisius de Reggio (Guido de Bayso), author of *Commentarii supra Decretorum volumina* (Venice, 1480); he would therefore understand that the reference is to the Decretum, in which *d.* stands for *distinctio* (books I and III of the Decretum are divided into *distinctiones*), and *c.* for canon. If he wished to look up the reference, he would easily discover that his edition of the Decretum included the Archdeacon's gloss, which claims that an elderly simpleton may be pardoned because of his age (D 1).

So far, so good; but as soon as we propose to analyze the humor of this episode, we run into a number of conflicting interpretations of it. Why did Rabelais spin a simple joke out into four chapters of largely incomprehensible legal references? Mainly because of his love of *copia* in all domains (Plattard), his fondness for what I call trivial pursuit? Or is there a moral lesson to be learned here? If so, it is far from obvious, inasmuch as for Screech (1964) Bridoye is a Christian fool worthy of respect who entrusts his decisions to God, for Derrett an apparent old bumbler whose self-defense is actually quite well thought out, for Duval (1983) a fundamentally ambiguous character, and for Céard (1996) an object lesson for Panurge about patient study before coming to a decision.

The two most detailed analyses are those of Derrett and Screech, which are diametrically opposed. Derrett, who was convinced that Rabelais intended his reader to follow up each and every lawbook reference in order to perceive the joke, thinks that Bridoye's old-simpleton persona is part of what is in fact a clever defense. Screech, who dismisses the lawbooks altogether and claims that Rabelais is using only legal tags from commonplace collections (in this case "Senectus . . . sapientiam auget" ["old age increases wisdom"]), thinks that the humor of this particular reference lies in Bridoye's citing an authority that would claim his physical weakness was offset by superior wisdom; "yet it is precisely for lack of wisdom that he has been arraigned" (177). This sounds plausible, and indeed one of the attractions of Screech's thesis is that his Bridoye is considerably funnier than Derrett's.

Because a good deal of Derrett's learned argumentation is simply over my head, and because nearly all critics of the *Tiers Livre* refer to Screech's article, rather than to Derrett or Nardi, the following discussion will most often cite Screech's views. He essentially proposes four bases for the episode's humor. First, Bridoye's stupidity leads him to quote passages that prove the opposite of what he thinks they do, as in the example just given, and as when he quotes *Gaudent brevitate moderni* in an absurdly prolix praise of brevity (S 7).

Second, Bridoye, like so many other Renaissance simpletons, is unaware that language is sometimes used metaphorically, as it is in the expression *alea judiciorum* on which the entire episode is based. He decides lawsuits with the use of actual dice, thinks Brocadium Juris was the name of his law professor, and assumes that the much-discussed term *Muscarii* refers to the "jeu de la mousche" (S 23). He reminds us of the numerous characters in farce who take literally expressions like "vendre ses oeufs au prix du marché" ("to sell one's eggs at [to] market price"), "parler à trait" ("to speak with deliberation/to an arrow"), or "manger de l'oie" ("eat goose"), with hilariously disastrous results (see chapter 2).

Third, Bridoye's mind-set is so obsessively legal that he compulsively quotes legal authorities to support banalities like *pecuniae obediunt omnia* ("everything obeys money," S 22) or "le temps meurist toutes choses" ("time ripens all things," S 26). He also quotes maxims originating in the Bible, like *Vinum laetificat cor hominis* ("Wine rejoices the heart of man," S 30) or *Beatius est dare quam accipere* ("It is more blessed to give than to receive," S 46), not from the Bible but from their legal context. Bridoye is undoubtedly the most impressively law-obsessed character between Philocleon and Perrin Dandin.

And fourth, Screech emphasizes the comedy of Bridoye's word-associations, which are still further evidence of his simplemindedness: the word *maturitas*, for instance, triggers a flood of legal references which have nothing to do with the matter in hand (S 28). A few of these references are charmingly obscene, as when Bridoye excuses his poor eyesight with a reference to a legal argument over whether a man with only one testicle is qualified for military service (S 2).

Although Screech's purpose in this article was not specifically to analyze the episode's comedy, he does produce a charming picture of Bridoye the obscurantist (legal *brocards* were considered old-fashioned by 1546), literal-minded, reference-obsessed, but essentially harmless old dodderer. Can anything be added to this picture?

Commentators on these chapters seem not to have noticed some quite obvious comedy. Bridoye uses his Moliéresque refrain: "vous aultres messieurs" ("you gentlemen") a total of twenty-two times, and almost every use of it implies a snide comment about what *all* judges routinely do. He first explains (chap. 39) that by *alea judiciorum* he means "les dez . . . des jugemens . . . des quelz dez vous aultres messieurs ordinairement usez en ceste vostre court souveraine, aussi font tous aultres juges" ("The dice . . . of judgments . . . which dice you gentlemen ordinarily use in this sovereign Court of yours; so do all other judges"). That is to say, the decisions of *all* judges suggest that they might as well have used dice. Next, in answer to the question of exactly how he goes about it, he replies: "Je fays comme vous aultres messieurs. . . . Ayant bien veu, reveu, leu, releu, paperassé, et feueilleté les . . . " ("I do as you gentlemen do. . . . Having well seen, reviewed, read, reread, papered, and leafed through the [list of thirty-seven technical names for legal documents]"), "et aultres telles dragées et espisseries" ("and other such goodies and spices"). That is to say, *all* judges pile up incredible quantities of useless documents.

Similarly, in the remainder of chapter 39, we learn that "vous aultres messieurs" favor the *défendeur* (defendant) over the *demandeur* (plaintiff), prefer lawsuits with lots of bags full of documents, use small dice for cases with very many such bags and large dice for those with fewer bags, and (as above) finally deliver stupid judgments. In chapter 40 we find that *all* judges find excuses for delaying the resolution of a case, are liable to be unhealthy and short-lived, think only about money, and drag their feet as much as possible. Chapters 41 and 42 add a few more lines to the portrait: "vous aultres messieurs" are usually old, foolish enough to believe silly legends about baby bears, and finally find delaying strategies even in a *flagrante crimine* case. Bridoye, like a more celebrated successor, embodies the law; no wonder this comprehensive indictment appealed to Racine and to Beaumarchais.

Bridoye's placement of tags within his monologue is also interesting. In the earlier part of the episode they usually come at the end of a series of references, as if to mock the listener/reader—why should we bother to decipher all these abbreviations if the essential point is stated, quite simply, in the tag? When Bridoye begins his story about Perrin Dandin, in chapter 41, the tags are more apt to precede the references. Part of the comedy here is in the contrast between the legal citations, that is, written texts, and the tags, which are oral rather than written (the maxims of the

Disticha Catonis and similar works were intended to be read aloud and learnt by heart). Like so many of Rabelais's episodic characters, Bridoye creates himself through his speech, but he is the only one whose oral *copia* consists largely of written references, so that the contrast between his torrent of verbiage and its ostensibly written content is itself comic.

An obvious question then arises (but I have never seen it asked): how does Bridoye pronounce § and ff.? Just try saying out loud:

> *ut ait gl. VI. q. I c. Si quis. g. de cons. d. V. c. I. fi. et est no. per doct. C. de impu. et aliis subst. l. ult. et l. legitimae. ff. de stat. hom. gl. in l. quod si nolit. ff. de edil. ed. l. quis. C. ad le. Jul. maiest. Excipio filios à moniali susceptos ex monacho, per gl. in c. Impudicas. xxvii. q. I.*

This may be one answer to another question raised by Screech's article; if, as Screech claims, all of Bridoye's references are to be found in the commonplace anthologies of legal tags, what is the point of the actual legal references we have been at such pains to elucidate? Derrett would reply that we must always go to the actual passage in Code, Digest, or Decretals to get the joke, but I am not convinced.

Plattard is certainly right to stress Rabelais's simple delight in accumulation and repetition, but the piling up of references surely has other purposes. It enables Bridoye to demonstrate dramatically that he is neither a humanist nor an up-to-date lawyer; Stein points out that "the indiscriminate use of *regulae iuris*, both civil and canon, had by the sixteenth century become a scandal" (162). Granted that he quotes civil law more often than canon law: forty-five references to the Digest, twenty-four to the Codex, two to the Institutes, and four to the Authentica, as against fourteen to the Decretum, twelve to the Decretals, one to the Clementines, and five to the Sixtus. But he also quotes commentary and gloss almost as often as text: five references each to Bartolus and "Speculator," four to Baldus, two each to Alberic da Rosata and Barbatia, one each to Ludovicus Romanus, Alexander Tartagno, Pope Innocent IV, Salicetus, Cardinalis, Joannes de Prato, Antonio de Butrio, and Giovanni d'Andrea, plus a striking thirty uses of *gl.* for "gloss." His very first reference, quoted above, is not to a text but to a note by the Archdeacon on the Decretum. This even-handed acceptance of civil and canon law, text and gloss as equally valid, is of course anathema to the humanists, and we note that he quotes only commentators of the thirteenth to the fifteenth century; he is unaware of recent humanist commentary on the law books and never mentions Budé, Alciati or Tiraqueau.

Despite the flood of Latin that Bridoye pours out so fluently, it is also clear that his Latin is not up to humanist standards. He garbles *manducet* into *manige ducat*, and apparently thinks that *alea* (in *alea judiciorum*) is plural when it is in fact singular: the die (and by extension the hazard or uncertainty), not the dice. These are faults even more egregious than his literal-minded use of dice (which will be excused, we recall, by Pantagruel himself in chap. 43).

To Rabelais's intended intellectual, legally literate reader, there must have been several layers of joking in these references. Sometimes Bridoye begins his set-speech by stating the point first:

> Les dez . . . des jugemens, *Alea iudiciorum,* des quelz est escript par *doct. 26 q. II. c. Sors l. nec emptio. ff. de contrah. empt. l. quod debetur. ff. de pecul. et ibi Barthol.* . .

The reader tempted to consult, respectively, the Decretum and two passages from the Digest will find that (like most of Bridoye's references, according to Derrett), these are correct, but have nothing to add to Bridoye's initial statement, so that looking them up was a waste of time.

Although there is an immediately obvious comic point here (Bridoye is a literal-minded idiot who thinks that *alea* is an actual die or dice rather than a metaphor), I suggest that in many cases, if the reader follows up the reference, several different things may happen. She may find that the reference works against Bridoye's point instead of for it; or that the reference has no connection with Bridoye's point apart from a common keyword; or that the reference implies a tactless comment on the men sitting in judgment on Bridoye (Screech). And in a number of cases, Screech may well be right that the comedy arises from the absolute banality of Bridoye's tags, which can be found not only in legal commonplace books but in proverb collections, the *Disticha Catonis*, in literature and in everyday speech. I also suggest that there are likely to be more allusions to Budé, Tiraqueau, and other contemporary jurists than have yet been unearthed.

Plattard and Derrett are surely correct in saying that a legal expert would get the most fun out of this episode. There is treasure trove here awaiting a knowledgeable scholar whose library contains all the relevant sixteenth-century editions, of civil and canon law in their old-fashioned format, and of commentators on both laws quoted by Rabelais. I have tried to show that even a little familiarity with sixteenth-century law greatly increases its comic potential. Bridoye, like Janotus de Bragmardo (whom he resembles quite strikingly), is a stupid and (to a humanist) despicable character who is rendered inoffensive by his own hilarious speech. In G 20 the uproarious laughter of the bystanders, at the end of Janotus's harangue, is a clear signal to the reader. There is no such laughter at the end of chapter 42 of the *Tiers Livre*, but I contend that Rabelais's reader has been receiving comparably clear signals throughout the episode.

This chapter has attempted to justify the claim that taking the trouble to decipher Rabelais's legal references is worth the effort. We cannot, alas, recapture the mind-set of Rabelais's intended reader, able spontaneously to laugh as heartily at Bridoye as he did at the Saint-Victor Library, but we can considerably enlarge our appreciation of law-based humor in the four books. The chapter has also tried to show that law, like medicine, is both more interesting and more entertaining than has been realized. A few episodes in Rabelais (the Chiquanous, the Papimanes) are incomprehensible without some knowledge of law; many more become funnier the more we know about the legal context. Thaumaste is not hilarious until we recognize where the debate-by-signs originated; Panurge's *perplexitas* in the *Tiers Livre* is legally, as well as morally, laughable; and Bridoye turns out to be both fundamentally reprehensible and delightfully comic.

Envoi

Rire, c'est survivre

RAYMOND DEVOS

It is not by chance that a book with a theatrical title ends with the flamboyantly dramatic Bridoye. Perhaps more than any of Rabelais's picturesquely comic secondary characters, Bridoye is "on stage." His cousin Janotus de Bragmardo is physically described (even if largely by negatives, G 18), but all we learn about Bridoye in TL 39 is that he is "on mylieu du parquet assis" ("sitting there in the middle of the place appointed for the hearing"), and that he says he's too old to see the dice properly. The remainder of chapters 39–42 is essentially his dramatic monologue, barring a few questions by Trinquamelle to urge him along.

I have referred a number of times to the letter to Odet de Châtillon, in which the Hippocratic doctor is at once rhetorician, actor, and stage manager. If medicine, for Hippocrates, is a "farce à trois personnages," Rabelais's four books could be called a farce (or a "tragicque comoedie") with a cast of dozens. Many mem-

bers of this cast are actors, Thaumaste, the Sybil and the fool
are mimes, Gymnaste a *bateleur* (in G 35), and Panurge (in
Pantagruel) a very efficient stage-manager. Life as drama is one
of the Western world's oldest metaphors, used by Erasmus in the
Praise of Folly, Vives in his *Fable about Man*, Shakespeare, Corneille,
Cervantes, and many others, but Rabelais's instinct for theater,
as I tried to show in chapter 2, goes much deeper than a moral-
izing desire to emphasize that all the world's a stage. Most "theatrical" episodes carry a humanist message, but they none the less
function very effectively as theater. I would also claim that besides
being a skilful creator of comic characters, Rabelais was himself a comic character, as broadly defined by Zack Bowen: "comic
characters have a morality which is complete, in the sense that
their principles are generally clear and coherent enough so that
they do not face soul-wrenching moral decisions" (Z. Bowen, 3).

This book began by urging a reading of Rabelais focused on
his multiplicity. Subsequent chapters, it may be objected, concen-
trated on specific aspects of his comic art, and thus detracted from
this multiple focus. If I were Rabelais, no doubt I could have found
a way to discuss simultaneously literature, humanism, rhetoric,
medicine, and law, which would have been fairer to my author.
Lacking this ability, I have at least tried wherever possible to point
out links between and among these disparate topics.

How does the Rabelais portrayed here differ from the Rabelais
presented by, say, Duval, Schwartz, Tournon, and Blanchard?
We are all agreed that he was an Erasmian Evangelical humanist, and that his comedy often accompanies serious reflections on
religion, politics, education, and ethics. I share Duval's conviction that religion was very important to him, although I think
Duval goes too far in making Pantagruel into a consistent figure
for Christ. I agree with Tournon that verbal pyrotechnics were
also very important to him, though not, I believe, more important

than humanist messages. Blanchard's view that Menippean satire in general, and Rabelais in particular, are fundamentally pessimistic about the capacities of humanism, is, I think, mistaken. Blanchard bases his theory on what Nauert and Grendler have to say about fifteenth-century Italian humanists; but whereas they may well have been conscious that their Renaissance was winding down, French intellectuals of the mid-sixteenth century were (even if dismayed at political and religious developments) still heartily confident in the power of humanism to liberate and to heal. Schwartz's deconstructionist position seems to me even more unfair to Rabelais, who really did want to transmit a clear humanist message to his readers, and who would have been depressed to learn that his text could be read as fundamentally ambivalent.

I hope that my Rabelais, at the end of this book, is perceived as a humanist for whom comedy and serious purpose were inseparable, and whose love of theater colored his views on humanism, rhetoric, and even medicine and law. He entered laughing, in the Prologue to *Pantagruel*, and he exited laughing (if we assume that the end of the *Quart Livre* was the last thing he wrote). Far from agreeing with La Fontaine ("Le Rieur et les Poissons") that

> Dieu ne créa que pour les sots
> Les méchants diseurs de bons mots

> God created, but only for fools,
> The wretched people who tell jokes,

he saw laughter as an essential weapon for the orator and the doctor, essential defense against hypocrites and bigots, and (like Raymond Devos) an essential lifeline for survival in difficult times.

As Evelyn Waugh said of Wodehouse, "He has made a world for us to live and delight in," and like Wodehouse's world, Rabelais's is also intended to reassure us. Tyrants may threaten and aunts may tyrannize, Charles V or the Nazis may overrun Europe, but laughter will always provide a sure refuge, an island of sanity in a dangerously mad world. Perhaps if today's princes, politicians, and educators were better able to enter and exit laughing, our world would be a more congenial place.

Appendix I

CIVIL AND CANON LAW

I CIVIL LAW

(Compiled by order of Emperor Justinian [527–565 C.E.])

1) *Institutiones*. Elementary manual for first-year law students, in four books. Only two references by Bridoye.
2) *Codex*. 534 C.E. Twelve books of titles and law. l.i.C. de sentent. quae pro ea quod = Codex VII. 47.1 (l. = lex). l.recepticia, C. de constit. pecun. = Codex IV.18.2. "Constituta pecunia" is in the title index, "Receptitia actione" in the law index.
3) *Digest* or *Pandects*. 533 C.E. Decisions of jurists. Fifty books, often in three volumes in the sixteenth century: Digestum Vetus, twenty-four books; Infortiatum, fourteen books; Novum, twelve books. ff. de re milit. l. qui cum uno = Digestum Novum 11.16 (or Digest 47.16 in modern editions). De re mil. is title (rubric), qui cum uno is law. References are easy to trace if Rabelais names the law or title, otherwise very tedious (see Screech).
4) *Novellae* or *Authentica* or *Volumen*. Later enactments by Justinian, and other material. Nine Collationes with numbered Tituli. Some are letters from Justinian to Belisarius et al., sometimes with month but not year.

II CANON LAW

1) *Decretum* of Gratianus, 1139–48. Three parts: I (on nature and sources of law, ecclesiastical offices and conduct) has 101 distinctions with canons. II (Christian behavior, penal law, church property, religious orders, marriage, penance) has thirty-six causes with questions and canons. Question 3 of cause 33 is a separate section, De penitentia. III (sacraments and doctrine) is titled De consecratione and has five distinctions. d.lxxxvi c. tanta = I, dis. 86, canon beginning Tanta. xxxiii, q.II ult = II, causa 33, qu. 2, last para. de cons. d. 5 c.j.fi. = III, dis. 5, canon 1, end. p. = de penitentia. Rubric palaea = additions by Paucapalaea.

2) *Decretals* of Gregory IX, composed by Raymond de Penafort, 1234. Five books: judex, judicium, clerus, conubium, crimen. Divided into tituli and rubricae; tituli into capitula into paragraphi into versiculi. c.fin.de sortil. = *Decretals* V, titulus 21: "De sortilegiis," capitulus 3 (last). Easy to find via title index.

3) *Liber Sextus*, 1294. Five books corresponding in content to the five books of *Decretals*. de reg. iur. in VI = Sext. V, De reg. iur., Regula 54. Most titles are numbered and divided into capituli, but De reg. iur. is a separate title at end, with regulae instead of capituli.

4) *Clementinae*, 1317. Prepared by Boniface VIII, publ. by John XXII. Also five books with the same plan.

5) *Extravagantes* of John XXII. 1325, 14 tituli. Never quoted by Bridoye.

6) *Extravagantes communes*. Never quoted by Bridoye.

Appendix II

§	paragraph, in Decretum, Digest, or Institutes
Alber. de Ros.	Albericus de Rosate, 14th-century jurist, author of a well-known *Lexicon utriusque Juris*
Alex.	Alexander Tartagno de Imola, 15th-century jurist, commentator on both laws
Anto. de Butrio	Antonio da Budrio, 15th-century Bologna canonist
Archid.	Archdeacon, i.e., Baisius de Reggio (Guido de Bayso), author of celebrated commentaries on the Decretum
arg./Arg.	*argumentum*
Autent/autent.	4th and latest volume of Civil Law, variously titled Novellae, Authentica, or Volumen
Bal./Bald.	Baldus, famous post-glossator, 1323–1400
Barbatia	André Barbatia, 15th-century jurist
Barthol./Bar./Bart.	Bartolus of Sassoferrato, famous post-glossator, 1313–1357
C./Cod.	Codex, second volume of Civil Law
c.	canon, in the Decretum, or capitulum, in the Decretals
c. fin.	last canon or capitulum
Card.	Cardinalis, i.e. Franciscus Zabarella (1360–1417), Italian canonist
Cle.	Clementinae, 1317, fourth major volume of Canon Law

coll.	*collatio*, in Authentica/Novella/Volumen
de reg. jur.	either *de diversis regulis juris*, title of Digest (Novum col. 1898), or *de regulis juris*, last title of Liber Sextus
D./d./dist.	*distinctio*, in Decretum I or III
de cons.	*de consecratione*, title of Decretum Book III
Doct./doct.	Doctors (of Canon Law)
eod. tit.	in the same title
extra.	Decretals (and not Extravagantes, as claimed by most critics)
ff.	Digest (Pandects)
fin.	see c.
gl./glos.	gloss
hic no.	note this
i.	*id est*
Innoc./Inno.	Pope Innocent IV
in princ.	at the beginning
Instit./instit.	Institutes
Io. de Pra.	Johannes de Prato, 15th-century Florentine jurist
j.	number 1
Joan. And.	Giovanni d'Andrea
l.	*lex*, in Codex or Digest
le./leg.	*legem* or *lege*
lib. vi./VI	Liber Sextus
Lud. Ro.	Ludovicus Romanus, i.e. Pontanus, d. 439; commentator on Codex and Digest

no./not.	note
p.	*de penitentia* (Decretum II.33)
q.	*quaestio*, in Book II of Decretum (but preceding no. refers not to *quaestio* but to *causa*)
Salic.	Salicetus, i.e. Bartolomeo Saliceto, 14th–15th century Bolognese commentator on civil law
Spec.	*speculator*, i.e., Guilhelmus Durandus, commentator on Canon Law
tit.	*titulus*
ult./ulti.	*ultimus/um/o*

Notes

1. Abel Lefranc's views on Rabelais are too well known to need support here. For the other authors, see Bibliography.

2. The only critic to emphasize multiplicity of genres in Rabelais, to my knowledge, is Demerson (1995, chap. 3).

3. A similar kind of gratuitous goofiness is found in the lyrics of W. S. Gilbert and in Marx Brothers movies (and readers over fifty years old may remember a wonderful British radio program called "The Goon Show").

4. It is to be hoped that no readers of this book share the opinion expressed by Alfred Glauser in 1966 (75), that there are no women in Rabelais's four books because women are not funny. We know now that women can not only read Rabelais, but they can write about him, sometimes entertainingly.

5. Violence in Rabelais is a complex and interesting subject, but not immediately to my purpose here; see the discussion in Demerson 1992.

6. *Baiser* in modern French means "to have sex with," but as far as I can tell it did not acquire this meaning until after the sixteenth century.

7. Unless otherwise specified, all Rabelais quotations are from the critical edition by Mireille Huchon (abbreviation RH), and all translations from Donald Frame.

8. Anne Lake Prescott reminds me that much science fiction on television manages to be both authentic narrative and ironic self-mockery. Rabelais would have enjoyed it.

9. There is an "espée baise-mon-cul à deux mains" in Noël Du Fail's *Propos Rustiques* (131); one also thinks of Uncle Fred's great sponge Joyeuse (*Uncle Fred in the Springtime*, chap. 10).

10. Florence Weinberg protests that Pantagruel is actively "cooperating" with God by holding the mast firmly in place, as well as by his prayer, and that on numerous occasions the dialogue implies quite frenzied actions by frere Jean and the sailors.

11. I am grateful to Anne Lake Prescott for this reference.

12. See note 19.

13. I must protest against Floyd Gray's statement that the enormous portmanteau words describing the wounds of the participants in this battle are unpronounceable (Gray 1974, 176). With a little practice, they can be pronounced—and can be counted on to make the listeners laugh.

14. Two quite different explanations have been suggested for this phrase: 1) the line is a special-effects cord used in a theatrical performance; 2) it is a fishing line, and Panurge is about to play Dindenault as a fisherman plays a hooked fish (Frame). The former seems to me more likely.

15. See my discussion of this play in "Le théâtre du cliché," *Cahiers de l'Association Internationale des Etudes Françaises* 26 (1974): 33–47. There are also a number of what I call sexual-action plays, in which the metaphor (*rembourrer le bas*, *écurer le chaudron* and so on) has obvious sexual connotations. Rabelais may have known the best of these, Gringoire's *Raoullet Ployart* of 1512, where the metaphor is the cultivation of a vineyard, and the heroine tries out two workmen called respectively Dire and Faire. Cf. B. Bowen, "Metaphorical Obscenity in French Farce, 1460–1560," *Comparative Drama* 11 (1977–78), 331–44.

16. My translation.

17. At the Sixteenth Century Studies Conference in St. Louis in December 1993, Donald Perret of Emerson College staged a superb performance of this monologue; it is now available on video.

18. I am grateful to Anne Lake Prescott for this reference.

19. When feasible, I give the numbers of jokes in my anthology *One Hundred Renaissance Jokes*, inasmuch as it is much easier to find them there than to go to the original source.

20. Ingrid Rowland recently discovered a small collection of extremely obscene German humanist poems, which Rabelais could not have known but which provide still further evidence of the mind-set of the time.

21. Florence Weinberg makes the following intriguing suggestion: "*beuged* could be a sixteenth-century German word (now "[ge-]beugt") meaning bowed down, humped over, crouched (as in genuflecting) or perhaps squatting as in shitting. Sixteenth-century

German often dropped the "ge-" prefix. This word, together with "-cribrationes," would mean "squatting discussions [discussions while squatting] of the shitters."

22. Antoine de Lève was one of Charles v's generals. He invaded Provence, which could be described as "the color of red wood" after it was burned by the invading forces in 1536.

23. Merlinus Coccaius is the pseudonym of Teofilo Folengo, author of the *Baldus* (see Chapter 2), in which devils play a sizeable role.

24. Accursius, author of the best-known late medieval gloss on Roman law, was often the butt of the humanists; cf. chapter 6.

25. Frame translates "by S.C.," the initials of Symphorien Champier, who published a treatise with this title, but that seems a waste of the paragraph sign.

26. Wayne Rebhorn's provocative *The Emperor of Men's Minds: Literature and the Renaissance Discourse of Rhetoric* (1995) reached me too late for me to treat in detail here. His interesting evidence that Renaissance rhetoric could be seen as subversive, disturbing, potentially destructive and sexually ambiguous has not shaken my conviction that for Rabelais it represented the best of the Classical (both literary and moral) heritage.

27. My translation.

28. See note 6.

29. For the history of this definition, see Monfasani, article III: "Episodes of Anti-Quintilianism in the Italian Renaissance: Quarrels on the Orator as a *Vir Bonus* and Rhetoric as the *Scientia Bene Dicendi.*"

30. My translation.

31. So Frame; but *orateurs* surely here means "those who pray," not "orators."

32. *Expérience* in French can mean both "experience" and "experiment," rendering translation difficult.

33. My translation.

34. This is the only translation of Platina into English; unfortunately, it has no page numbers.

35. My translation.

36. My translation.

37. An interesting recent article by Thomas Greene, "Rabelais and the Language of Malediction" (see Bibliography), stresses the simultaneously aggressive and healing qualities of Rabelaisian comedy.

38. Because it would be enormously time-consuming to expand and explain all the abbreviated words in these Latin titles, I shall assume that most readers are not sufficiently interested in them; a few samples are explained in more detail later.

39. My colleague Tom McGinn tells me that *ius gentium* does not necessarily mean "natural law," but something more like "the way in which human society tends to be organized."

40. Both Derrett and Screech number the legal citations they discuss, so I give both numbers to facilitate reference for readers who wish to pursue them.

41. It is unfortunate that two excellent recent critical editions, M. Huchon's of the *Oeuvres complètes* (RH), and Jean Céard's of the *Tiers Livre*, repeat the old error that *extra* means the *Extravagantes*.

42. According to Florence Weinberg, there is a very funny rendition of this story in the introduction to the fourteenth-century *Libro de buen amor* by Juan Ruiz.

Bibliography

EDITIONS OF RABELAIS

Rabelais, François. *Gargantua.* Ed. Gérard Defaux. Paris: Livre de Poche, 1994.

———. *Gargantua.* Ed. M.A. Screech. Geneva: Droz, 1970.

———. *Les horribles et espoventables faictz & prouesses du tresrenommé Pantagruel Roy des Dipsodes, filz du grand geant Gargantua.* Lyons: Claude Nourry, n.d. [1531/1532].

———. *Oeuvres.* Ed. Abel Lefranc et al. 6 vols. Paris: Champion, 1913–.

———. *Oeuvres complètes.* Ed. Guy Demerson. Paris: Seuil, 1973.

———. *Oeuvres complètes.* Ed. Mireille Huchon. Paris: Gallimard, 1994.

———. *Oeuvres complètes.* Ed. Pierre Jourda. 2 vols. Paris: Garnier, 1962.

———. *Pantagruel.* Ed. Gérard Defaux. Paris: Livre de Poche, 1994.

———. *Pantagruel.* Ed. V.-L. Saulnier. Paris: Droz, 1946.

———. *Le Quart Livre des faicts et dicts Heroiques du bon Pantagruel.* Paris: Michel Fezandat, 1552.

———. *Quart Livre.* Ed. Robert Marichal. Geneva: Droz, 1947.

———. *Tiers liure des faictz et dictz Heroiques du noble Pantagruel.* Paris: Chrestien Wechel, 1546.

———. *Tiers Livre.* Ed. M.A. Screech. Geneva: Droz, 1964.

———. *Tiers Livre.* Ed. Jean Céard. Paris: Livre de Poche, 1995.

———. *La vie très horrificque du grand Gargantua père de Pantagruel.* Lyon: Fr. Juste, n.d. [1534/1535].

OTHER RENAISSANCE TEXTS

Aneau, Barthélemy. *Alector ou le coq: histoire fabuleuse.* Ed. Marie Madeleine Fontaine. 2 vols. Geneva: Droz, 1996.

Anonymous. *Fierabras, Roman en prose de la fin du XIVe siècle publié d'après les manuscrits Fonds fr. 4969 et 2172 de la Bibl. Nat. à Paris.* Ed. Jean Miquet. Ottawa: Editions de l'Université d'Ottawa, 1983.

———. *Mensa philosophica: In hoc Opusculo tractatur de his quibus utimur in mensa.* Cologne, n.p., 1500.

————. *Mer des Histoires.* n.p., 1488.

Arlotto, Piovano. *Motti e facezie del Piovano Arlotto.* Ed. G. Folena. Milan: Ricciardi, 1953.

Aubailly, Jean-Claude, ed. *Deux jeux de Carnaval de la fin du Moyen Age: La Bataille de Sainct Pensard à l'encontre de Caresme et le Testament de Carmentrant.* Geneva: Droz, 1978.

Bebel, Heinrich. *Heinrich Bebels Facetien: Drei Bücher.* ed. Gustav Bebermeyer. Leipzig: Hiersemann, 1931.

Bouchard, Alain. *Les grandes croniques de Bretaigne nouuellement Imprimees a Paris.* Paris: Galliot du Pré, 1514.

Bouchet, Jean. *Les Annales d'Aquitaine. Faicts et gestes en sommaire des roys de France et d'Angleterre, Pays de Naples & de Milan.* Poitiers: Abraham Mounin, 1644.

Bracciolini, Poggius. *Opera omnia.* Ed. Riccardo Fubini. 2 vols. Torino: Bottega d'Erasmo, 1964.

Cortesi, Paolo. *[De cardinalatu].* *Ad Episcopum Urbis Romae.* Rome: Castro Cortesio, 1510.

Erasmus. *Erasmus on His Times.* Ed. Margaret Mann Phillips. New York: Harper & Row, 1967.

————. *The Colloquies of Erasmus.* Tr. Craig. R. Thompson. Chicago: University of Chicago Press, 1965.

Folengo, Teofilo. *Opus Merlini Cocaii.* n.p.: 1522.

————. *Le Maccherone.* Ed. Alessandro Luzio. Bari: Laterza, 1911–1927.

Gaguin, Robert. *La Mer des chroniques & miroir hystorial de france jadis compose en latin par religieuse personne frere Robert Gaguin. . . Lequel traicte de tous les faitz aduenis* [sic] *depuis la destruction de Troie la grant.* n.p., 1525.

————. *Le premier volume des grans croniques de france. . . Auecques la Cronique frere Robert Gaguin contenue a la cronique Martinienne.* Paris: Fr. Regnault, n.d.

Gast, Johann. *Convivalium sermonum liber.* Basel: n.p., 1541.

Guillerm, Luce, et al., eds. *Le miroir des femmes, II: Roman, conte, théâtre, poésie au XVIe siècle.* Lille: Presses Universitaires de Lille, 1984.

Koopmans, Jelle, ed. *Recueil de sermons joyeux (XVe–XVIe siècles).* Geneva: Droz, 1988.

Lemaire de Belges, Jean. *Concorde des deux langages.* Ed. Jean
    Frappier. Paris: Droz, 1947.
————. *Epitres de l'amant vert.* Ed. Jean Frappier. Lille: Giard, 1948.
————. *Les Illustrations de Gaule et Singularitez de Troye, par maistre
    Iean le Maire de Belges.* Lyon: Iean de Tournes, 1549.
Luscinio, Ottomaro [Othmar Nachtigall]. *Joci ac sales mire festivi.*
    n.p.: 1524.
More, Thomas. *Responsio ad Lutherum.* In John M. Headley, ed., *The
    Complete Works of St. Thomas More.* Vol. 5. New Haven: Yale
    University Press, 1963.
Panormita, Antonius. *Antonii Panormitae de dictis et factis Alphonsi
    regis Aragonum libri quattuor.* Basil: Ex officina Heruagiana,
    1538.
Perceforest, Roy. *La Treselegante Delicieuse Melliflue et tresplaisante
    hystoire du tresnoble victorieux excellentissime Roy Perceforest/
    Roy de la grant Bretaiane* [sic]/ *fundateur du franc palais/ et du
    Temple du Souuerain dieu.* 6 vols. in 3. Paris: n.p., 1531.
Poliziano, Angelo (probably a false attribution). *Detti piacevoli.* Ed.
    Tiziano Zanato. Rome: Istituto della Enciclopedia Italiana,
    1983.
Pontano, Giovanni. *Ioannis Ioviani Pontani De sermone libri sex.* Eds.
    S. Lupi and A. Risicato. Lugano: Thesaurus Mundi, 1954.
Pulci, Luigi. *Morgante.* Ed. Davide Puccini. 2 vols. Milan: Garzanti,
    1989.
Ravisius Textor. *Officina, sive Theatrum histor. et poeticum.* Basil:
    Sumptibus Ludovici Regis, 1617.
Tissier, André, ed. *Recueil de Farces (1450–1550).* 11 vols. in print.
    Geneva: Droz, 1986.
Verville, Béroalde. *Le moyen de parvenir.* Eds. Hélène Moreau and
    André Tournon. Aix-en-Provence: Université de Provence,
    1984.

RABELAIS, HUMANISM, AND RHETORIC (Chapters 3 and 4)

Backus, Irena. *The Disputations of Baden, 1526 and Berne, 1528:
    Neutralizing the Early Church. Princeton Theological Seminary
    Studies in Reformed Theology and History* vol. 1, no. 1, Winter
    1993.

Baron, Hans. *The Crisis of the Early Italian Renaissance: Civic Humanism and Republican Liberty in an Age of Classicism and Tyranny.* 2 vols. Princeton: Princeton University Press, 1955.

Balavoine, Claudie. "L'essence de marjolaine, ou ce qui, de l'adage, retint Erasme." In Lafond, Jean, ed., *Formes brèves de la prose et le discours discontinu aux XVIe et XVIIe siècles,* 159–83. Paris: Vrin, 1984.

Best, Thomas W., ed. *Eccius dedolatus: A Reformation Satire.* Lexington: University of Kentucky Press, 1971.

Bowen, Barbara C. "Facétie/*sententia*/apophtegme: les *Divers Propos Memorables* de Gilles Corrozet." In Piotr Salwa and E. D. Zolkiewska, eds., *Narrations brèves: Mélanges de littérature ancienne offerts à Krystyna Kasprzyk,* 229-236. Warsaw: University of Warsaw, 1993.

——. "Festive Humanism: The Case of Luscinius." *Explorations in Renaissance Culture* 9 (1993): 1–18.

——. "Roman Jokes and the Renaissance Prince, 1455–1528." *Illinois Classical Studies* 9 (1984): 137–48.

——. *Words and the Man in French Renaissance Literature.* Lexington: French Forum Monographs, 1983.

Bowen, Barbara C., ed. *One Hundred Renaissance Jokes: An Anthology.* Birmingham, Alabama: Summa Publications, 1988.

Buda, Gulielmo. *Gulielmi Budaei Parisiensis, Consiliarii Regii, De asse et partibus eius libri V.* Lyon: Seb. Gryphe, 1542.

Burke, Peter. "The Renaissance Dialogue." *Renaissance Studies* 3 (1989): 1–12.

Crane, William G. *Wit and Rhetoric in the Renaissance: The Formal Basis of Elizabethan Prose Style.* New York: Columbia University Press, 1937.

Domenichi, Ludovico. *Facetie, motti et burle di diversi signori.* Venice: Leoncini, 1574.

France, Peter. *Rhetoric and Truth in France: Descartes to Diderot.* Oxford: Clarendon Press, 1972.

Franklin, A. L. A. *Histoire de la bibliothèque de l'abbaye de St.-Victor à Paris.* Paris: n.p., 1865.

Freeman, Michael. "Gilles Corrozet et les débuts littéraires de Pierre de Larivey." *Bibliothèque d'Humanisme et Renaissance* 48 (1986): 431–38.

Fumaroli, Marc. *L'âge de l'éloquence: rhétorique et "res literaria" de la Renaissance au seuil de l'époque classique.* Paris: Champion, 1980.

de la Garanderie, Marie-Madeleine. "L'harmonie secrète du *De asse* de Guillaume Budé." *Bulletin de l'Association Guillaume Budé* 4e série no. 4 (déc. 1968): 473–86.

Grafton, Anthony, and Lisa Jardine. *From Humanism to the Humanities: Education and the Liberal Arts in 15th Century and 16th Century Europe.* Cambridge: Harvard University Press, 1986.

Gray, Hanna. "Renaissance Humanism: The Pursuit of Eloquence." *Journal of the History of Ideas* 24 (1963): 497–514.

Grendler, Paul F. *Schooling in Renaissance Italy: Literacy and Learning, 1300–1600.* Baltimore: Johns Hopkins University Press, 1989.

Holborn, Hajo, ed. *On the Eve of the Reformation: Letters of Obscure Men.* New York: Harper & Row, 1964.

Jeanneret, Michel. *Des mets et des mots: banquets et propos de table à la Renaissance.* Paris: Corti, 1987.

Kenny, Neil. *The Palace of Secrets: Béroalde de Verville and Renaissance Conceptions of Knowledge.* Oxford: Clarendon Press, 1991.

Kohl, Benjamin G. "The Changing Concept of the *studia humanitatis* in the Early Renaissance." *Renaissance Studies* 6 (1992): 185–209.

Kristeller, P. O. *Renaissance Thought: The Classic, Scholastic and Humanist Strains.* New York: Harper & Row, 1961.

Kushner, Eva. "Le dialogue en France au XVIe siècle: quelques critères génologiques." *Revue Canadienne de Littérature Comparée* Spring 1978: 141–53.

[Lacroix, Paul.] *Catalogue de la Bibliothèque de l'Abbaye de Saint-Victor au seizième siècle rédigée par François Rabelais.* Paris: Techener, 1862.

Lauvergnat-Gagnière, Christiane. *Lucien de Samosate et le lucianisme en France au XVIe siècle: athéisme et polémique.* Geneva: Droz, 1988.

Lipking, Joanna B. "Traditions of the *facetiae* and Their Influence in Tudor England." Ph.D. dissertation, Columbia University, 1970.

Maillard, J.-F. "Aspects de l'encyclopédisme au XVIe siècle dans le

Traicté des chiffres annoté par Blaise de Vigenère."
Bibliothèque d'Humanisme et Renaissance 44 (1982): 235–68.

Margolin, Jean-Claude. "De la digression au commentaire: pour une lecture humaniste du *De asse* de Guillaume Budé." In Grahame Castor and Terence Cave, eds., *Neo-Latin and the Vernacular in Renaissance France*, 1–25. Oxford: Clarendon Press, 1984.

Mehl, James V. "Characterizations of the 'Obscure Men' of Cologne: A Study in Pre-Reformation Collective Authorship." In Thomas F. Mayer and D. R. Woolf, eds., *The Rhetorics of Life-Writing in Early Modern Europe: Forms of Biography from Cassandra Fedele to Louis XIV*, 163–85. Ann Arbor: University of Michigan Press, 1995.

———. "From Humanist Satire to Reformation Polemic in the *Eccius Dedolatus* (1520)." Paper given at the Renaissance Studies Association annual conference, Dallas, April 1994.

———. "Language, Class, and Mimic Satire in the Characterization of Correspondents in the *Epistolae obscurorum virorum*." *Sixteenth Century Journal* 25 (1994): 289–305.

Monfasani, John. *Language and Learning in Renaissance Italy: Selected Articles*. Brookfield, Vermont: Variorum, 1994.

Moss, Ann. "Printed Commonplace Books in the Renaissance." In Alexander Dalzell et al., eds., *Acta Conventus Neo-Latini Torontonensis*, 509–18. Binghamton, New York: Medieval and Renaissance Texts and Studies, 1991.

Nauert, Charles. "The Clash of Humanists and Scholastics: An Approach to Pre-Reformation Controversies." *Sixteenth Century Journal* 4 (1973): 1–18.

Overfield, James H. "A New Look at the Reuchlin Affair." *Studies in Medieval and Renaissance History* 8 (1971): 165–207.

———. *Humanism and Scholasticism in Late Medieval Germany*. Princeton: Princeton University Press, 1984.

Randall, Michael. *Building Resemblance: Analogical Imagery in the Early French Renaissance*. Baltimore: Johns Hopkins University Press, 1996.

Rebhorn, Wayne A. *The Emperor of Men's Minds: Literature and the Renaissance Discourse of Rhetoric*. Ithaca, New York: Cornell University Press, 1995.

————. "'The Emperour of Mens Minds': The Renaissance Trickster as *Homo Rhetoricus*." In David Quint et al., eds., *Creative Imitation: New Essays on Renaissance Literature in Honor of Thomas M. Greene*, 31–65. Binghamton, New York: Medieval and Renaissance Texts and Studies, 1992.

Rowland, Ingrid D. "Revenge of the Regensburg Humanists, 1493." *Sixteenth Century Journal* 25 (1994): 307–22.

Rummel, Erika. *The Humanist-Scholastic Debate in the Renaissance and Reformation*. Cambridge: Harvard University Press, 1995.

Schiffman, Zachary Sayre. *On the Threshold of Modernity: Relativism in the French Renaissance*. Baltimore: Johns Hopkins University Press, 1991.

Servet, Pierre. "*Alector* et le roman d'aventures médiéval." *Réforme, Humanisme, Renaissance* 39 (1994): 45–73.

Stephens, Walter. *Giants in Those Days: Folklore, Ancient History, and Nationalism*. Lincoln: University of Nebraska Press, 1989.

Tomarken, Annette H. *The Smile of Truth: The French Satirical Eulogy and Its Antecedents*. Princeton: Princeton University Press, 1990.

Trinkaus, Charles. *In Our Image and Likeness: Humanity and Divinity in Italian Humanist Thought*. 2 vols. London: Constable, 1970.

Wilson, K. J. "Ascham's *Toxophilus* and the Rules of Art." *Renaissance Quarterly* 29 (1976): 30–51.

Wilson, Thomas. *The Arte of Rhetorique (1553)*. Ed. Robert Hood Bowers. Gainesville, Florida: Scholars' Facsimiles and Reprints, 1962.

RABELAIS AND MEDICINE (Chapter 5)

Alberini, Massimo. *Storia del pranzo all'italiana: Dal triclinio allo snack*. Milan: Rizzoli, 1966.

Antonioli, Roland. *Rabelais et la médecine*. Geneva: Droz, 1976.

Arano, Luisa Cogliati, ed. *Tacuinum sanitatis: The Medieval Health Handbook*. New York: Braziller, 1976.

Berriot-Salvadore, Evelyne. "La question du scepticisme scientifique dans le *Tiers Livre* et le *Quart Livre*." In James Dauphiné and Paul Mironneau, eds., *Rabelais, A propos du Tiers Livre: Actes des troisièmes Journées du Centre Jacques de Laprade tenues au Musée national du château de Pau les 8 et 9 décembre 1995,* 22–30. Biarritz: J & D Editions, 1995.

Blond, Georges, and Germaine Blond. *Festins de tous les temps: histoire pittoresque de notre alimentation.* Paris: Fayard, 1976.

Bowen, Barbara C. *"Porcus troianus* et paon doré: l'exotisme culinaire de la Renaissance." In E. Berriot-Salvadore, ed., *Les représentations de l'Autre du Moyen Age au XVIIe siècle: Mélanges en l'honneur de Kazimierz Kupisz,* 109–17. Saint-Etienne: Publications de l'Université de Saint-Etienne, 1995.

———. "Rabelais et le propos torcheculatif." In François Marotin and Jacques-Philippe Saint-Gérand, eds., *Poétique et Narration: Mélanges offerts à Guy Demerson,* 371–80. Paris: Champion, 1993.

———. "Rire est le propre de l'homme." *Etudes Rabelaisiennes* 21 (1988): 185–90.

Canappe, Jean, ed. *Opuscules de divers autheurs medecins, Redigez ensemble pour le proufit & utilité des Chirurgiens.* Lyon: Jean de Tournes, 1552.

Cardanus, Hieronymus. *De sapientia libri quinque . . . Eiusdem De consolatione libri tres . . .* Aureliopoli: Apud Petrum & Jacobum Chouët, 1624.

———. *Hieronymi Cardani Mediolanensis, De propria vita liber.* Amsterdam: Apud Joannem Ravesteinium, 1654.

———. *Les Livres de Hierosme Cardanus . . . intitulez de la Subtilité . . . Traduits de Latin en François par Richard le Blanc.* Paris: Simon Caluarin, 1584.

Céard, Jean. "La diététique dans la médecine de la Renaissance." In Jean-Claude Margolin and Robert Sauzet, eds., *Pratiques et discours alimentaires à la Renaissance: Actes du Colloque de Tours de mars 1979,* 21–36. Paris: Maisonneuve et Larose, 1982.

[Champier, Bruyerin.] *De re cibaria libri XXII . . . Io. Bruyerino Campegio Lugdun. authore.* n.p., 1560.

Champier, Symphorien. *Castigationes seu emendationes Pharmacopolarum, siue Apothecariorum.* Lyon: Jean Crespin, 1532.

————. *Symphonia Galeni ad Hippocratem . . . Item, Clysteriorum Campi*. n.p., 1528.

Colin, Sebastian. *Bref dialogue contenant les Causes, Iugemens, Couleurs & Hypostases des Vrines*. Poitiers: Marnef, 1558.

————. *Declaration des abvz et tromperies qve font les Apothicaires, fort vtile & necessaire à vn chascun studieux & curieux de sa santé, composée par Maistre Lisset Benancio*. Lyon: chez Michel Ioue, 1556.

Conrad, Lawrence I., et al. *The Western Medical Tradition, 800 b.c. to a.d. 1800*. Cambridge: Cambridge University Press, 1995.

Cosman, Madeleine Pelner. *Fabulous Feasts: Medieval Cookery and Ceremony*. New York: Braziller, 1976.

Cruciani, Fabrizio, ed. *Il teatro del Campidoglio e le feste romane del 1513*. Milan: Edizioni Il Polifilo, 1968.

de Rocher, Gregory. *Rabelais's Laughers and Joubert's Traité du Ris*. University: University of Alabama Press, 1979.

Dixon, J. E. G. "The Treatment of *morbus Gallicus* in Rabelais." *Etudes Rabelaisiennes* 25 (1991): 61–77.

Erasmus, Desiderius. "Encomium medicinae." In *Opera omnia* vol. 1, part 4: 145–86. Amsterdam: North-Holland, 1972.

Estienne, Charles. *La dissection des parties du corps humain diuisee en trois liures*. Paris: Simon de Colines, 1546.

Fernel, Jean. *Universa Medicina*. Coloniae Allobrogum: Apud Samuelem de Tournes, 1679.

Fontaine, Marie Madeleine. "Quaresmeprenant: l'image littéraire et la contestation de l'analogie médicale." In James A. Coleman and Christine M. Scollen-Jimack, eds., *Rabelais in Glasgow*, 87–112. Glasgow: Glasgow University Printing, 1984.

Fracastorius, Hieronymus. *Hieronymi Fracastorii Veron. Liber I, De Sympathia & Antipathia rerum*. Lugduni: Apud Gulielmum Gazeium, 1550.

French, R. K. "Berengario da Carpi and the Use of Commentary in Anatomical Teaching." In A. Wear et al., eds., *The Medical Renaissance*, 42–74. Cambridge: Cambridge University Press, 1985.

Fuchs, Leonard. *Medendi methodus* (Haguenau, 1531): *Methode ou brieve introduction, pour parvenir à la congnoissance de la vraye & solide Medecine, Composee par M. Leonard Fuchs, & traduite*

en François par maistre Guillaume Paradin. Lyon: Jean de
Tournes and G. Gazeau, 1552.

————. *Paradoxorum libri tres, in quibus sane multa à nemine hactenus
prodita, Arabum aetatisque nostrae medicorum errata non tan-
tùm indicantur, sed & probatissimorum autorum scriptis, firmis-
simisque rationibus ac argumentis confutantur*. Paris: Apud
Carolam Guillard, 1555.

Gocklenius the Elder, Rudolph. *Hermolai Barbari, Patritii Veneti,
Scientiae Naturalis Compendium. Cui adjuncta est Rodolphi
Goclenij Profess. Marpurg. Physiologia De Risu et Lacrumis*.
Marpurgi: Excudebat Paulus Egenolphus, 1597.

Greene, T. "Rabelais and the Language of Malediction." In Jean-
Claude Carron, ed., *François Rabelais: Critical Assessments*,
105–20. Baltimore: Johns Hopkins University Press, 1995.

Joubert, Laurent. *Traité du Ris, contenant son essence, ses causes, et mer-
veilleux essais, curieusement recerchés, raisonnés et observés*.
Paris: Nicolas Chesneau, 1579; reprint Geneva: Slatkine,
1972.

————. *Treatise on Laughter*. Tr. Gregory de Rocher. University:
University of Alabama Press, 1980.

Landi, B. "Barbaromastix, sive Medicus, dialogvs elegantiss." *Novae
Academiae Florentinae opuscula. Aduersus Auicennam, &
medicos neotericos, qui Galeni disciplina neglecta, barbaros colunt*, 3–60. Lyon: Seb. Gryphium, 1534.

Leonicenus. *De Plinii et aliorum medicorum erroribus liber*. Basel: n.p.,
1529.

Mancinus, Celsius. *Celsi Mancinii Ravennatis. . . Libri III. I. De
Somniis, ac Synesi per somnia. II. De Risu, ac ridiculis. III. De
Synaugia Platonica*. Frankfurt: Ex Officina M. Zachariae
Pathenij, 1598.

Mcadoo, Jane. "Du Bellay's 'Hymne de la surdité' or the Puzzle of
the Third Ossicle." *Renaissance Studies* 8 (1994): 198–204.

Ménager, Daniel. *La Renaissance et le rire*. Paris: Presses
Universitaires de France, 1995.

da Messisbugo, Cristoforo. *Banchetti composizioni di vivande e
apparecchio generale*. Ed. Fernando Bandini. Venice: Neri
Pozza, 1960.

Nancelius, Nicholas. *Nic. Nancelii Trachyeni Noviodunensis, apud Turones Medici, de Immortalitate animae, velitatio adversus Galenum*. Paris: Jean Richer, 1587.

Nilles, Camilla J. "Revisions of Redemption: Rabelais's Medlar, *Braguette* and Pantagruelion Myths." *Renaissance et Réforme* 25 (1989): 127–37.

Nutton, Vivian. "Humanist Surgery." In A. Wear et al., eds., *The Medical Renaissance*, 75–99. Cambridge: Cambridge University Press, 1985.

————. "The Rise of Medical Humanism: Ferrara, 1464–1555." *Renaissance Studies* 11 (1997): 2–19.

Paré, Ambroise. *Les Oeuvres d'Ambroise Paré*. 9th ed. Lyon: Veuve Rigaud, 1633.

Platina 1528. *Platine de honeste volupté. Sensuyt le liure de Platine tresutile & necessaire a toutes gens*. Tr. Didier Christol. Lyon: n.p., 1528.

Platina 1967. *Platina de honesta voluptate: The First Dated Cookery Book (Venice: L. Aguila, 1475)*. Tr. Elizabeth Buermann Andrews. St. Louis: Mallinckrodt Chemical Works, 1967.

Regimen sanitatis en françoys. Souuerain remede contre lepydimie. Traictie pour congnoistre les urines. Remede tresutile pour la grosse verole. Lyon: Claude Nourry, 1514.

Roy, Emile. "Un régime de santé du XVe siècle pour les petits enfants, et l'hygiène de Gargantua." In *Mélanges offerts à Emile Picot* I, 151–58. Paris: Société des Bibliophiles, 1913.

Ryan, Lawrence V. "*Erasmi Colloquia*: the Banquet Colloquies of Erasmus." *Medievalia et Humanistica* n.s. 8 (1977): 201–15.

Saulnier, V.-L. "Médecins de Montpellier au temps de Rabelais." *Bibliothèque d'Humanisme et Renaissance* 19 (1957): 425–79.

Screech, M. A. "Aspects du rôle de la médecine dans la philosophie comique de Rabelais." In J. A. G. Tans, ed., *Invention et imitation: études sur la littérature du XVIe siècle*, 39–48. The Hague and Brussels: Van Goor Zonen, 1968.

————. "Medicine and Literature: Aspects of Rabelais and Montaigne." In Peter Sharratt, ed., *French Renaissance Studies (1540–1570): Humanism and the Encyclopedia*, 159–69. Edinburgh: Edinburgh University Press, 1976.

Screech, M. A., and Ruth Calder. "Some Renaissance Attitudes to Laughter." In A. H. T. Levi, ed., *Humanism in France at the End of the Middle Ages and in the Early Renaissance*, 216–28. Manchester: Manchester University Press, 1970.

Scully, Terence. *The Art of Cookery in the Middle Ages*. Woodbridge: Boydell Press, 1995.

Siraisi, Nancy G. *Medieval and Early Renaissance Medicine: An Introduction to Knowledge and Practice*. Chicago: University of Chicago Press, 1990.

Wear, A., et al., eds. *The Medical Renaissance of the Sixteenth Century*. Cambridge: Cambridge University Press, 1985.

Wheaton, Barbara Ketcham. *Savoring the Past: The French Kitchen and Table from 1300 to 1789*. Philadelphia: University of Pennsylvania Press, 1983.

RABELAIS AND LAW (Chapter 6)

Arresta Amorum, cum erudita Benedicti Curtii Symphoriani explanatione. Lyon: Gryphe, 1533.

d'Auvergne, Martial. *Les Arrêts d'Amour de Martial d'Auvergne*. Ed. Jean Rychner. Paris: Picard, 1951.

Barat, J. "L'influence de Tiraqueau sur Rabelais." *Revue des études Rabelaisiennes* 3 (1905): 138–55, 253–75.

Budé, Guillaume. *Annotationes in quattuor & viginti pandectorum libros*. Paris: R. Estienne, 1535.

Céard, Jean. "Le jugement de Bridoye." *Cahiers Textuel* 15 (1996): 49–62.

Defaux, Gérard. "Plaidoyer pour l'histoire: Rabelais, les *Brocardia juris*, Démosthène et l'antiquaille." *Revue d'Histoire Littéraire de la France* 77 (1977): 723–48.

Demerson, Guy. "Rabelais et la violence." *Europe* 70 (1992): 67–79.

Derrett, J. Duncan M. "Rabelais's Legal Learning and the Trial of Bridoye." *Bibliothèque d'Humanisme et Renaissance* 25 (1963): 111–71.

Duval, Edwin M. "The Juge Bridoye, Pantagruelism, and the Unity of Rabelais's *Tiers Livre*." *Etudes Rabelaisiennes* 17 (1983): 37–60.

Garin, E., ed. *La Disputa delle arti nel quattrocento*. Florence: Vallecchi, 1947.

Goyet, Francis. "L'origine logique du mot *maxime*." In Marie-Luce Demonet-Launay and André Tournon, eds., *Logique et Littérature à la Renaissance: Actes du Colloque de la Baume-les-Aix, Université de Provence, 16–18 septembre 1991*, 27–49. Paris: Champion, 1994.

Kelley, Donald R. *Foundations of Modern Historical Scholarship: Language, Law, and History in the French Renaissance*. New York: Columbia University Press, 1970.

———. *History, Law and the Human Sciences: Medieval and Renaissance Perspectives*. London: Variorum Reprints, 1984.

Maclean, Ian. *Interpretation and Meaning in the Renaissance: The Case of Law*. Cambridge: Cambridge University Press, 1992.

Marichal, R. "Rabelais et la réforme de la justice." *Bibliothèque d'Humanisme et Renaissance* 14 (1952): 176–92.

———. "René Dupuy Seigneur de Basché et les Chicanous." *Bibliothèque d'Humanisme et Renaissance* 11 (1949): 129–66.

Nardi, Enzo. *Rabelais e il diritto romano*. Milan: Giuffré, 1962.

Robinson, O. F., T. D. Fergus, and W. M. Gordon. *An Introduction to European Legal History*. London: Professional Books, 1985.

Salutati, Coluccio. *De nobilitate legum et medicinae; De verecundia*. Ed. E. Garin. Florence: Vallecchi, 1947.

Saulnier, V.-L. "Pantagruel au large de Ganabin, ou la peur de Panurge." *Bibliothèque d'Humanisme et Renaissance* 16 (1954): 58–81.

Schiller, A. Arthur. *Roman Law: Mechanisms of Development*. The Hague: Mouton, 1978.

Screech, M. A. "Eleven-Month Pregnancies: A Legal and Medical Quarrel à propos of *Gargantua* chapter 3: Rabelais, Alciati and Tiraqueau." *Etudes Rabelaisiennes* 8 (1969): 93–106.

———. "The Legal Comedy of Rabelais in the Trial of Bridoye in the *Tiers Livre de Pantagruel*." *Etudes Rabelaisiennes* 5 (1964): 175–95.

———. "Medicine and Literature: Aspects of Rabelais and Montaigne (with a Glance at the Law)." In Peter Sharratt, ed., *French Renaissance Studies (1540–1570): Humanism and the Encyclopedia*, 156–69. Edinburgh: Edinburgh University Press, 1976.

Stein, Peter. *Regulae juris: From Juristic Rules to Legal Maxim.* Edinburgh: Edinburgh University Press, 1966.

Tiraquellus, Andreus. *Andreae Tiraquelli . . . Commentarii, De nobilitate, et de iure primigeniorum.* Basel: Froben, 1561.

——. *De legibus connubialibus, et iure maritali.* Basel: Froben, 1561.

STUDIES ON RABELAIS

Amory, Frederic. "Rabelais's Hurricane Word-Formations." *Etudes Rabelaisiennes* 17 (1983): 61–74.

Bakhtin, Mikhail. *Rabelais and His World.* Tr. Helene Iswolsky. Cambridge: MIT Press, 1968.

Baraz, Michaël. *Rabelais et la joie de la liberté.* Paris: Corti, 1983.

Berry, Alice Fiola. "'Les Mithologies Pantagruelicques:' Introduction to a Study of Rabelais's *Quart Livre.*" *Publications of the Modern Language Association* 92 (1977): 471–80.

Blanchard, W. Scott. *Scholars' Bedlam: Menippean Satire in the Renaissance.* Lewisburg, Pennsylvania: Bucknell University Press, 1995.

Bowen, Barbara C. "Rabelais and the Library of Saint-Victor." In B. C. Bowen and Jerry Nash, eds., *Lapidary Inscriptions: Renaissance Studies for Donald A. Stone, Jr.,* 159–70. Lexington, Kentucky: French Forum Monographs, 1991.

——. "Rabelais and the Rhetorical Joke Tradition." In Raymond La Charité, ed., *Rabelais's Incomparable Book: Essays on His Art,* 213–25. Lexington, Kentucky: French Forum Monographs, 1986.

——. "Rabelais's Unreadable Books." *Renaissance Quarterly* 40 (1995): 742–58.

——. "Rire est le propre de l'homme." *Etudes Rabelaisiennes* 21 (1988): 185–90.

Brault, G. J. "The Significance of Eudemon's Praise of Gargantua (Rabelais, I.15)." *Kentucky Romance Quarterly* 18 (1971): 307–17.

Butor, Michel, and Denis Hollier. *Rabelais ou c'était pour rire.* Paris: Larousse, 1972.

Cave, Terence. *The Cornucopian Text: Problems of Writing in the French Renaissance.* Oxford: Clarendon Press, 1979.

Céard, Jean. "L'histoire écoutée aux portes de la légende: Rabelais, les fables de Turpin et les exemples de saint Nicolas." In Robert Aulotte, ed., *Etudes seiziémistes offertes à M. le Professeur V.L. Saulnier,* 91–109. Geneva: Droz, 1980.

———. "Rabelais et la matière épique." In *La Chanson de geste et le Mythe carolingien (Mélanges René Louis),* 1259–76. Saint-Père-sous-Vézelay: Musée Archéologique Régional, 1982.

———. "Rabelais, lecteur et juge des romans de chevalerie." *Etudes Rabelaisiennes* 21 (1988): 237–48.

Charitos, Stéphane A. "Un monstre du rire et un rire monstrueux: directions pour une étude sur François Rabelais et Georges Bataille." *Romance Notes* 28 (1988): 217–25.

Clark, Carol. *The Vulgar Rabelais.* Glasgow: Pressgang, 1983.

Coleman, Dorothy Gabe. *Rabelais: A Critical Study in Prose Fiction.* Cambridge: Cambridge University Press, 1971.

Defaux, Gérard. *Pantagruel et les Sophistes: contribution à l'histoire de l'humanisme chrétien au XVIe siècle.* The Hague: Nijhoff, 1973.

Demerson, Guy. *L'esthétique de Rabelais.* Paris: SEDES, 1996.

———. "Les facéties chez Rabelais." In Guy Demerson, *Humanisme et facétie: Quinze études sur Rabelais,* 35–54. Orléans: Paradigme, 1994.

———. "*Géant* de Chroniques et *géants* de Chronique: Rabelais entre Jean Bouchet et Erasme (à propos d'un article de RHR et d'un livre récent)." *Réforme, Humanisme, Renaissance* 37 (1993): 25–50.

———. *Rabelais.* Paris: Fayard, 1991.

———. "Rabelais et la violence." *Europe* 70 (mai 1992): 67–79.

———. "Tradition rhétorique et création littéraire chez Rabelais." *Etudes de Lettres* 2 (1984): 3–23.

Duval, Edwin M. *The Design of Rabelais's Pantagruel.* New Haven: Yale University Press, 1991.

———. "The Medieval Curriculum, the Scholastic University, and Gargantua's Program of Studies (*Pantagruel,* 8)." In Raymond C. La Charité, ed., *Rabelais's Incomparable Book,* 30–44. Lexington: French Forum, 1986.

———. "La messe, la cène, et le voyage sans fin du *Quart Livre.*" *Etudes Rabelaisiennes* 21 (1988): 131–41.

————. "Pantagruel's *chanson de ricochet* and Rabelais's *art et manière d'escrire histoires.*" In Barbara C. Bowen, ed., *Rabelais in Context: Proceedings of the 1991 Vanderbilt Conference*, 21–38. Birmingham, Alabama: Summa Publications, 1993.

————. "Panurge, Perplexity, and the Ironic Design of Rabelais's *Tiers Livre.*" *Renaissance Quarterly* 35 (1982): 381–400.

Freccero, Carla. *Father Figures: Genealogy and Narrative Structure in Rabelais.* Ithaca, New York: Cornell University Press, 1991.

Gaignebet, Claude. *A plus hault sens: l'ésotérisme spirituel et charnel de Rabelais.* Paris: Maisonneuve et Larose, 1986.

Gauna, Max. *The Rabelaisian Mythologies.* London: Associated University Presses, 1996.

Gilman, Peter, and Abraham C. Keller. "Rabelais, the *Grandes Chronicques*, and Jean Lemaire de Belges." *Etudes Rabelaisiennes* 29 (1993): 93–104.

Glauser, Alfred. *Rabelais créateur.* Paris: Nizet, 1966.

Glidden, Hope H. "Rabelais, Panurge, and the Anti-Courtly Body." *Etudes Rabelaisiennes* 25 (1991): 35–60.

Gray, Floyd. *Rabelais et le comique du discontinu.* Paris: Champion, 1994.

————. *Rabelais et l'écriture.* Paris: Nizet, 1974.

Hansen, Bjorn Bredal. *La peur, le rire et la sagesse: Essais sur Rabelais et Montaigne.* Copenhagen: Munksgaards, 1985.

Jeanneret, Michel. *Le défi des signes: Rabelais et la crise de l'interprétation à la Renaissance.* Orléans: Paradigme, 1994.

Kinser, Samuel. *Rabelais's Carnival: Text, Context, Metatext.* Berkeley: University of California Press, 1990.

Kritzman, Lawrence D. "La quête de la parole dans le *Quart Livre* de Rabelais." *French Forum* 2 (1977): 195–204.

La Charité, Raymond C. "The Framing of Rabelais's *Gargantua.*" In Emanuel J. Mickel, Jr., ed., *The Shaping of Text: Style, Imagery and Structure in French Literature: Essays in Honor of John Porter Houston*, 45–57. Lewisburg: Bucknell University Press, 1993.

La Charité, Raymond C., ed. *Rabelais's Incomparable Book: Essays on His Art.* Lexington, Kentucky: French Forum, 1986.

Lefebvre, Henri. *Rabelais.* Paris: Editeurs Français Réunis, 1955.

Lewis, John. "Pantagruel Reconsidered: Rabelais's First Fictional

Chronicle as Paradigm." *Etudes Rabelaisiennes* 25 (1991): 7–21.

Masters, G. Mallary. *Rabelaisian Dialectic and the Platonic-Hermetic Tradition*. Albany: SUNY Press, 1969.

Ménager, Daniel. *Rabelais en toutes lettres*. Paris: Bordas, 1989.

Moreau, François. "La bibliothèque de l'Abbaye de Saint-Victor (*Pantagruel*, chapitre VII)." *Littératures* 19 (1988): 37–42.

Nakam, Géralde. "Rire, angoisse, illusion." *Europe* 70 (1992): 21–35.

Naudon, Paul. *Rabelais franc-maçon*. Paris: Editions La Balance, 1954.

Nilles, Camilla J. "Reading the *Ancien Prologue*." *Etudes Rabelaisiennes* 29 (1993): 127–38.

Plattard, Jean. *L'oeuvre de Rabelais (sources, invention et composition)*. Paris: Champion, 1967.

Poutingon, Gérard Milhe. *François Rabelais: bilan critique*. Paris: Nathan, 1996.

Quesnel, Colette. *Mourir de rire d'après et avec Rabelais*. Montréal and Paris: Bellarmin/Vrin, 1991.

Randall, Michael. *Building Resemblances: Analogical Imagery in the Early French Renaissance*. Baltimore: Johns Hopkins University Press, 1996.

Rigolot, François. *Les langages de Rabelais*. Geneva: Droz, 1972.

———. "Rabelais, Misogyny, and Christian Charity: Biblical Intertextuality and the Renaissance Crisis of Exemplarity." *Publications of the Modern Language Association* 109 (1994): 225–37.

Saintsbury, George. *A History of the French Novel* vol. 1. London: Macmillan, 1917.

Saulnier, V.-L. *Le Dessein de Rabelais*. Paris: SEDES, 1957.

———. *Rabelais II, Rabelais dans son enquête: Etude sur le Quart et le Cinquième livre*. Paris: SEDES, 1982.

Schwartz, Jerome. *Irony and Ideology in Rabelais: Structures of Subversion*. Cambridge: Cambridge University Press, 1990.

Screech, M. A. *Rabelais*. Ithaca, New York: Cornell University Press, 1979.

———. *The Rabelaisian Marriage: Aspects of Rabelais's Religion, Ethics and Comic Philosophy*. London: Edward Arnold, 1958.

———. "Sagesse de Rabelais: Rabelais et les 'bons christians'." In

Jean Céard and Jean-Claude Margolin, eds., *Rabelais en son demi-millénaire: Actes du Colloque International de Tours (24–29 septembre 1984)*, 9–15. Geneva: Droz, 1988.

Smith, Paul. "Le Prologue du *Pantagruel*: une lecture." *Neophilologus* 68 (1984): 161–69.

————. *Voyage et Ecriture: Etude sur le Quart Livre de Rabelais.* Geneva: Droz, 1987.

Tetel, Marcel. *Etude sur le comique de Rabelais.* Florence: Olschki, 1964.

————. "Rabelais et Folengo." *Comparative Literature* 15 (1963): 357–64.

————. "Rabelais et Folengo: De patria diabolorum." In Jean Céard and Jean-Claude Margolin, eds., *Rabelais en son demi-millénaire: Actes du Colloque International de Tours (24–29 septembre 1984)*, 203–11. Geneva: Droz, 1988.

Thuasne, Louis. *Etudes sur Rabelais.* Paris: Bouillon, 1904; reprint Paris: Champion, 1969.

Tournon, André. *"En sens agile:" Les acrobaties de l'esprit chez Rabelais.* Paris: Champion, 1995.

Weinberg, Florence M. "Platonic and Pauline Ideals in Comic Dress: 'Comment on vestit Gargantua'." *Illinois Classical Studies* 9 (1984): 183–95.

————. "Rabelais's Isle de Ruach (*Quart Livre*, 43–44)." *Romance Languages Annual* 1995: 203–7.

————. *The Wine and the Will: Rabelais's Bacchic Christianity.* Detroit: Wayne State University Press, 1972.

————. "Written on the Leaves: Rabelais and the Sibylline Tradition." *Renaissance Quarterly* 43 (1990): 709–30.

STUDIES ON LAUGHTER

Adolf, Helen. "On Medieval Laughter." *Speculum* 22 (1947), 251–53.

Allen, Steve. *The Funny Men.* New York: Simon and Schuster, 1956.

Allen, Steve, and Jane Wollman. *How to Be Funny: Discovering the Comic You.* New York: McGraw-Hill, 1987.

Bain, Alexander. *The Emotions and the Will.* 3rd ed. London: Longmans, 1888.

Baudelaire, Charles. "De l'essence du rire." In *Oeuvres Complètes* II: 525–43. Paris: Gallimard, 1976.

Bowen, Zack. *Ulysses as a Comic Novel*. Syracuse, New York: Syracuse University Press, 1989.

Chapman, Antony J., and Hugh C. Foot, eds. *Humour and Laughter: Theory, Research and Applications*. London: John Wiley, 1976.

Douglas, Mary. *Implicit Meanings: Essays in Anthropology*. London: Routledge and Kegan Paul, 1975.

Eastman, Max. *Enjoyment of Laughter*. London: Hamish Hamilton, 1937.

Eckardt, A. Roy. *Sitting in the Earth and Laughing: A Handbook of Humor*. New Brunswick, New Jersey: Transaction Publishers, 1992.

Favre, Robert. *Le rire dans tous ses éclats*. Lyon: Presses Universitaires de Lyon, 1995.

Feibleman, James. *In Praise of Comedy*. New York: Macmillan, 1939.

Flieger, Jerry Aline. *The Purloined Punch Line: Freud's Comic Theory and the Postmodern Text*. Baltimore: Johns Hopkins University Press, 1991.

Freud, Sigmund. *Jokes and Their Relation to the Unconscious*. Tr. James Strachey. New York: Norton, 1960.

Gregory, J. C. *The Nature of Laughter*. London: Kegan Paul, 1924.

Greig, J. Y. T. *Psychology of Laughter and Comedy*. London: Allen and Unwin, 1923.

Gutwirth, Marcel. "Réflexions sur le comique." *Revue d'esthétique* 17 (1964): 7–39.

Hobbes, Thomas. *The Elements of Law Natural and Politic*. Ed. J. C. A. Gaskin. New York: Oxford University Press, 1994.

Kant, Immanuel. *Kant on Laughter: Kant's Critique of Aesthetic Judgement*. Tr. J. C. Meredith. Oxford: Clarendon Press, 1911.

Kline, L. W. "The Psychology of Humour." *American Journal of Psychology* 18 (1907): 421–41.

Menon, V. K. Krishna. *A Theory of Laughter*. London: Allen and Unwin, 1931.

Leacock, Stephen. *Humor: Its Theory and Technique*. New York: Dodd, Mead, 1935.

Ludovici, A. M. *The Secret of Laughter*. London: Constable, 1932.

McDougall, William. "A New Theory of Laughter." *Psyche* 2 (N.S.) (1922): 292–303.

Ménager, Daniel. *La Renaissance et le rire*. Paris: Presses Universitaires de France, 1995.

Monro, H. *The Argument of Laughter*. Melbourne: Melbourne University Press, 1951.

Morreall, John. *Taking Laughter Seriously*. Albany: SUNY Press, 1983.

Morreall, John, ed. *The Philosophy of Laughter and Humor*. Albany: SUNY Press, 1987.

Raskin, Victor. *Semantic Mechanisms of Humor*. Dordrecht: Reidel, 1985.

Schopenhauer, Arthur. *The World as Will and Idea*. Tr. R. B. Haldane and J. Kemp. 2nd ed. London: Kegan Paul, 1891.

Screech, M. A., and Ruth Calder. "Some Renaissance Attitudes to Laughter." In A. H. T. Levi, ed., *Humanism in France at the End of the Middle Ages and in the Early Renaissance*, 216–28. Manchester: Manchester University Press, 1970.

Spencer, Herbert. "Physiology of Laughter." In *Essays Scientific, Political, Speculative*. London: C. A. Watts, n.d.

Swabey, Marie Collins. *Comic Laughter: A Philosophical Essay*. New Haven: Yale University Press, 1961.

Sypher, Wylie, ed. *Comedy: Laughter (Henri Bergson), An Essay on Comedy (George Meredith)*. New York: Doubleday, 1956.

Tiersma, Peter M. *Language-Based Humor in the Marx Brothers Films*. Bloomington: Indiana University Linguistics Club, 1985.

OTHER WORKS CITED

Appia, Henry. "O rare P.G. Wodehouse!" *Etudes Anglaises* 26 (1973): 22–34.

Genette, Gérard. *Palimpsestes: la littérature au second degré*. Paris: Seuil, 1982.

Hay, Denys. *Annalists and Historians*. London: Methuen, 1977.

Parker, Patricia. *Literary Fat Ladies: Rhetoric, Gender, Property*. New York: Methuen, 1987.

Schor, Naomi. *Reading in Detail: Aesthetics and the Feminine*. London: Methuen, 1987.

Index

One of the foremost scholars in sixteenth-century French and Romance language studies, BARBARA C. BOWEN is professor of French and comparative literature at Vanderbilt University. She is the current president of the Renaissance Society of America and is the author of several previous monographs, including *Words and the Man in French Renaissance Literature* (1983).

ENTER RABELAIS, LAUGHING

was composed electronically using
Granjon types, with displays in
Granjon, Bauer Bodoni, and Type Embellishments One.
The book was printed on 60# Natural Smooth paper
and was Smyth sewn and cased in Pearl Linen
by Braun-Brumfield, Inc.
The dust jacket was printed in three colors by
Vanderbilt University Printing Services.
Book and dust jacket designs are the work of Tom Ventress.
Published by Vanderbilt University Press
Nashville, Tennessee 37235